The Making of the Professional Actor

Design for a Theatre open to the air, the sun and moon.
Frontispiece to Edward Gordon Craig's *The Theatre Advancing*
(Constable, 1921)

ADRIAN CAIRNS

The Making of the Professional Actor

A History, an Analysis and a Prediction

with a Foreword by

JEREMY IRONS

PETER OWEN

London & Chester Springs PA

PETER OWEN PUBLISHERS
73 Kenway Road London SW5 0RE
Peter Owen books are distributed in the USA by
Dufour Editions Inc. Chester Springs PA 19425–0007

First published in Great Britain 1996
© Adrian Cairns 1996

A catalogue record for this book is available
from the British Library

ISBN 0–7206–1002–8

Printed and made in Great Britain by
Biddles of Guildford and King's Lynn

Dedication

To the memory of my father, William Cairns (1891–1967), who 'showed virtue her own feature', and would have smiled at another book in the family;

and to Edward Gordon Craig (1872–1966), whom I once met for an afternoon's chat which made me 'feel smilingly all over'.

Know thyself

> – Motto said to have been inscribed over the entrance to the Temple Theatre at Delphi, circa fourth century BC

All the world plays the player

> – Motto said to have been displayed on the signboard of Shakespeare's Globe Theatre, Southwark, 1599

A good theatre company is a metaphor of a possible society

> – Peter Hall, 1974

The essence of theatre is within a mystery called 'the present moment'. . . . So what is our aim? It is a meeting with the fabric of life, no more and no less

> – Peter Brook, 1993

Acknowledgements

In a book of this scope full acknowledgements are sometimes difficult to assess or to trace, but every effort has been made to contact those sources indicated in the text. If any have been missed, I offer apologies, and hope that copyright holders who have any queries will contact the publisher.

I would especially like to thank Christopher Robinson, Keeper of the Theatre Collection at Bristol University's Drama Department, for his unfailing courtesy and patience whenever I called upon him for help; also Elwyn Johnson, Associate Principal at the Bristol Old Vic Theatre School, for his encouragement and with whom many of the descriptions and ideas in the book were discussed during countless pub-lunch breaks.

Grateful thanks are offered to the following for permission to quote from the works indicated: Reed Books and the Methuen imprint for *Brecht on Theatre* (1964), edited by John Willett; John Willett, *The Theatre of Bertolt Brecht* (1967); Peter Brook, *There Are No Secrets* (1993); *The Revels History of Drama in English*, Vols. VII and VIII (1978); Jean Benedetti, *Stanislavski: A Biography* (1988); Edward Braun, *Meyerhold on Theatre* (1969) and *The Director and the Stage* (1982); Yoshi Oida, *An Actor Adrift* (1992). Crown Publishers Inc., New York, for Piscator material in *Actors on Acting*, copyright 1970 by the editors Toby Cole and Helen Krich Chinoy. David Whitton, *Stage Directors in Modern France* (MUP, 1987). Heinemann Publishers (Oxford) Ltd, for Michel Saint-Denis, *Training for the Theatre* (1982), also published by Theatre Arts Books, New York. The Athlone Press for Dr Michael Sanderson, *From Irving to Olivier* (1984). Professor Christopher Balme of Munich University for items on Strehler's *Faust* project. Routledge Publishers for *Copeau: Texts on Theatre* (1990), edited and translated by John Rudlin and Norman H. Paul; Iain Mackintosh, *Architecture, Actor and Audience* (1993); Richard Schechner, *The Future of Ritual* (1993); Thomas Richards and Jerzy Grotowski, *At Work with Grotowski on Physical*

Actions (1995). Element Books for James Roose-Evans, *Passages of the Soul: Ritual Today* (1994). Peters Fraser and Dunlop for Ronald Hayman, *Artaud and After* (OUP, 1977). Cambridge University Press for Allardyce Nicoll, *English Drama 1900–1930* (1973); John Rudlin, *Jacques Copeau* (1986); Herbert Blau, *By Means of Performance* (1990); Yvonne Daoust, *Roger Planchon* (1981). Clive Barker and *New Theatre Quarterly.* Thames and Hudson for Jean-Louis Barrault, *Memories for Tomorrow* (1974, trans. Jonathan Griffin).

Last, and anything but least, I would like to thank my editor at Peter Owen Ltd, Stephen Stuart-Smith, for his eagle eye over textual details which had slipped past my attention.

Contents

Contents

Foreword

Adrian Cairns, apart from being an actor, was one of my teachers at the Bristol Old Vic Theatre School. His experience both as an actor and as a teacher, and his practice of considered thought, make this an invaluable book at a time when Government and Local Authorities seem confused as to what actors' training should be, let alone what their role should be in contemporary society. This uncertainty has caused, in many cases, withdrawal of an educational subsidy towards actors' training.

Mr Cairns's book examines the history of actors' training, leading to an analysis of the present situation as well as a prediction of the actor's role in the future and the method of training we should work towards to accommodate this.

The Making of the Professional Actor should be required reading, not only for those decision makers who hold the responsibility of subsidizing the next generation of actors, but for any prospective, student, or professional actor. It is a vital addition to the current debate.

Jeremy Irons

Introduction

This is not a book on how to become a professional actor. Only experience can bring that; it cannot be learned from any manual, nor for that matter, from any vocational course whether carrying degree status or not. Courses may give a useful grounding, but only in the proving-fire of public and paid work will the professional be forged. It usually takes anything from five to ten years of employment for the process to settle itself; and thereafter, the refinements continue with each role for the rest of the professional's life. The purpose of the historical perspective on the development of the actor given in Part One is to set the scene for the general influences on acting and acting styles in this century which are discussed in Part Two; and to help indicate the continuing tendencies likely to prove future developments which are hazarded in Part Three. Because it reflects the social changes of its time, the actor's craft and his training may well proceed in a spiral manner – rather like the cycles of civilization, or indeed the DNA molecule itself. It will both repeat itself, and place the new on top of the old. The theatre – that 'fabulous invalid' – is constantly dying and, at the same time, being reborn.

Actor training in Britain today

In the past, apprenticeship on the job was the way in which most actors got their professional training. Although a fictional

character, Nicholas Nickleby comes to mind as he joined Vincent
Crummles and his company on tour at Portsmouth in 1838. A
young gentleman with some education, a wardrobe of his own,
reasonable looks, a knowledge of sword-handling and the basic
social graces, who is looking for an occupation 'to see the world
to advantage in', might well have considered the theatrical profession. So, at least, thought Mr Crummles looking for 'a novelty'
to boost his business. '"But I don't know anything about it,"
rejoined Nicholas, whose breath had been almost taken away by
this sudden proposal. "I never acted a part in my life, except at
school." "There's genteel comedy in your walk and manner, ju-
venile tragedy in your eye, and touch-and-go farce in your laugh,"
said Mr Vincent Crummles. "You'll do as well as if you had
thought of nothing else but the lamps from your birth down-
wards."'

After the Second World War, with the advent of so-called 'kitchen-
sink' drama on both stage and film (and ever more increasingly
with the development of the television 'soaps'), class background
and the social graces of speech and behaviour were no longer
any sort of criteria for the acting profession. They still had their
place in the classical repertoire, but if anything they became a
hindrance in management offices where 'casting to type' was as
much sought after as acting ability. The 'all-round actor', of course,
may play any role convincingly; but this is not an observation
which directors, as a rule, will entertain when they have plenty
of choice from what they would regard as 'the real thing'. Moreover,
as most acting for the camera has become tantamount to behav-
ing as in real life (however much that may be 'the art which
conceals art'), the matter of training is not always considered
that essential. Anyone can do it, as witness the employment of
well-known boxers and cricketers in pantomime; and in any case,
the English love an amateur. Indeed, the claim to have had no
training is sometimes brandished in interviews with pride as if it
carried some kind of inverted élitism.

It may be that special abilities will come into their own again,
distinguishing the professional from the amateur. Future writers
for theatre and screen – some already doing so today – will demand more than simple truthfulness of playing: they will expect
high degrees of expertise in ancillary skills such as singing and

acrobatic movement, mime and all kinds of dance, unarmed combat and tumbling, and of course, in some period work, the ubiquitous fencing. The old actor-priest may even return as the new guru, showing ourselves to ourselves; for as Peter Hall once commented, 'Acting is not imitation, it is revelation. Actors in performance reveal their inner selves.' Now *that* does take professional skill.

The main trouble about actor training in Britain today is that there is too much of it. Even a cursory glance at Sara Duncan's well-researched *Guide to Careers and Training in the Performing Arts* (Cheverell Press, 1993) confirms the point. It would seem that this surplus is also true in the USA, but we will come to that later. The supply far exceeds the demand for new blood in a profession already vastly overcrowded; consequently there is considerable frustration and unhappiness in many students who have career hopes but little or no chance of realizing them, even if they have talent.

Despite this well-known gloomy picture, the efforts of so many dedicated training establishments are not altogether wasted. Since the very early days of Tree's Academy and Elsie Fogarty's Central School, it has been recognized that a training for acting can also be a training for life – that is to say, a more fulfilled personal life, both physically and mentally, whether it is spent in the theatre or in any other vocational career. Would that this were better appreciated by the Department for Education and Employment when looking at course priorities.

In the economic and artistic climate of the 1990s, it is likely that more and more drama students will be accepted by the vocational schools more for their ability to pay the tuition fees than for their talent alone. This may result in the acceptance of second and third choices on the waiting list. Talent, of course, is a very difficult thing to assess in embryonic form. Mistakes of judgement can easily be made, and are made, whether by individuals or committees. But in the fiercely competitive process of even getting in to a drama school of any quality, criteria for entry have to be set. These criteria differ enormously, and are always difficult to agree upon, even by 'experts'. The most unlikely aspirant, in fact, may turn out to be 'star material' after three years of training. Thus, allowing that the theatre, reflecting life, requires all human variations, the factor most likely to weigh in choosing applicants, after some basic proof of performing potential, will be their financial standing. Their funding will usually be private, sometimes with contributory help from educational or charitable bodies.

However, today, with ever-increasing fees and basic maintenance expenses, grants by official institutions – often themselves under considerable financial constraint – are becoming more and more inadequate, so that the pressure on the student to find his or her own way of supplementing the inadequacy is now beginning to have a serious effect on the courses themselves.[1] The traditionally romantic view that it is possible to 'work your way through college' is rarely tenable any more. Overseas students, in particular, are inclined to harbour this comfortable illusion that by working hard at some menial (or even specialized) task during evenings, night-times, weekends and college vacations, they will be able to survive. A very few, indeed, do succeed in achieving this, though at what cost to their health and the actual training is rarely assessed. But year by year, the stratagem is getting more and more difficult. This is not only because the fees and the cost of living constantly rise, but also because courses have become more intensive. The working week of the average drama student can be much heavier than many may think. A twelve-hour day will not be unusual, and of course, weekends and public holidays are in no way sacrosanct. The student has to be accustomed to a routine reflecting the demands of the profession. Show business, whether classical or commercial, is a hard business, demanding nothing less than 'all' from its dedicated servants. Drama students, in particular, usually have unbounded energy in pursuit of their goal. Ambition is the spur in their competitive race; and the more they are asked to do, the more they like it. The problem for the curriculum planner at most drama schools is finding the time to fit everything in; and, conversely, controlling the amount scheduled to a wise and rational balance. Yet whatever the official planning, the individual students will invariably opt to stretch themselves further and take on more. It is little wonder that responsible drama schools insist on prospective students producing a doctor's certificate to indicate their fitness to undertake such a strenuous regime.

However admirable some of this may be, the fact remains that there are too many vocational schools, not to mention all the others, which are training too many students for a profession which cannot possibly employ more than a fraction of them. The result is a 'shameful and uncoordinated mess', according to an article in *The Stage* (8 October 1992), which points out the ineptitude, cynicism, personal pain and hopelessness, and of course, economic madness, that is involved. Back in 1975, it was hoped that this situation was at last to be remedied by the setting up of the National Council for Drama Training (NCDT), following a Gulbenkian Enquiry into 'Going on the Stage'. Only those schools accredited for a five-year period by an Accreditation Panel responsible to the Executive of the Council would be truly acceptable as training bodies. But the operation of these visiting panels, supposedly to be made up as equally as possible of 'experts' from management, the Actors Union, and the training field itself, proved to be unsatisfactory, and even at times irresponsibly inept. The NCDT was soon reduced to being little more than a 'rubber stamp': it was useful to those Local Education Authorities who wanted to shed the responsibility for deciding which drama schools merited discretionary grants. But even that purpose is now in doubt. Moreover, the accreditation system constantly begs the question as to what and whose standards are being applied. It is assumed that there is agreement over those standards throughout the NCDT body at large, which is certainly far from being the case. It might have been hoped that the NCDT would have adhered to the very highest possible standards and accredited only about ten schools in the country as a reasonable number to supply the needs of the profession for new blood, but it never had the courage, nor the power, to do this.

On the other hand, how desirable is it to try and restrict intake into the profession at all? The issue seems to go beyond the heartache and the ostrich-like disregard of actual requirements. In a free-market democracy, the profession might well wish to retain the right to employ untrained talent and amateur 'personalities' as it does now, despite Union objections, and with such risky judgement being on its own head. Also 'in-service training' (as apprenticeship is now called) will always retain its own value and short-cut effectiveness; but it can never have the time nor special facilities necessary for the broader scope and ideals of a full 'accredited training'.

The ideals of the latter have long been expressed in this century – as we shall see – in the various curricula that were first established by Copeau, Stanislavski, Brecht and their later disciples. Naturally, some of these curricula have shaped those currently adopted by leading schools, although it must be noted that the original ideals were too often short-lived in practice, because of lack of sufficient financial support. As ever, they await full implementation by a more enlightened further education administration. But this, as we have seen, is increasingly unlikely. Currently only one in six Local Education Authorities provides full grants (*Observer*, 10 July 1994), and the number of beneficiaries is decreasing yearly.

With discretionary grants for the training of actors fading fast, some top drama schools are now looking for mandatory grants for their students by seeking degree status for their courses. This, of course, will put them in direct competition with those universities (including the many former polytechnics) which also offer degree courses in Drama and Theatre Studies, including Acting. As far as student numbers are concerned – always a very real issue for the profession – the situation grows increasingly out of hand. Currently, many *postgraduate* drama degree holders from the universities are applying for true vocational training at the accredited theatre schools, and have done so, indeed, for many years. But instead of the required (and necessary) three-year minimum vocational training programme (or perhaps for some more experienced students, two years), the postgraduate is likely to be offered – if anything at all – a mere one year's further training on a mandatory basis. Nearly all the vocational schools are agreed that this is very unsatisfactory, and can even be counter-productive: for it allows just enough time to break down bad habits but no time to put good ones together again. Thus for many on degree courses, and even for those new graduates at the accredited schools, whose former curriculum will presumably have to be adjusted, the postgraduate grant situation will remain unchanged.

It has to be recognized that however desirable a drama degree may be for a culturally-informed background, and for obtaining other employment – for example, as a teacher – when the actor is 'resting', it is of no use whatever for getting a job in the professional market-place. The pragmatic training programme required for preparing the actor, even throughout three years, can ill afford dilution for academic degree purposes (as we can see from those many postgraduate students applying for further training). One other difficult factor which the drama schools currently offering or seeking degree status for their courses will have to reckon with is that the mandatory grant will be considerably less than their current or former fees. Unless the difference can be made up by the student privately, then staffing and facilities (and again, most likely, standards) will suffer accordingly. It will not be simply a case of robbing Peter, the tax-payer, to pay Paul his mandatory vocational grant, but of continuing to rob Paul privately before he can take up his place.

In a pertinent article written in May 1995, Clive Barker points to how previous processes of validation for actor training have been breaking down.[2] For example, there are no longer any of the criteria originally set by HMI and CNAA; a school like East 15, not accredited by the NCDT, can nevertheless obtain validation from the University of East London; a BA in Drama at Bristol University might be a cheaper option that a BA in Acting at the Bruford School; and a B-Tech course, or a GNVQ/DVE, may not actually qualify the student for anything at all. It is all very confusing, both for those seeking a career and for those seeking to give some sort of vocational training. In reviewing a new 1995 Report in the same issue of *New Theatre Quarterly*, Barker writes:

> ... perhaps the mass of detailed evidence marshalled by the authors of this report might succeed in making national and local authorities wake up to the perilous state of training for the theatre today.
>
> Beneath the figures, tables, and graphs of this report lie all the individual stories of hardship and, too often, insurmountable difficulties which stand in the way of the would-be performer today.... Whether anyone in authority will take heed is a moot point.[3]

The best way to avoid the current dilemma – and probably the only just and workable one – would seem to be the establishment of direct central funding for nationally accredited courses. Only in this way can there be any guarantee of maintaining quality and non-discriminatory access to training. This, indeed, was the recommendation of the Arts Council's Anthony Everitt in a report to both the Department of Education and the Department for National Heritage in March 1993. The government subsequently confirmed that it will be reviewing the grants situation. However, the problem of defining standards of accreditation and ensuing accountability would remain.

What is it about an actor's life – pressured as it is – that makes it an attractive prospect to so many? The answer is not far to seek. Acting as a career appears to offer a fairly easy realization of an exciting lifestyle which, with a bit of luck, may include money and adulation. No academic examinations (at least, none until this degree business began to proliferate) are considered primarily relevant – they are useful but not essential – and there is no bar to any physique or type when the intention is to mirror life. In no other profession is it made so easy to turn a blind eye to personal failure. Whatever the actor's inadequacies, the big chance is always just around the corner. 'It is only in the theatre that an individual may still consider himself an active participant even if he only works for a few weeks or months in any one year.'[4] This get-out clause has considerable attraction for young people worried about making a success of their lives. They read frequently of the star who either 'made it overnight' or made it after years of apparent failure as an unrecognized bit-player. The door of hope is never shut as it is so often shut in other walks of life. The romance of that hope – and the rougher the interim years the sweeter the romance – is much beloved of journalists and the media. From Cinderella getting to the Ball to the understudy who replaces the sick star, the myth of the instantly realized dream-ambition has enormous potency. Adolescence is a time of impatience; everything seems to take so long to happen; a short cut is immensely attractive. Some see the theatre and allied media as possibly offering such a short cut. If lucky they get into a theatre school, only to discover just how much work, application, self-discipline, intelligence and cultural background is actually required to meet the competition from others with the same idea. Not to mention the strain of finding the money to survive the course.

The American training scene

For some time now in the USA, actor training has been largely conducted by University or College Theatre Departments, well over a thousand of them, many offering degree programmes. The commercial sector also has an active life, with hundreds of schools in cities throughout the country, and thirty principal ones divided between New York and California (nearly all in Los Angeles with a couple or so in San Francisco). You pay your money and you take your choice, and there are plenty of books offering analysis and advice as to how you should do so, as in Britain; and as always in such exercises, there are just a handful of top contenders.

The best, it might be assumed, are run in conjunction with a fully professional theatre. Yale is an example of this, as is the Goodman Theatre and School of Drama in Chicago; but there are at least a dozen other campuses spread throughout the country which have a high reputation, and their own theatre building available to visiting companies. New York has several famous commercial schools which are at least adjacent to professional activity, such as the Juilliard at the Lincoln Center, what used to be called the Circle-in-the-Square Theatre School (though names and venues frequently change), and the old Neighborhood Playhouse School of Theatre. There are, of course, many other reputable commercial teaching studios in New York. Probably one of the earliest of them all and surviving today is the American Academy of Dramatic Arts on Madison Avenue, which was founded way back in 1884 (as the Lyceum Theatre School of Acting) and received charters from NYU in 1899 and 1952; and which extended to the West Coast in the 1980s with a Pasadena branch. An up-to-date and exhaustive list of training venues for the whole country is available from the American Theatre Association, 1010 Wisconsin Avenue NW, Washington, DC 20007. One of the latest schools in New York is the New Actors Workshop School of the Theatre, which offers a two-year professional actor training programme ('government approved for foreign students'). It is headed by a triumvirate of well-known teacher/directors: Mike Nichols (eight Tonys and an Oscar), George Morrison (ex-Yale, Strasberg, Juilliard) and Paul Sills (teacher son of Viola Spolin, who ran

Story Theatre, Games Theatre and his own company).

The USA led the world in establishing the first university degree in theatre arts at Pittsburgh's Carnegie Institute of Technology in 1914. Influential Yale followed in 1925. Britain took
until 1947 to create its first Department of Drama at the University of Bristol; and now there are at least thirty-three institutions
in Britain offering a BA degree in Drama, not to mention countless more where Drama is part of a combined study. But in the
article by Clive Barker mentioned earlier – 'What Training – for
What Theatre?' – he usefully addresses the current dilemma, which
has become increasingly evident in both the USA and Britain.
What is the use of spending money giving professional training
for so many actors when only a very few will find work at the
end of it, and when in any case the future nature of that work is
likely to differ greatly from the past – a past on which most of
the training is based? How is actor training to be best rational-
ized for the future? He notes quizzically that one bookseller's
catalogue 'contains 25 books on teaching acting, and I have heard
of none of them'. Although Clive Barker is an ex-Theatre Workshop professional actor and director, and author of the highly
practical *Theatre Games* (1977), he is also a university peda-
gogue. He talks of 'the narrow concerns of the acting school'
being opened out by Drama Departments. Well, yes; but professional pragmatism soon narrows down the 'course modules'
or syllabus of concerns again, if only because of pressures on the
timetable and the money available. Nevertheless, Barker is right
when he suggests that the aim should be for 'contextual knowledge'.

The USA has experienced for some time, and for longer than
in Britain, the way in which training pathways which began by
being quite separate are now overlapping. British theatre schools
like the RADA, LAMDA, Central and the rest, were created strictly
for the vocational training of the professional actor; and British
universities, including the former polytechnics, carried out academic education of a non-vocational kind (unless it be for teaching). Today, the two paths are crossing, though they are by no
means merged either in Britain or in the USA. Instead of the
cross-fertilization that Barker would like to see happen, one of
the unhappier results of the dual pathways in recent years has
been that 'bright young bloods', well informed theoretically and

hot from their university degrees, have gone directly into the profession and *then* learnt their business at the expense of working
professional actors, designers and lighting people, not to mention
paying audiences. Certain star-names have been very bitter about
this. Whether the same sort of thing has happened in the USA, I
do not know, but I suspect something similar to be the case. On
the other hand, eventually such raw talents have often created
exciting and original work, earning a justified reputation where
other less gifted persons, forged by the commercially-compromised
conditions of the profession, have failed to deliver. But as Albert
Hunt (quoted by Barker) so neatly put it, the avant-garde is all
too ready to repeat the past and 're-invent the same mistakes'.

Whatever the arguments against town and gown joining forces,
and experience tells of many, the ideal of a practising professional
theatre with a training faculty attached and working with it still
pertains. Whether attempted by Stanislavski or Copeau, or Saint-
Denis at the Old Vic, and whether failing after a few years or
not, this has always been the best answer. Barker points out that
in the USA and continental Europe, actors are now as likely to
quote on their CVs the privately-run master classes and 'workshops' they have attended as much as any school or faculty which
they may have attended. In Britain, too, this is now becoming
more commonplace, due no doubt to the failing grant-systems
and the prohibitive cost of attending most accredited schools.
Prospective actor-students are seeking training where they can
just about afford it, and this means schools with shorter courses
and ones with less full-time restrictions, yet still offering some
sort of 'show-case' for agents and employers at the end. The
attraction is obvious, and there is no shortage of advertisements
from those ready to supply such training, for they require no
special accreditation to set up shop. 'Master-classes' are a particular magnet as students can then identify their training with a
successful and famous name – as if, in just a few hours, they can
imbibe the experience of a lifetime through mere contact. The
'master', incidentally, can rarely choose the students who might
be the ones that could best benefit from his or her wisdom.

Finally, as much for American training as for British, Barker
asks 'How can we best acquaint the student with the context
within which to start work?' and 'Can we work to discover a

basic common core . . . an irreducible training programme?' It is the purpose of this book to go some way towards answering those questions.

But such questions have only recently arisen. Back in the beginning – not the more distant beginning in ancient Greece and Rome but the European Middle Ages – the worries were more those of the priest than the performer. The making of the professional actor began as an expedient initiative by the Church.

PART ONE: The Past

The drama's incomparable vividness – its pictures painted in the human medium of the actors – lends to the past the actuality of the present... Of what does the past consist? Essentially... of the things we have done with; while what is still alive for us and within us is therefore not to be reckoned in that sort of past at all.

Harley Granville-Barker, *The Use of the Drama*
(Lectures at Princeton University, USA, 1944)

1

The Religious and the Secular in Medieval Acting

There are two different strands of early development which gave impetus to the rebirth of the professional player in medieval Europe. These were the official Christian religion and primitive festivals, respectively. On the one hand, acting became a necessary element in the interpolated *quem quaeritis* trope of the liturgical service;[1] on the other hand, it continued from earliest recorded history in the seasonal and agricultural rites held as a traditional part of village and town life. The first uses the mode of drama as a kind of audio-visual aid to Christian education and celebration; the second uses it in a less partisan way to express the great existential facts of Nature and our tragi-comic human situation, employing accrued traditions from much folklore and local legend, combined with coarse symbolic analogies.

From our knowledge of primitive races and early civilizations, it would appear that the witch-doctors and magicians, the shamans and priests, were the first 'actors'. These were the tribal 'professionals'. But the players in the old English Mummer Plays, and in the Christian Mysteries, Miracles and Moralities, were more the equivalent of today's local amateurs, out of which secular tradition a kind of professional expertise slowly snowballed. It was the local priest who organized them, directed the proceedings, held the 'book' (as probably the only educated one among them), and, on occasion, took part, for example, as the 'Doctor' (of theology) in *Everyman*; and no doubt as 'God' – at the risk of hubris – when the Mystery cycles indicated His appearance high on the wagon.

Incidentally, the terminology which describes the different types of medieval play usually requires some clarification. As an instance, scholars do not seem to agree on the origin of the word 'Mystery'. In France, where the religious impetus to dramatic expression in the musical elaboration of the liturgy would seem to have started – Limoges provides the earliest known *quem quaeritis* trope, dated between 923 and 934 – the term used for plays dramatizing the biblical stories is *mystères*. This is probably the most commonly accepted meaning of the Mystery cycles in England, where the earliest known texts date from the mid-fifteenth century, although no doubt composed at least a century earlier. They concerned, after all, the mysteries of Creation and Redemption, and in particular, they were most often performed on the Feast of Corpus Christi which celebrates the mystery of transubstantiation in the Eucharist, as well as the mystery of the Risen Lord.

However, many other titles were applied from time to time, and fairly indiscriminately, to these 'theatrical events'. In self-evident Latin they occur thus: *ludus*, *historia*, *officium*, *similitudo*, *miraculum*, *representio*, and most particularly, *misterium*. This last refers to a person's trade or business (as witness Othello's heated command to Emilia to go about her 'mystery'), and has the obvious connection with the fact that it was the various Trades Guilds who were responsible for staging appropriate stories in the cycles. This seems to me the most attractive interpretation. The 'Morality plays' speak for themselves; and 'Miracle plays' are virtually non-starters, since the destructive ardour of the Reformation has left us very few. The Corpus Christi cycles are more often thought of as Mystery plays than Miracles, although it can be argued that they deal with the miracle of the Resurrection. There are French examples in 'The Miracles of Our Lady', a collection of forty plays preserved in two small manuscript volumes dating from 1380.[2] But mostly the genre would have been drawn from the dramatizing of miraculous incidents in the lives of the saints, although the one survivor in an English text, pointed out by John Barton, is not hagiological, being an oddity entitled *The Conversion of Sir Jonathas the Jew by the Miracle of the Blessed Sacrament*, dated 1461.[3]

A separate 'actor type' from those members of Trades Guilds who played in the religious cycles was the individual entertainer.

He was part of that village, town, or court festival strand of development indicated earlier. He was the one with 'a talent to amuse', the clown, the juggler, the buffoon, the 'all-licensed fool' and ballad singer who must always have been there, even through the Dark Ages. Another separate phenomenon was the itinerant 'band of players'. In many cases they had initially come together in the employment and under the protection of royalty or aristocracy to perform Interludes – 'a kind of crude comedy of manners sauced with some not-too-serious social criticism'[4] and no doubt used to relieve the indulgence of a long banquet as the equivalent of modern cabaret. But the band of players found that when not required by their master they could, with permission, tour their entertainments and earn for themselves an all-the-year-round living. Moreover, they began to recognize the value of original and fresh material. Anyone who could write – or purloin – stories for performance found themselves with a saleable product (be it comical, tragical, historical, pastoral, or any of those mixtures of the same outlined by Polonius): collections could be made in the market-place, or the inn courtyard where the booth theatres were set up for profit, and ultimately, even at the entrance doors to James Burbage's first custom-built 'Theatre' in 1576, and its immediate successors. The players found that the product needed some protection as the 'property' of the Company concerned, open as it was to the practice of 'pirating' by a competent shorthand thief in the audience. The need for dramatic copyright had arrived, although incredibly, despite efforts by Dion Boucicault in the mid-nineteenth century, it was 1911 before an act of Parliament established a copyright law.

More and more, in the sixteenth century, these bands of players began to have need, not only of their own more public place in which to perform, but also of their own writers to provide them with material which would enable them to compete with other companies for the public favour. Such writers obviously had to be educated people. Where were they to come from? The aristocratic protectors might occasionally indulge their own dilettante talents for the amusement of their friends or of the Court; but, for the most part, the players would have to rely on the scholars – above all, on witty young men from the universities who were in need of some cash. The written drama, other than Mummer plays and Mysteries, had existed previously, of course, in classical times. The Latin texts of Plautus, Terence and Seneca were used by the schools and universities in the sixteenth century as academic exercises to teach the language and, inevitably, they were sometimes revived by students in theatrical form for their entertainment value. Then some schoolmasters, like Nicholas Udall and William Stevenson, began to write pieces in the vernacular to please themselves, modelled on the ancient rules of dramaturgy, but which nevertheless initiated the genuine native product. The law students and others who followed their example were quick to develop the art of writing plays. Intoxicated with the flowering of the English language, young men like John Lyly, Thomas Nashe, George Peele and Robert Greene created the foundations for the first golden age of our national drama. It was natural for these new writers (Lyly excepted) to become closely involved with the companies of actors for whom they wrote, and even to act themselves; and when the more talented and popular solo clowns and singers also joined with the actors, the two main strands we have mentioned intertwined, and the 'profession', much as we still know it, was born. Also born was the 'star attraction', whether player or writer or both.

In the performances given by medieval city guilds and at country festivals, the 'actors' were not yet separate from their audience as being a different professional breed. They were all merely people or citizens of the same place, who probably knew each other, and were in willing collusion to 'suspend disbelief' and accept the fiction enacted, just as children would play a game. Playacting was part of a social ritual which focused their common experience. As with many amateurs and their audiences today, there would have been little question of criticizing the performances for technique. Their acting, like their speech, was in the direct vernacular of their mutual lives. The idea of 'art' or 'culture' as being separate activities would probably not have occurred. The event was all, and its own justification.

The boy players of Tudor times, however, and those older students at university, were required to declaim their Terence and Seneca with a certain clarity and understanding, and no doubt with appropriate gestures for each emotion and situation. Criticism of the 'correct' way of performing begins to have its place. The willing collaboration of player and audience was not the order of the day here. It became one thing to be examined in the Latin and another to perform the action of a Latin play for the fun of it, commanding an audience. 'Entertainment' had begun to separate itself from mere instruction; and 'technique' from simple accurate repetition.

2

The Elizabethan Actor Turns Pro

For the last half of the sixteenth century, from the indigenous *Gammer Gurton's Needle* (c. 1552) and *Gorboduc* (1562) to *Hamlet* in 1600, the written drama developed at such an explosive pace that within fifty years a degree of human observation and psychological comment had informed it in a way that would not be matched again for nearly three hundred years. Certainly the heights of dramatic art exemplified by Shakespeare – that Everest among the Himalayas of genius represented by Marlowe, Jonson, Webster, Ford, Dekker, Middleton and the rest – could only afterwards descend to the foothills of mock heroics, sentimental moralities and coarse melodramas. There were exceptions, of course, when a few short years at the end of the seventeenth century were enlivened by the wit and perception of such writers as Etherege, Dryden, Wycherley, Congreve and Farquhar; and again towards the end of the eighteenth by the lonely, immaculate sophistication of Sheridan. But for nearly another century still, that was about it. However, it was not so with the actors whose craft had some catching up to do.

By the 1590s the Elizabethan actor had become a true professional. Indeed, he was almost forced to become one by the outstanding quality and fecundity of the Tudor dramatists mentioned above. A leading actor, Edward Alleyn, and his business associate, Philip Henslowe, opened a season at the Rose Theatre in February 1592, in which the company played six days a week for about eighteen weeks, presenting twenty-three different plays and giving a total of one hundred and five performances.[1] What this meant in terms of standards of acting can only be conjectured. Certainly the acting would have been broad in movement and gesture with clearly delineated emotions. Above all, with such a length and wealth of text to learn and deliver, voice and speech had to be powerful, musical and well-articulated. The best actors would be 'naturals', as we term an inborn talent today, who learnt mostly by doing the job; but who would also have the traditions established in the religious cycles to consider, as well as the academic strictures imposed from Latin example, and some would have received an apprenticeship as boy players. These boy players were a tradition in their own right from as early as 1528, when the boys of St Paul's played the Plautian prototype of *The Comedy of Errors* to Wolsey's household, to the end of the century when Rosencrantz's complaint about that 'aery of children, little eyases' shows what a threat they still were to the adult professional companies.

From their inception, the professionals had been in trouble with the City of London magistrates, especially their more puritanical representatives. But in 1583, Elizabeth arranged for the formation and support of her own company of players – the Queen's Men. With such an example and pressure from the Crown, the City had to give in, and in the following year they failed to maintain their previous prohibition against companies performing within the City boundaries (although these would only have been open-air performances in inn yards). Back in 1576, James Burbage had taken the precaution of building his first 'theatre' outside the city walls, in Finsbury Fields (near the current Shoreditch High Street), where Middlesex magistrates were less hostile. This was followed by the Curtain nearby; and then in 1588, Henslowe built the Rose on Bankside, south of the Thames and also outside city jurisdiction. Within ten years it was joined by the Swan and the Globe. It was as well they were all outside the city, for with the plague of 1594 and the obvious dangers in any public gatherings, the magistrates' power to restrict theatrical activities was somewhat revived. However, three years later the Privy Council of the Crown took matters into its own hands and licensed just two companies to perform: the Admiral's Men (with Alleyn) and the Chamberlain's Men (with Richard Burbage, Shakespeare and

Kempe). The former played at the Rose, the latter at the Theatre. Then in December 1598, Cuthbert Burbage (elder brother of Richard by one year) dismantled the old Theatre and rebuilt it as the Globe on Bankside near to the Rose. Henslowe and Alleyn countered the move by building their own new theatre, the Fortune, modelled on the Globe, which they opened in the autumn of 1600. A new play was produced by both companies at an average of one a fortnight. In the three seasons of some 115 playing weeks, the Admiral's Men purchased fifty-eight new plays, of which Dekker's *The Shoemaker's Holiday* is probably the best remembered; the Chamberlain's Men had probably staged as many, including Jonson's *Every Man in His Humour* and many of Shakespeare's earlier works – in fact, more than half his total output had been performed before 1600.[2]

The Chamberlain's Men (who became the King's Men after Elizabeth's death in 1603) continued to act until the theatres were closed in 1642. In the first quarter of the century they rose to unchallenged supremacy over all other companies in London, of which there were by now some twelve or fifteen, continuing to stage Shakespeare and Jonson, among many others. A full-blooded age required full-blooded plays – and actors. The rich Jonsonian 'humours' took more than mere naturalism in their performance (*Volpone* was staged in 1606); and the passionate Revenge tragedies of Webster, Ford, Tourneur, Middleton, et al., if not always more than life-size, certainly expressed their themes with a high intensity of language and action.

In 1609 the King's Men tried a bold experiment which was to have a lasting effect. They took over from one of the rival boy companies (the Children of the Revels) the small, private, indoor Blackfriars Theatre. Entry prices were more expensive, so the broad social spectrum of the Elizabethan audience began to be curtailed. The theatre was more intimate, so the style of acting began slowly to be modified. Moreover, in addition to Shakespeare and Jonson, three new dramatists of exceptional talent now strengthened their repertoire even further. The well-to-do sons of a judge and a bishop respectively, Francis Beaumont (1584–1616) and John Fletcher (1579–1625) jointly produced *Philaster* in 1610, and *The Maid's Tragedy* in about 1611; and the melancholy John Webster (c. 1575–1634), possibly an ex-actor who came late to writing for the stage, had his *The Duchess of Malfi* produced at the Blackfriars in 1614. The new venture was not only an artistic success but a commercial one as well. The company 'took £1000 a winter more at the Blackfriars than they had formerly taken at the Globe'.[3]

Beaumont and Fletcher proved very prolific, with at least fifty-four plays jointly or individually ascribed to them, with possible additional collaboration from Philip Massinger (1583–1640). Apart from their lively burlesque at the Elizabethan stage in *The Knight of the Burning Pestle* (first performed without success by children in 1607 but revived to cheers by the King's Men in 1635), most of their pieces were either trite little comedies, tidy romances or semi-tragedies, all coarsely plotted to send an audience away happy, and which appealed to the shallow side of Court life. So much so, indeed, that Shakespeare and Jonson were ousted as favourites. Plays were no longer being performed for a cross-section of all the people.

Another significant change which came out of the 1609 experiment at the Blackfriars concerned the staging of plays. Inigo Jones (1573–1652), the renowned architect and artist, designed many Court masques; and it seems likely that his scenic innovations of painted drops, wing flats, and eventually a rising and falling curtain framed in a proscenium arch, were employed, if only partially, at the Blackfriars. Being indoors, of course, a means of lighting had also to be considered. The most obvious was candle-light, using chandeliers with, perhaps, footlights and other onstage aids to illumination. Already the rudiments of the nineteenth-century theatre were here, awaiting their further development after 1660.

It is interesting to note, in view of continuing contemporary variations on the Actors Company (first formed by Ian McKellen, Edward Petherbridge, Caroline Blakiston and others in 1972), that at least four of the actors with the King's Men (Richard Burbage, Shakespeare, Heminge and Condell) held shares in their own company. Whilst today's motive is undoubtedly more artistic freedom and 'the right to work', rather than personal commercial gain (indeed, today's actors will be very fortunate if they succeed in breaking even), the 'Sharers' in the seventeenth-century company made fairly substantial sums. It is this business aspect of the actor's profession which eventually provided the principal reason for actors being able to change their social status from rogues to gentlemen, cemented by the knighthood of an affluent Irving, and following him, several other actor-managers. Today there is a school of thought which wants to reverse this historical process, making the actor once again an 'outsider', free to act as a critical burr on the body politic, and be a revolutionary force fermenting in the social *status quo*, rather than an accepted and respected servant of the establishment.

An actor's training in the early seventeenth century still involved an apprenticeship: boys from ten to sixteen years of age were lodged and boarded with an actor who was responsible for teaching them and who also received their pay of about fifteen shillings (Elizabethan money-value) a week.[4] Part-timers, or 'hired men' who played minor roles on a more or less regular basis, received about five to ten shillings a week according to their ability and the amount of work they were given to do. This was quite a good fee when compared to the one shilling a day a carpenter or other artisan might expect.

At the beginning of 1625, the year in which Charles I began his reign, at least thirty-five men and an unknown number of boys were employed by the King's Men, which speaks strongly of their prosperity. But with recurring plagues from 1636 onwards, the continued and extremely vocal opposition of the Puritans, and their ultimate control of Parliament after the outbreak of the Civil War in 1642, 'the devil's chapels in London' were eventually closed. The company of the King's Men was dissolved. The theatres were mostly destroyed. The actors hung on for a while hoping to return to the more harmless business of only killing men in stage tragedies, but with renewed prohibitions in 1647 and 1648, they found themselves 'rogues' once more, and only able to pursue their profession – which they occasionally did – under threat of disturbance by soldiers and consequent imprisonment.

William Beeston was one of those illegally active during the interregnum at a private theatre, the Salisbury Court; and some of the 'old' actors – Michael Mohun, Charles Hart, John Lacy – sometimes tried their luck at one of the last remaining open-air theatres, the Red Bull. Also continuing to be much given to banned theatrical matters was Sir William D'Avenant (1606–68), reputedly Shakespeare's illegitimate son, but more likely his godchild. He was a dramatist who wrote Court masques like those of Ben Jonson, whom he succeeded as Poet Laureate in 1638; and he was knighted by Charles I in 1643 for fighting on the King's side. Somehow he got permission to stage his *The Siege of Rhodes* in 1656, probably by insisting that it was 'musical recitative' and not 'a play'. There appeared in this a Mrs Coleman, wife of the composer, who although she was unable to learn the script and therefore had to read from her copy, must nevertheless be dubbed the 'first English actress'.

3

Enter the Actress:
Restoration Liberation and Eighteenth-
Century Developments in Acting

The history of what happened when Charles II was restored to his throne in 1660 has been widely described. D'Avenant and another courtier and playwright, Thomas Killigrew (1612–83), were licensed to set up two companies and erect two theatres. After diverse temporary accommodation for the companies, Drury Lane was built in 1663 and the Dorset Garden in 1671, providing renewed premises for the remnants of the old acting profession and a solid springboard for newcomers. Among these were Thomas Betterton – destined to become the new star in the firmament – and Underhill, Kynaston and Noakes who were mostly used by D'Avenant, whilst the older actors like Mohun and Lacy were employed by Killigrew. But of course the most powerful new attraction was found with the actresses, also freshly licensed, who now emerged on the stage. Reputedly the first of these 'legitimate' ladies was Mistress Katherine Corey, who is said to have played Desdemona in Killigrew's production of *Othello* at the temporary Theatre Royal in Vere Street. Other actresses who soon became famous – or notorious – were Anne Marshall, Mary Knapp, Mary Saunderson (who married Betterton in 1662) and the ubiquitous Nell Gwynn. Later 'stars' of note were Elizabeth Barry and Anne Bracegirdle.

The audience for these new players was largely an aristocratic one, with a sprinkling of coachmen and city plebeians. The average citizen was still under the influence of Puritan prohibition. It was a decadent kind of theatre, both rough and elegant at once, in which gallants, masked ladies, fops and whores, vied with the actors for attention, and in which only the broadest of acting styles could survive. Heroic verse dramas, brittle mannered comedies full of sexual innuendo, and spectacular scenic effects were the most popular fare. To begin with, the old plays by Shakespeare, Jonson, Webster, Middleton, and Beaumont and Fletcher were revived; but soon there were new names to be seen and heard, illustrious in hindsight, but at the time grist to the theatrical mill and a noisy audience greedy for novelty. Dryden was first on the scene, then Shadwell, Etherege, Wycherley and Otway (*Venice Preserved*, with Betterton and Mrs Barry, was seen at Dorset Garden in 1682). Even a successful new play was lucky to run more than three to six days. A revival would run even less. For the actors this must have meant a hard life, with the endless chore of line-study or revision, with rehearsals every morning, performances every afternoon except Sundays, and sometimes special performances for the Court at night. Alongside their reputation for hard drinking, jealous quarrels, love affairs, and the fashionable casual indifference to any reality but money, it may be judged how much time there was for subtlety in their work. Nevertheless, reputations for compelling histrionic skill were made, and the box-office attraction of the 'star system' was fully established.

With the death of Charles II in 1685, the theatre lost a friend in high places, but its renaissance was to continue. The Restoration period proper had come to an end, but for the purposes of dramatic history it is usually extended to include at least three other playwrights of classic quality: William Congreve (1670–1729), Sir John Vanbrugh (1664–1726) and George Farquhar (1678–1707). Congreve's five plays were all written in the 1690s; Vanbrugh, busy with many architectural and other enterprises, had an equally small output of which only two plays were entirely by himself (*The Relapse*, 1696, and *The Provok'd Wife*, 1697); and Farquhar, who only began to write at the turn of the century, was to die at the age of twenty-nine in dire poverty, having completed six plays, the last of which, *The Beaux' Stratagem*, was performed at the Queen's Theatre in the Haymarket only a few days before his death. (Colley Cibber, possibly enamoured of dramatic coincidence, reports that he died during the third performance – the author's benefit night.)

Yet there was an important sense in which Charles's death did end the theatrical period. Without his personal interest, the close ties between the Court and the stage waned; times were unsettled, audiences fickle, and the actors were constantly at war with the managers, especially 'an old snarling lawyer' named Christopher Rich who gained complete control of Drury Lane by 1693. Betterton had become the great actor figurehead, the Olivier of his day, and he led the actors to form their own company at Lincoln's Inn Fields, where they opened in 1695 with Congreve's *Love for Love*, and remained there successfully until 1705.

But styles were changing, not because of playwrights or actors, but from an increasing demand by the solidly growing merchant and trade class – the new middle-class audiences – who wanted plays closer to their own lives and sentiments. Thomas Shadwell (c. 1642–92) had made an early step in the new direction with a play called *The Squire of Alsatia* in 1688; and Farquhar, of course, took the action of his plays away from London into the provinces where rustic innkeepers and chambermaids, charitable ladies, country gentlemen and justices, farm boys and recruiting sergeants were the natural denizens. Farquhar might have led the changed drama of the eighteenth century to new heights, but with his early death it was not to be. His natural heirs did not arise until Goldsmith with *She Stoops to Conquer* (1773), and Boucicault with *London Assurance* (1841). In the early 1700s it was Colley Cibber (1671–1757) and Sir Richard Steele (1672–1729) who answered the climate of the theatrical times with their sentimental and vaguely moralistic comedies, turning laughter from cynicism to benevolence, and switching brittle social comment into the doldrums of urban respectability.

Acting in the Restoration theatre was essentially declamatory – an oratorical, highly artificial way of speaking, with its own strict rules of delivery, including set gestures for each emotion, especially in the heroic tragedies.[1] Potency of voice was all, or nearly all. Clearly a pleasing and expressive countenance helped, and the precise use of stance and movement showed whether you knew your trade. The closest examples of such a technical attitude today are probably found in the traditional oriental theatre companies; for instance, the Japanese Noh company seen at the National Theatre in 1990. Problems of psychological characterization, so prominent in this century, were virtually unknown; although no doubt the natural instinct of the better performers unconsciously employed observation of human foibles under stress. For the rest it was a matter of speaking the lines as set down rather than attempting to interpret between them. But as Edwin Duerr comments in a dry aside, although the Restoration actor might have failed to fully understand a role, he could nevertheless act it, unlike some modern actors who fail to act a play even though they can understand it perfectly.[2]

It was not that 'naturalism' had not been conceived – both Congreve and Dryden comment on it – but that it was not 'artistic' to be exactly like life. Dialogue had to be 'designed', not merely reproduced; which is why Dryden did not like prose for his serious heroic dramas; and Congreve, though in prose, nevertheless agreed with him that characters should be 'something larger than life', and he wrote scathingly of those crude farces where there was 'imitation of common persons and ordinary speaking'. Neither dramatist would have understood that those few actors – like Mountfort, Hart, Kynaston, a little known comedian called Benjamin Johnson, and one John Verbruggen – who were striving to impersonate characters according to real life, were actually the key to the next two and a half centuries of development in the player's art.[3]

The history of acting in eighteenth-century England (and France) was to become, in fact, only the initial battlefield in the opposition of 'art and nature' (Hamlet's advice to the Players always excepted), and of the concepts of acting as a controlled presentation according to certain accepted conventions or as a 'free' expression of the actor's own being (a kind of 'happening' in which he retains his own identity). The argument still goes on as 'illusion versus reality' and it is still to be finally fought out, although one suspects that we are faced here with two irreducible archetypes which must always co-exist, with mere historical changes of emphasis. The very fact that one has to write 'free' and 'happening' in inverted commas shows that the words are not quite what they seem to infer: there are always the restrictions of form and content and people and places chosen which give the 'free' and 'unrehearsed' intent the lie. The dichotomy of 'art and nature' has always sounded better in theory than it has appeared in practice. It is a poor and vague division of concepts; and when radical desperation has forced the one or the other into single, exclusive expression, the result – as the twentieth-century world of the arts has witnessed frequently – is often absurdity. Further discussion of this central issue – the intriguing dilemma of the artist *vis-à-vis* his work and the world around him – will appear later in the text. For now, it is enough to note that a tentative, although at times passionate, start was made by eighteenth-century actors to give expression to the concept of 'naturalism'; moreover, their efforts were now being eagerly discussed in print. This was an innovation by Steele in his *Tatler* No. 35 of 1709, and others soon followed suit. The Critics had arrived.[4]

Betterton died in 1710, and in that same year an expedient writer, Charles Gildon, published his *Life of Betterton*, through which he hoped to convey to other actors 'such Instructions, that if they are perfectly understood, and justly practised, will add such Beauties to their Performances, as may render his Loss of less Consequence to the Stage'. It is hardly a biography, in fact, as only six from one hundred and seventy-six pages deal with Betterton's life, the rest being devoted to 'Rules' which 'might form a System of Acting'. He claims it as being the first such book in English to lay down such a System. Dull though much of the book must seem to any reader today, telling, for example, that your right and not your left hand should be applied to the bosom when speaking of yourself, its main interest is that it was written during a period of transition, and it is, in fact, a kind of fulcrum point in the theory of acting, summarizing much of the classical techniques of oratory and gesture, taken from ancient Rome (Quintilian's *Institute Oratoria*, c. AD 90) and rediscovered in the sixteenth century, and looking forward to new developments which aimed at keeping naturalism in view to the extent of actually looking 'within to find/Those secret Turns of Nature in the Mind'.[5]

It is an ironic fact that the 'personality actor', the one who is always basically him- or herself in whatever role, and whom we might expect to represent the 'natural' side of the art-versus-nature controversy, was in the eighteenth century the exemplar of the classical modes of haughty speech and exaggerated gesture, with his eyes more likely to be out front with his audience than paying any attention to his fellow actors. Barton Booth (1681–1733) was such a one, who more or less inherited Betterton's mantle, and together with Cibber and Thomas Wilks, managed Drury Lane for some twenty years after his initial success there in Addison's *Cato* in 1713. Another was James Quin (1693–1766). These were ranged against two brilliant new 'character actors', actors whose own personality seemed sunk in that of their roles, and whose naturalness to life brought a tremendous – and lucrative – excitement to the theatre almost precisely together from the year 1741. Their names were Charles Macklin (c. 1699–1797) and David Garrick (1717–79).

Macklin (born McLaughlin) was the senior of the two by some eighteen years, and indeed long outlived Garrick to reach the age of ninety-eight, a most unusual longevity for the times. He served a ten-year apprenticeship in the provinces before coming to Drury Lane; and for another seven years he appeared there with the old-style actor Quin, gradually becoming a favourite with the public. In 1741 he became deputy manager of the theatre and used his new position to propose a revival of *The Merchant of Venice* (Shakespeare's original having been dropped since the beginning of the century in favour of a comic adaptation). Quin was to play Antonio with Macklin as Shylock. At rehearsals, it is said, he merely walked through his part without interpretation, but it also seems that Quin and the other actors got wind of his intention to play Shylock as a serious character, minutely observed to the life from daily visits to the Exchange in the City, and from coffee-house conversations with members of the Jewish race. He was mocked for conceit and presumption but persevered with his project. The production opened on 14 February 1741, and at the age of forty-two or thereabouts, Macklin's naturalistic interpretation became the talk of the town.

Garrick in that year was only twenty-four. He had not done a great deal previously, and although he had had a play of his performed at Drury Lane in the previous year (*Lethe: or Aesop in the Shades*), he could not get work there. But he had been friendly with Macklin and was influenced by the latter's ideas about natural speech and gesture. Garrick worked hard in private to perfect the new technique (also performing at Ipswich under the stage name of Mr Lydall); so that when he went to

Goodman's Fields, a theatre in the suburbs of London, to play
the lead in Cibber's version of *Richard III* on 19 October 1741,
he seemed to spring upon the scene fully-fledged, one of those
'overnight successes' so beloved of journalists and the public. He
followed up Richard with no less than nineteen other leading
roles in the next seven months, mostly widely different in character and age, even playing Lear and a schoolboy on the same
night.[6] He stunned his audiences, not only with versatility and a
truthfulness to life, but also with the dynamic energy with which
he imbued each scene. Macklin thought he rather overdid it, which
was probably right; and poor old Quin said dejectedly: 'If the
young fellow is right, I and the rest of the players have been all
wrong.'[7]

For his next season (1742–3) Garrick was invited to Drury Lane;
in 1746 he moved to Covent Garden; and in the following year
he took over the joint management of Drury Lane. By 1750,
only nine years after his début, Garrick and his style were supreme, remaining so until his retirement in 1776 (having first
disposed of his moiety of the Drury Lane patent for £35,000 to
Sheridan and others – no doubt as carefully planned as his début
and all his roles). He had succeeded in ridding the stage of chairs
for the élite in the audience, and stopping their habit of claiming
money back if they left at the end of the first act. Also he had
replaced the formal drop-cloth and wings with some built-up settings, and had developed the control and subtlety of stage lighting. But for all Garrick's innovations, it must not be imagined
that his 'naturalism' had reached anything like twentieth-century
standards. Art was still 'nature heightened' by a considerable degree
of obvious technique. Actual imitation of everyday speech and
behaviour, 'the art which conceals art', was not due for at least
another century with some of T. W. Robertson's plays, and some
would say not until much beyond that with the advent of *cinéma-
vérité* and television fictional-documentaries like *Cathy Come Home.*

It is difficult to judge which came first in eighteenth-century
experience: the theory or the practice of 'natural' acting. It is
probably true to suggest that they grew together, feeding on each
other. Yet apart from Gildon's remarks and several from Aaron
Hill in the 1730s, the practice of Macklin and Garrick was mostly
ahead of written theory. In the twenty-five years from 1750 to

1775 Duerr notes at least ten works in English, mostly with the stress on elocution and the manner of speech, including essays by Thomas Sheridan, the dramatist's father, and James Boswell.[8] But only the aforementioned Aaron Hill (1685–1749), and an unconnected namesake, John Hill (c. 1716–75), have any importance.

Aaron Hill had been a manager of Drury Lane from 1709 to 1711 when only in his mid-twenties. He had been suggesting that actors 'should not act, but really be' as early as 1716; and he had written one of the first domestic dramas with no attempt at heroics, a piece set in England called *The Fatal Extravagance* (Lincoln's Inn Fields, 1721). He seems to have been somewhat eccentric – he named one of his children 'Julius Caesar' – and was called both 'a bore' and 'a genius'; but he certainly loved the theatre and took great pains to try and reduce 'the players' gross ignorance of their art'. He wanted more feeling and truth from them, and in 1733 he expressed a desire to establish 'an academical theatre, for improving the taste of the stage, and training up young actors and actresses'. In 1740, encouraged by a successful adaptation from Voltaire, he tried formulating his new system of acting in a poem called 'The Actor's Epitome'. But this provided little more than a description of ten different passions. In 1746 he expanded his poem, re-titling it 'The Art of Acting', perhaps trying to keep up with the now famous demonstrations of naturalness by Macklin and Garrick, and explaining that it was 'only the outlines of a sketch of a new system which the author is preparing in prose'. He was as good as his word, producing 'An Essay on the Art of Acting' shortly before his death three years later; but he decided against printing it because he felt that he would now never see an actor better than Garrick to exemplify such a system. It was published posthumously in 1754 and 'variously printed, rearranged and published anonymously until near the end of the nineteenth century'.[9]

Unlike Aaron Hill, John Hill was not a theatre man first and last. His interests ranged very widely indeed, mostly scientific, and he wrote voluminously about them all. He was very much a jack of all trades yet master of none, including acting. His place in the history of the development of acting comes from his being the anonymous translator, in 1750, of Remond de Saint-Albine's *Le Comédien*, first published in Paris in 1747. Then in 1755, doubtless because of *The Actor*'s initial success, he rewrote it, virtually as a new book of his own. He deleted, paraphrased, reorganized and added new material which quoted the English examples of Garrick, Barry, and four leading actresses of the time at Drury Lane. In his Introduction he states that 'The intent of this treatise is to shew what acting truly is; to reduce to rules a science hitherto practised almost entirely from fantasy . . . '[10] He is much concerned that the actor should study to *understand* the playwright's characters and their given circumstances; and that he should develop that *spirit*, or fire, which alone makes a scene 'live' rather than appear acted. Observation and consideration, he says, are the true instructors. In all this, he clearly anticipates a certain amount of Stanislavski and twentieth-century acting principles. But the theory was one thing, the practice another; and it was to take the profession – and the public – many crowded seasons and not a few reversals to the old ways before these theoretical advances were consolidated. Elocution remained the *sine qua non* of acting.

The French theatre was experiencing much the same contrast and argument about acting styles at this time, exemplified in the rivalry of its two leading actresses, Madame Clairon (1723–1803) and Marie-Françoise Dumesnil (1713–1803). Clairon was the classical stylist with well-trained voice and body in perfect control; whereas Dumesnil showed the passion within, and an emotional truth which drew tears rather than mere admiration. Diderot saw that both elements were necessary to the whole actor.[11] The argument was to repeat itself at the end of the nineteenth century in the persons of Bernhardt and Duse.

The last half of the eighteenth century in English theatre certainly belonged to the actors rather than the playwrights – Goldsmith and Sheridan always excepted, although their very limited output was largely within a mere six-year period in the 1770s. In the 1774–5 season at Drury Lane and Covent Garden, ninety-eight full-length plays were presented between them. Actors were very much on the repertory treadmill (in its true English sense) with practically no opportunity to do any study in depth; moreover, they largely rehearsed on their own, regardless of others, and with no artistic director to harmonize the whole. The business of the stage manager was practical, not interpretive. After

Garrick had retired in 1776, there was a six-year low-ebb period with no really outstanding name until the two great Kembles took over: Sarah Kemble (1755–1831), otherwise better known by her married name of Mrs Siddons, and John Philip Kemble (1757–1823), her younger brother.

After a disastrous start to her London career, made at Drury Lane but completely overshadowed by the final blaze of Garrick's farewell performances, Mrs Siddons spent six years in the provinces, chiefly at Bath, forging her tremendous potential ability into becoming one of the greatest English tragic actresses. In 1782, aged twenty-seven, she was invited back to Drury Lane by Sheridan and this time, despite only two company rehearsals of Southerne's *The Fatal Marriage* (1694), she triumphed in the role of Isabella, a character affording good opportunities for displaying the full gamut of suffering and madness. She followed up her success at once with other tragic leads such as Jane Shore and Belvidira in *Venice Preserved*, until in 1785 she reached the apogee of her talent with a performance of Lady Macbeth, which drew more from the role than had ever been seen before. In her remaining seventeen years at Drury Lane (although she continued to act at intervals until 1812), she could always be relied upon to fill the house with her Lady Macbeth, the supreme accomplishment among the seventy-four other roles which she interpreted during her career there. Today we should almost certainly place her acting style in the category denigrated as 'ham', relying as it did on precisely designed elocution and gesture; but like Dumesnil in France, Siddons brought also the added sensibilities of fine intelligence and passionate feelings that surpassed the technical manner of expression, creating a living experience of the text. She was, in fact, a demonstration of Diderot's 'paradox of acting' – the whole artist who combines finesse of technique with profound emotional power.[12]

Those who saw and heard Mrs Siddons would not forget her as easily as they might her good-looking brother, who was all show and little matter. John Philip Kemble had a beautiful voice by all accounts, but also a monotonous and formal one, and although he always made sense of what he said, he rarely seems to have made it exciting. He approached acting rather as though it was mathematics: indeed, Hazlitt called him the 'Euclid of the stage'.[13] The 'grand manner' was all, though it was as static with him as it was dynamic with his sister. But nevertheless, the public seemed to like him – his was 'high art', however unnatural – and in 1788 he was appointed manager at Drury Lane. Between them, the two Kembles reigned supreme, reversing the movement towards naturalism taken earlier in the century, and reviving the declamatory art of Booth and Quin – with, perhaps, some finer and more intelligent feeling – as though it represented an advance upon the 'unartistic', easygoing ways of Garrick. In 1794 they were joined by a third member of the family, a younger brother of considerable charm, Charles Kemble (1775–1854), who played the romantic juveniles. In 1803, all three moved over to Covent Garden as part-proprietors, and in 1817 Charles inherited the management of that theatre. The fact that he did not do very well there was largely due to the arrival three years earlier at Drury Lane of 'the sun's bright child', the actor whose flamboyant genius provided the English theatre with one of its most enduring legends.

4

The Early Nineteenth Century: Acting in the Grand Manner

Edmund Kean (c. 1789–1833) learnt the business of acting from the age of ten when he recited in public. From 1804 until 1813 he was a strolling player in the provinces; then in January 1814, aged about twenty-six, he burst on the Drury Lane stage after only one rehearsal with a fiery, artful portrayal of Shylock which astounded the audience every bit as much as Macklin's version seventy-three years earlier. Once again, a new and highly personal dynamism was to blow away the cobwebs which had gathered round the careful formalities of style to which theatre connoisseurs had grown accustomed. The Kembles were still respected, but critics like Hazlitt – of whom it was said that Kean was scarcely less of a godsend than he was to Kean – were forced to admire the originality and force, combined with occasional naturalness and profound flashes of illumination, which Kean brought to such roles as Sir Giles Overreach (in Massinger's *A New Way to Pay Old Debts*) and the major Shakespearian leads. Drury Lane, which had been at the point of financial collapse, revived its fortunes with an average attendance of 2305 per night for the first 68 nights Kean performed. As a well-known cartoon of the time showed, he metaphorically carried the theatre on his back. His work was highly individual and passionate, and although he lacked Kemble's intelligence and grace he prepared his cunning effects as carefully and was by no means the impulsive improviser some stories are inclined to suggest. He provided his audiences with a revelatory experience which they did not forget, and that, after all, is what gives the so-called ephemeral art of theatre its true significance. But his gypsy nature and licentious ways led to social ostracization, and eleven years after his London début he had to flee to the United States in 1825 for an extended tour. Things were never quite the same after his return.

The early-nineteenth-century theatre was not conducive to the development of naturalism in acting. The size of the principal theatres had grown ever larger. Covent Garden's capacity was now 3103 and Drury Lane's 3611 – 'a wilderness of a place' as Mrs Siddons called it. Only the broadest acting style could hope to 'carry' in such places. Lighting had improved with the introduction of gas-jets in 1817, but although they could be manipulated in strength, they must have created an ugly 'unreal' glare which demanded much compensatory make-up, thus adding a further distancing from naturalism. The smaller 'illegitimate' theatres were actually denied the case of natural dialogue altogether, as the two London patent or legitimate playhouses mentioned above retained their theoretical monopoly until the 1843 Act for Regulating Theatres. The illegitimate auditoriums were obliged to employ only placard expressions and song-lyrics to make their dramatic points. Hence the rise of popular 'melo-drama' which audiences in the first half of the century so enjoyed, and which provided stiff opposition for any natural art of the theatre. Ironically, it was in scenic effects that naturalism found its favoured development, and there was little that a naturalistic actor could do against the appeal of such set pieces as 'The Storming of the Bastille' or 'The Battle of Trafalgar' – except overplay to regain attention!

Nevertheless, it was Kean's great rival and Victorian successor William Charles Macready (1783–1873) who managed to preserve something of the integrity of tragic acting in a studied, intelligent, unified and truthful – if not entirely natural – style. He believed that there was 'only one best' way, and laboured to achieve it by more frequent rehearsal than was customary at the time. His is the famous retort to the actor who said it would be all right on the night: 'Sir, if you cannot do it in the morning, you cannot do it at night.' He believed that concentration rather than mere exhibition 'told' in an actor: and of course he was right. Apart from the obligatory Shakespeare, he also appeared in contemporary plays, one of the most durable of which in this shallow dramatic age was Bulwer Lytton's *Money* (1840), something of a prototype for later work by Robertson, Jones, Pinero, Granville Barker and Galsworthy. Macready was a cross-grained, strangely unwilling leader of his profession. In February 1851, having been vociferously acclaimed for his farewell performances at the Haymarket of Lear and Macbeth, he wrote in his *Journal* (edited by J. C. Trewin, Longmans, 1967) a final 'Thank God' to his acting career and lived quietly for another twenty-two years.

The general debility of drama in the first half of the nineteenth century was not for want of playwrights trying to be great. The trouble, as Allardyce Nicoll pointed out, was Shakespeare. Nearly all the great romantic poets – Byron, Keats, Shelley, Wordsworth, Coleridge – saw themselves inheriting his mantle, so that his example proved the greatest hindrance to the development of prose drama. But their efforts were virtually all closet-dramas, to be read rather than acted. There was much more true theatricality in the numerous hack melodramas, nautical romances, Gothic horror tales, farces and spectacles of the day than in these heavy-handed imitations in the death-moulded style of another age. There were a handful of playwrights who tried to find a middle course between the two. Lytton was one, Knowles another, but the most notable was Dion Boucicault (1822–90), a prolific actor-dramatist whose long career was divided between London and New York, and the second of whose plays, *London Assurance* (1841), brought him an immediate and justified success. Its long-run revival in London during 1970–72 was proof of its lasting quality (and of the excellence of Ronald Eyre's subtle adaptation, which places it in a tradition of English comedy between the Restoration, Sheridan and Wilde). There was a further successful revival in 1989 in a production by Sam Mendes, with Paul Eddington and Angela Thorne in the roles of the foppish Sir Harcourt Courtly and the exuberant Lady Gay Spanker. The play was originally written to commission in only thirty days, and in his Preface Boucicault regrets that 'his first appearance before the public had to be in this out-of-breath style; but I saw my opportunity at hand – I knew how important it was not to neglect the chance of production – the door was open – I had a run for it, and here I am'.[1]

London Assurance was not only an auspicious chance for Boucicault but also for its commissioners, whom it rescued – at

least temporarily – from debt. These were the then joint managers of Covent Garden, Madame Vestris (1797–1856) and her
second husband, Charles Mathews, the younger (1803–78), who
played Dazzle in the piece. Madame Vestris's first marriage at
the age of sixteen to one Armand Vestris had folded in 1820
when he left her, but she continued to be known as 'Madame' to
her companies, whom she ruled with a rod of iron. After an
early career as a popular singer in light opera, and several successful
years in Paris, she found her *métier* back in London, where she
not only played burlesque and the fashionable ladies of high comedy,
but also demonstrated a firm talent for management. She had
good taste in costume and a flair for contrasting the stilted farces
of James Planché (1796–1880), who, like Boucicault, wrote many
pieces for her, with carefully furnished sets in a realistic manner.
London Assurance had one of the first recorded box-sets, complete with part-ceiling, and also amazed its first audiences with
real instead of stage properties. In 1831 Vestris opened the small
Olympic Theatre, determined to raise standards in the 'illegitimate' theatre. Mathews was one of her actors there who showed
'charm and delicacy' in comedy roles; she married him in 1838.
They went together to New York, then returned to Covent Garden where they staged some brilliant productions, including *London Assurance* in 1841. Later they moved to the Lyceum, but
despite her apparently fascinating personality and ambitious scenic innovations their seasons led to financial disaster, in the midst
of which she died. Mathews' career continued with distinction
for many years, but he lacked her pioneering spirit. Her memory
was revived in 1973 with the publication of a luxuriously produced and illustrated full-length biography by Clifford J. Williams.

For all the ideals toward a new realism initiated by the Vestris
management, acting for the most part remained a matter of 'the
beautiful tones and correct gestures taught at the newly founded
Musical and Dramatic Academy in 1846'.[2] Before looking further to trace the slow emancipation of 'natural' acting from its
'artistic' strait-jacket after 1850 in England, it is worthwhile glancing
briefly across the Channel to what was happening in France between 1825 and 1850, and particularly at the formulations for a
science of expression made by François Delsarte (1811–61). France,
like England, had been torn between the 'old-fashioned' classical

mode of playwrighting and acting, and the new styles. Eugène Scribe (1791–1861) had grasped the idea that audiences would enjoy well-told stories with topical ditties and plenty of surprises and suspense – in fact, a thoroughly 'theatrical' entertainment – and the French had a word for it: vaudeville. Vaudeville was a kind of French equivalent to our own 'illegitimate' theatre of the time, later to be described as Music Hall, and surviving, of course, in the USA where it defines the genre, along with Variety. Scribe devised a formula technique for the pieces of early vaudeville, starting with a situation and simply fitting characters and complications to it, not unlike the improvised tradition of the Italian Comedy or *commedia dell'arte,* though probably without the latter's performing genius. By 1827 Scribe had written nearly a hundred such pieces, and his output would extend to nearly five hundred before the end of his life. He became a kind of play-factory for the stages of France; and by way of the ubiquitous advertisement 'adapted from the French', also for the stages of England. Not surprisingly, his pieces were trashy and mechanical, but they were also a dominating influence.

If Scribe could do this for the writing of plays, why should Delsarte not evolve similar scientific and 'sure-fire' procedures for the business of acting? Disappointed with his own faulty training, in 1839 he put together his first course in 'Applied Aesthetics' by which physical and vocal expression was precisely codified. He was particularly fond of dividing everything into trinities. Art is the revelation of life, mind and soul; the artist must move, interest and persuade; his means are language, thoughts and gesture; the actor represents man in relation to nature, humanity and divinity; and so on. E. T. Kirby keeps with the sacred trinity when he finds three frontiers of actor training in Delsarte's system: 'rhythmic gesture; kinesics, or the science of body language; and semiology, the science of signs'.[3] Delsarte's organized approach to acting has always found its most avid support in the USA, ahead of, and along with the Stanislavski-derived 'Method'. The acting profession as a whole, however, has found such systems less appealing, not to say daunting and restrictive. They are fine for giving teachers something to teach, but less useful to the performer in action. Nevertheless, Delsarte had some good things to say, some of them a long way ahead of their time, even to the point of anticipating Grotowski. For example: 'Nothing is more deplorable than a gesture without a motive'; the preliminary condition for all expression is flexibility (relaxation), and again, 'harmonic poise of bearing' (posture); in stillness or in motion, all theatrical presentation is a sign to be interpreted. His influence in the field of eurythymics and creative dance in this century has been extensive, although little acknowledged.

Back in England, another mid-century influence who has been done less than justice, according to Alec Clunes,[4] was Samuel Phelps (1804–78). As an actor he had the usual provincial apprenticeship advancing to Shakespearian leads at London's Haymarket, and playing Othello to Macready's Iago at Covent Garden. Then in 1843, with the abolition of the monopoly for the two 'legitimate' theatres, he took over the management of Sadler's Wells, and during the next nineteen years, battling hard against the odds, he produced all but four of the Shakespearian canon with care and imagination. His work at the Wells did much to redeem the English stage from its overall triviality, and a number of young actors whom he trained there were later to boast of the fact and themselves continue the tradition which he started.[5]

Another actor-manager who reached the head of his profession in the 1850s was Charles Kean (1811–68). At the small Princess's Theatre, then near Oxford Circus, he initiated a lavish style of pictorial realism and historical accuracy not only in Shakespeare, with a famous *Midsummer Night's Dream* of 1856, but in all types of drama from Sheridan's *Pizarro* to Byron's *Sardanapalus*. His father, the great Edmund Kean, having been only too conscious of his own untutored start in life, had sent him to Eton with hopes of something better than a stage career. But by 1833, Charles was at Drury Lane playing Iago to his father's Othello. Indeed, it was the latter's final appearance, for during the performance on 25 March he faltered and fell saying 'I am dying. Speak to them, Charles.' He survived another two months to die in his home at Richmond on 15 May. Charles had married Ellen Tree (1806–80), and together as joint-rulers at the Princess's they continued the reforms in production started by Garrick, Kemble and Macready; and at the same time, being affected by their contemporary, Phelps. One of their most significant innovations, at least historically, was 'the long run'. It meant that actors now had to learn to sustain the freshness of their work, and it also limited them in the number of their portrayals each season. In 1856, Mrs Kean gave the eight-year-old Ellen Terry her first engagement as the boy Mamillius in *The Winter's Tale*. Ellen Terry recalled in her memoirs the infinite pains given to every detail. Charles Kean was putting his classical education and refined taste to good theatrical account, and he was strongly backed by the fiery personality and industry of his wife. 'Rehearsals lasted all day, Sundays included, and when there was no play running at night, until four or five the next morning. I don't think any actor in those days dreamed of luncheon.'[6]

After 1850 the playwright slowly began to regain importance alongside the actor, even if the actor-manager did remain the controlling influence until well into the twentieth century. In 1852, Tom Taylor (1817–80) had collaborated with novelist Charles Reade (1814–84) on the popoular *Masks and Faces* (about the celebrated eighteenth-century actress Peg Woffington). Taylor wrote over a hundred well-constructed pieces of which *The Ticket of Leave Man* (1863) is still good enough to be occasionally revived. But it is to T. W. Robertson (1829–71) that we look as something of a nineteenth-century watershed in the revival of English drama. He is mostly recognized today as the 'Tom Wrench' of Pinero's *Trelawny of the 'Wells'*, written over a quarter of a century after his death. Robertson started as a child actor and jack of all trades in the old theatre traditions, wrote a few unsuccessful pieces, then achieved his first real fame at thirty-five with *David Garrick* (1864), which oddly enough, given its subject, was adapted from a French original. It contained elaborate descriptions for scenery and costumes together with copious stage directions. The actors were given specific instructions instead of being left, as was more usual, to their own devices. In fact, it is as much as a stage manager-cum-director as for being a playwright that Robertson is a significant figure. At the time of his first success, before he joined the Bancrofts who were to consolidate his ideas and fame, he wrote:

The Stage Manager is the man who should direct everything behind the scenes. He should be at one and the same time a poet, an antiquarian, and a costumier; and possess sufficient authority, from ability as well as office, to advise with a tragedian as to a disputed reading, to argue with an armourer as to the shape of a shield, or to direct a wardrobe-keeper as to the cut of a mantle. He should . . . be capable of handling crowds and moving masses as a major-general. He should possess universal sympathies, should feel with the sublime, and have a quick perception of the ludicrous. Though unable to act himself, he should be able to teach others, and be the finger-post, guide, philosopher and friend of every soul in the theatre. . . . Above all, he should be endowed with a perfect command of his own temper, and the power of conciliating the temper of others. The art of stage-management consists chiefly in a trick of manner that reconciles the collision of opposing personal vanities.[7]

This is Craig's 'ideal stage-manager' as he was to describe him in 1905;[8] it is how Peter Goffin saw him in an excellent little book published in 1953 called *The Art and Science of Stage Management*; and, of course, it gives – over a century ahead of its time – today's job description for an Artistic Director whether of the National Theatre or the smallest fringe company.

Tom Robertson was more than fortunate to have his next play, *Society* (1865), accepted by the actress-manager Marie Wilton (1839–1921) who had just opened the small Prince of Wales's Theatre, charmingly refurbished from its old nickname as the 'Dust Hole' in the unfashionable quarter near Goodge Street (formerly the old Queen's Theatre, and later, the Scala). She let him rehearse the play himself. In the company were her future husband, Squire Bancroft (1841–1926), and John Hare (1844–1921), and between them, for the next five years, they finally established a naturalistic school of acting and production in England – popularly labelled 'the cup and saucer drama', because it largely took place in the domestic milieu of society, and used real stage-properties. But it was still far from the fourth-wall realism of television and much of today's 'behaviouristic' acting. Pinero noted in 1929 that the Bancrofts did not confuse an *imitation* of life with a *reproduction* of it: 'the teacups and saucers were handled in such a way as to be entertaining to the occupants of the back row of the gallery'. In short, however natural, theatre and reality were not to be confused. *Society* became the talk of the town and was revived by the Bancrofts no less than three times. It was followed in 1856 by *Ours*, revived five times, then in 1867 by *Caste*, his best-known piece which is still revived from time to time today. *Play* in 1868 was less successful, but *School* in 1869 beat all the Bancrofts' previous performance totals. Finally, *M.P.* in 1870, with a mere single run of 156 nights, brought the grand total of performances by the Bancrofts of Robertson's plays to an impressive three thousand in six years. The Bancrofts were the first management to schedule regular mid-week and Saturday matinées. Robertson, who was allowed to 'stage-manage' all his own plays, became virtually the first of that new and separate breed in the modern theatre, the Artistic Director, implying the greater overall responsibilities now assumed by the formerly humble position of Stage Manager. He died at the early age of forty-two in 1871.

5

The Fin de Siècle Foundations of Modern Acting

The modern theatre was born, in the most literal sense, during the third quarter of the nineteenth century. Only Henrik Ibsen (1828–1906), as ever, was ahead of everyone else, and had written his first play, *Catilina*, by 1850. Strindberg was born in 1849, Pinero in 1855, Shaw and Wilde and Freud in 1856, Brieux and Antoine in 1858, Duse and Lady Gregory in 1859, Chekhov and Barrie in 1860, Hauptmann and Appia and Maeterlinck in 1862, Stanislavski in 1863, Yeats in 1865, Galsworthy and Pirandello in 1867, Gorky in 1868, Gordon Craig in 1872, Reinhardt in 1873, Maugham in 1874 and Copeau in 1878. In glancing through those names one cannot help being struck by the tremendous imaginative, emotional and intellectual range which they represent. They were destined collectively to infuse into the largely moribund drama of the nineteenth century a force and a power which would sweep the theatre – and, of course, actors with it – into the twentieth century with a challenging artistry, at once subtle and brash, comforting and disturbing, poetic and realistic. The repercussions of the explosion largely detonated by these names around the 1890s would last half-way into the new century. Their proselytizing and civilized influence was to mean that much more intelligence and sensitivity and cultural dedication than ever before would eventually be demanded of the 'straight' acting profession which, with a few star exceptions, had not until then been renowned for such qualities. Although it is quite arguable, even today, that an actor does not need to be brainy to be an expert performer (Shaw, for one, was devastating on the subject), nevertheless the actor's personal understanding and the degree of informed approach to his material will obviously be relevant and show in his work. Acting, by reason of its processes, is ultimately the character of the actor being made manifest.

However, the critic G. M. Lewes (1817–78), like Shaw something of an actor manqué, wrote with gentle remonstration that he could not bring himself 'to place the actor on a level with the painter or the author'; and that an audience is often applauding the part rather than the acting of it. 'They are apt to credit the actor with a power of intellectual conception and poetic creation to which he has really a very slight claim, and fail to recognize all the difficulties which his artistic training has enabled him to master.'[1] In his book *On Actors and the Art of Acting* (1875), Lewes analyses that special training; and he does it so well that in the historical perspective of acting theory he has something like the last word, despite the subsequent and better-known formulations of Stanislavski, Brecht, Saint-Denis et al. Contemporary books on acting contain no contradiction of Lewes's three main points. These are (1) that 'the very separation of Art from Nature involves ... calculation'; or, in other words, all art involves deliberate selection from life, and acting is no exception. The actor's sensitivity 'must tell him when he has hit upon the right tone and right expression, which must first be suggested to him by his own feelings. In endeavouring to express emotion, he will try various tones, various gestures, various accelerations and retardations of the rhythm; and during this tentative process his vigilant discretion will arrest those that are effective and discard the rest.' (2) Acting is symbolical, not actual. 'We do not admire a man for being old, but we may admire him for miming age.' In acting, we may admire the technique of communication separately from the communication itself; hence great performances may be given in bad plays, as has often been the case. Finally, as a corollary to the last point, Lewes adds (3) that because acting 'is a representative art, it cannot be created by intelligence or sensibility (however necessary these may be for the perfection of the art), but must always depend upon the physical qualifications of the actor, these being the means of representation', and particularly upon the 'primary requisite' of 'knowing how to speak'.[2]

This last point is surely fundamental, and Schools of Acting of whatever theoretical persuasion ignore it at their peril – or rather, at the peril of the public. The argument of the documentary-style director that the average person rarely 'speaks well' does not alter the prime requisite of clarity in communication. A regional accent, a foreign accent, a 'bad' accent, will be used by a good actor to reveal rather than disguise the character speaking. An audience lacking subtitling to interpret the action is a bored audience; and, indeed, a cheated one. It is sometimes assumed that truth of thought and feeling is sufficient to make a good actor. It is not. There is, of course, a case for the director of *cinéma-vérité* who not only prefers but requires people, children and animals simply to *be* themselves, as a supply of imagery and sound for the camera where later editing will contribute the artistry. There is a sense in which we are all actors unobserved, or would-be actors being observed. But the true actor, the artist-craftsman, the professional, must have in addition the trained and expert control of his equipment – bodily, vocal and imaginative – in order to express, *when it is required*, any aspect of true thought or feeling which all can recognize. Lewes rightly concludes that not only Shakespeare and other highly-mannered styles but also in even the most 'natural acting', in the most exactly simulated behaviour, the actor must still 'select and heighten' – and it is for his tactful judgement to determine how much.

Until quite far into the twentieth century (in fact, until the general development of radio, film and television – although some would say with considerable justification that these 'mechanical arts' made no basic difference), there is not much to be added to Lewes's analysis of acting as a solo craft. But in 1875 there was still much to happen in the development of ensemble work in the theatre. The rise of the producer or director, and the ever-improving techniques of set building, lighting and sound effects were to become an increasing challenge to the 'natural actor' to adapt accordingly, and in particular to be less selfish *vis-à-vis* other actors and the play as a whole.

A man who loathed the star-system as it was favoured in nineteenth-century Europe was Duke George II of Saxe-Meiningen (1826–1914). In 1866, when he became head of his family at the age of forty, he decided to improve the standard of plays at his court theatre. He had admired the productions of Charles Kean in London and now felt that he could do even better. He was very serious – in the German fashion – about 'the quality of actuality' in plays, especially the plays of the old standard repertoire. He had little interest in new ideas, new drama, or indeed the new 'natural acting'; his *métier* was to be found in exactly detailed staging, copying life at all points, and in the management of crowd scenes. He seems to have largely ignored the interpretation of theme and character, with the result that his productions *looked* natural but did not *sound* it. However, after eight years of careful preparation, four on his own and four with his company under the direction of Ludwig Chronegk (1837–91), he finally felt that he had achieved his aim and sent the Meininger, as the company became known, on an extended tour of Europe and Russia. Between 1874 and 1890 (when Chronegk's collapse from overwork virtually meant the collapse of the company) the Meininger had a sensational success wherever they appeared. After all, their painstaking work was *seen* for its effect, which has always appealed to audiences more than 'the art which conceals art'. In 1881 the Meininger gave fifty-six performances in London which helped consolidate those standards of naturalistic staging initiated in the late 1860s by Robertson and the Bancrofts. It also added to them the virtue of disciplined ensemble playing – the idea of company rather than individual stardom taking precedence – which was new to actors and audiences alike.

When the Meininger paid a second visit to Moscow in 1890 they were seen by the 27-year-old Konstantin Stanislavski, who was strongly influenced by them. He may also have seen a brochure published in Paris that same year called *Le Théâtre Libre*; at any rate, he had certainly heard about and been impressed by reports of the work being done by the theatre company of that name. It had been founded in 1887 by André Antoine, then a brilliant amateur like Stanislavski himself. It already had an off-shoot in Germany – the Freie Bühne set up by Otto Brahm in Berlin in 1889. Then in 1891, in England, the Dutchman J. T. Grein (1862–1935) set up the Independent Theatre company which gave performances of Ibsen's *Ghosts*, Zola's *Thérèse Raquin*, and in December 1892, Shaw's first play, *Widowers' Houses*. Stanislavski followed suit for Russia in 1898 when, together with Nemirovich-

Danchenko, he founded the Moscow Art Theatre.

Antoine, it may thus be seen, was a truly seminal influence on the development of modern acting, with his firm belief in the prime virtues of naturalism and truth in the theatre. The actors of the Théâtre Antoine (as the Théâtre Libre became known in 1897) did not 'recite' their parts, they 'lived' them. Moreover, every scene had its own rhythm to be found, subordinate in turn to the rhythm of the whole play. Some years later, Stanislavski was to write in similar terms. Antoine, too, had been impressed by the ensemble playing of the Meininger whom he had seen in Brussels in 1888, and saw the highest ideal of the actor as being found in such playing, in which the actor was 'a marvellously tuned instrument' and part of an orchestra conducted by the director. 'It is sufficient for him to have a purely physical and technical training, to make his body, face and voice more supple; and an intellectual training that will permit him to understand simply what the author would have him express.'[3] There is a touch of the oriental attitude to training there; and Shaw would certainly have gone along with it.

Before the end of the nineteeneth century, at least one actor-manager in England, Wilson Barrett (1847–1904), had tried going the whole hog and reduced Antoine's naturalism to its logical absurdity by employing real people instead of actors to appear as extras in one of his productions. The painful cry of the Player in Stoppard's *Rosencrantz and Guildenstern Are Dead* comes to mind: 'We're actors – the opposite of people!' But Wilson Barrett's experiment was an exception. It was soon argued that verisimilitude for its own sake was an empty exercise. Even the most naturalistic of plays required the art which conceals art, rather than actuality. Actors should search for a truthful interpretation, then having found it, they should 'transform their awareness of it into the theatrical'.[4] Moreover, naturalism was clearly not the only mode with which the 'classical' actor had to come to terms: from Greek tragedy to French farce, from heroic verse to the poetic mysticism of Maeterlinck and Yeats, there was a whole spectrum of dramatic styles which required the actor and his new colleague, the director, to be informed about in their historical context, and yet to make a choice. That choice remains the same today as it was at the end of the last century. Namely, whether to be presentational about *acting* a role, or representational, giving the illusion of *being* that role. Ironically, because the former is in a sense more honest than the latter, today's ultimate in 'naturalism' is for the actor to appear *as an actor*, alongside, as it were, his role. Brecht, Beck's Living Theatre company, Handke and Stoppard, have all followed this stratagem in some of their work 'to get nearer the truth'. Even in February 1992, the argument continued among critics. The superb revival of *Uncle Vanya* at the Cottesloe, with Ian McKellen as Vanya and Antony Sher as Astrov, caused Charles Spencer of the *Daily Telegraph* to complain that he felt he was watching individual actors *acting* and being brilliant, rather than characters *living* on stage in ensemble truthfulness. Other critics saw that truthfulness made manifest in courageous artistry stretched to its creative limits. You pay your money and take your choice.

On the whole, the star names of the 1890s chose the traditional mode of acting, that is, they 'presented' a role. Despite a reputation for 'realistic touches', Irving and Mrs Campbell were emphatically theatrical; and Forbes-Robertson, Martin Harvey, Benson and Tree, hardly less so. The controlling influence of a 'commercial theatricality' by the English actor-managers remained till the end of the century and considerably beyond, whatever the creeping insurgence of Ibsen, Strindberg, Wedekind and Chekhov from over the horizon might portend. As for that cheeky socialist upstart Shaw, the ex-critic who knew he could do better than what he saw from the stalls, he was a law unto himself – and would remain so for another fifty years.

Henry Irving (1839–1905), by sheer determined application – for none at first could have seemed less likely to succeed as an actor – became one of the great celebrities of the Victorian age. He first attracted attention in London in 1866, but had to wait until 1870 for his first real success as Digby Grant in *Two Roses* by James Alberry.[5] Then in 1871, at the age of thirty-three, he thrilled fashionable London society with his performance of Mathias in *The Bells* (adapted by Leopold Lewis). Irving never looked back. In 1878 he took over management of the Lyceum Theatre, where for the next twenty-one years, with Ellen Terry (1847–1828) as his leading lady, he maintained a high standard of production (although mostly ignoring any original new plays). Their partnership provided a constant topic for the talk of the town. His own acting never lacked many critics, but such was his prestige and dedicated integrity that, in 1895, he became the first actor to be knighted. This marked a watershed in the acceptance of the acting profession into respectable social status, instead of their long historical association with 'rogues and vagabonds'. Irving's last London production was Sardou's *Dante* in 1903.

Other great actor-managers of the late Victorian period included Johnston Forbes-Robertson (1853–1937) who had worked with Phelps, the Bancrofts and Irving, and who was reputedly one of the finest-ever Hamlets, but in the sing-song tradition of voice soon to become virtually extinct; Herbert Beerbohm Tree (1852–1917), a bizarre personality, with a romantic panache much beloved by his public; and George Alexander (1853–1918), for twenty-seven years the fashionable, polished, essentially commercial tenant of the St James's Theatre (sadly itself destroyed, despite objections from the House of Lords but not the Commons, by ruthless commercial interests in 1957). It was at the St James's under Alexander that the meteoric and flamboyant genius of Oscar Wilde (1856–1900) had two of his four great Society comedies performed – *Lady Windermere's Fan* in 1892 and *The Importance of Being Earnest* in 1895. Alexander and the other actor-managers, now only legends of the green room, bring the historical perspective of acting to its twentieth-century focus. Ellen Terry continued to perform until 1925; Benson survived in retirement till 1939, Mrs Campbell till 1940, and Martin-Harvey till 1944.

Before finally leaving the nineteenth century, it should be noted that it was in 1891 that actors first organized themselves as a trade union to try and protect their interests, particularly against managers who absconded with the box-office takings on tour. However, the British Actors' Association, as it was then called, was not very effective, despite practical co-operation from the socialist Granville-Barker in 1907. It was not until 1929 that the present British Actors' Equity Association came into being. Nevertheless, it was in the 1890s that the divisive philosophy which undermines the solidarity of Equity even today was first sown. Frank Benson and Robert Courtneidge, the earliest proposers of the Actors' Association, saw it less as a trade union than 'a co-operation between managers and artists'. It was only in this way that they could persuade Irving, and through him most other leading players, to support the project. It aimed to be the voice of the profession – both managers and actors – on legislative matters; and, it is true, to improve working conditions and dressing-room facilities. But essentially, it saw itself as confirming the status of a profession, akin to medicine and the law, rather than actors being workers in a capitalist industry along with miners and railwaymen. This dichotomy of class and of the nature of the actor's employment has been a continuing rift throughout Equity's history.[6]

It was in 1894 that the French actor Constant-Benoît Coquelin (1841–1909) published the final, reworked and enlarged version of his book about *The Art of the Actor* in which he put forward the proposition that the characteristic gift of the actor is to be at once an 'observed' and 'observing' self. The essential dualism in the nature of acting is defined by being private in public. 'Character,' says Coquelin, 'is the basis of everything in acting' and 'the inward study of characterization the most important of all studies'.[7] One may hazard whether the actors at ancient Delphi ever made the connection between their art and the motto reputedly emblazoned in the anteroom to the Temple of Apollo: 'Know thyself'. In any event, and at any time, the actor exhibits his own nature in re-creating a character for the stage. His task is not so much to 'live the part' as to make the part live through him. The creator and creation are inextricably mixed.

Mention of Coquelin's book prompts me to note some others published towards the end of the century: Gustave Garcia's *The Actor's Art* (London, 1882) attempted a rigid 'scientific' analysis 'incorporating his version of Françoise Delsarte's system' of gestures and expression to convey emotion; William Archer's *Masks or Faces?*, also published in 1888, was initially fired by 'a hot debate' between Irving and Coquelin on the relationship between the role played and the actor's personal involvement with it (in which Boucicault and a Dutch actor, Bouwmeester, also joined in); Percy Fitzgerald supported the 'old school' against the new 'gross realism' in his *The Art of Acting* (1892); J. A. Hammerton's *The Actor's Art* (1897) took a broader view in reporting the diverse views then current among leading players.[8]

A final footnote to the nineteenth century on this subject is offered by the critic C. E. Montague, when he wrote in 1899 that 'the truth of art is to be true less to facts outside you than to yourself stirred by the facts'.[9] From this it may be seen that current theories on acting are not quite so new as some might suppose.

PART TWO: The Present

He who would understand theatre at this moment cannot stand only on the stage. He must have one foot in the theatre, one outside.

Mordecai Gorelik, *New Theatres for Old* (1940)

6

The Edwardian Theatre and the
Establishment of Professional Training

As a term, 'Edwardian Theatre', like the 'Restoration Theatre', stretches beyond its strictly historical dates. Edward VII, 'King Teddie', reigned from 1901 until 1910; the theatrical period may be regarded as covering the years from 1890 until 1914. But in truth it goes far beyond that, reaching perhaps twenty years into the reign of George V, taking us to 1930. Allardyce Nicoll discerned 'an integral unit' in the first thirty years of the century. 'The evidence is varied, scattered and complex, but cumulatively it suggests that the theatrical change which occurred round about the year 1930 was, in fact, as great as any to be discovered in the stage's annals.'[1] That is a strong view from such a distinguished source, and only now coming into clearer perspective. The mantle of Pinero and Maugham had been assumed by early Priestley and Coward; and with Marie Lohr, Gerald du Maurier and Martin Harvey still onstage, so also were the young Gielgud, Richardson, Olivier, Thorndyke, Evans and Ashcroft.

But to return to the beginning of the century, popular drama was celebrating an apotheosis of its 1890s' renaissance, with Pinero reaching his zenith, and his knighthood, with *Mid-Channel* (1909); Barrie, impish and sentimental, delighting with *Quality Street* and *The Admirable Crichton* (both 1902), *Peter Pan* (1904), *What Every Woman Knows* (1908), and half a dozen other successes before the war; Shaw, at the height of his literary powers, forging his own didactic theatrical style, giving eleven of his plays at the Court Theatre in 1904–7 under the Barker-Vedrenne management, including *Man and Superman* (1905), *Major Barbara* (1905) and *The Doctor's Dilemma* (1906); Granville-Barker himself, that most progressive man of the theatre – actor, producer, manager, and now playwright – adding to his credit *The Marrying of Anne Leete* (1902), *The Voysey Inheritance* (1905), *Waste* (1907) and *The Madras House* (1910); Galsworthy entering the lists with three of his best plays in 1906–10, *The Silver Box*, *Strife* and *Justice*; and the witty, biting cynicism of Maugham, with *Lady Frederick* (1907), and no less than four plays running concurrently in London in 1908 (a record which, I believe, remained unequalled until Ayckbourn). Also active – and even popular – at the time were writers like Stephen Phillips and W. B. Yeats; and from abroad, Maeterlinck and Andreyev, dramatists who are very rarely revived today, their talents misled up the misty blind-alley of an ephemeral poetic symbolism.

Nevertheless, it was from abroad that the really significant guns were firing, or preparing to fire. Chekhov, the dramatist whose psychological truthfulness of observation has given actors their greatest challenge as well as professional joy, started the new century with *The Three Sisters* (1901) and *The Cherry Orchard* (1904), having given the Moscow Art Theatre its initial and enduring impetus with its revival of the earlier ill-fated *The Seagull* in 1898. Strindberg was in his last great period with the Intima Teatern in Stockholm; Reinhardt was at the Deutsches Theater in Berlin, an actor who in 1903 began to devote all his time to superbly organized productions; Copeau opened the Vieux Colombier in Paris in 1913; Pirandello in Rome, aged thirty-three in 1900, was preparing his literary scalpel to dissect the onion-like layers of illusion around our lives, which found such resonance in a disillusioned post-war generation in the 1920s. It took some time for their work to have any real influence on the theatrical scene in England, but once it was known it could not be ignored by those who cared about the art of the theatre.

One of the most significant advances in the making of the professional actor in England was initiated in the confident Edwardian age. For virtually the first time, two Schools were set up with the precise intention of serving the stage and those who had a vocational intention of going on it. 'The need for acting schools,' says Kenneth Richards, 'was felt to be a direct consequence of the old stock system's replacement by the long run.' The decay of stock companies deprived young actors of a valuable training ground, it was said; but others – with equal logic – pointed out that the stock system 'encouraged casualness of preparation and performance', relying on stage tricks to cope with the large number of roles which were played.[2] In 1904, Herbert Beerbohm Tree (later knighted in 1909) set up the Academy of Dramatic Art – later to become the RADA – with classes in his own theatre, which was then His Majesty's in the Haymarket. Only two years later, Elsie Fogarty created the Central School of Speech and Drama, then located in the upper rooms of the Albert Hall in Kensington. Before the founding of these two major Schools, there had been, of course, a training of sorts given by several individual teachers, and even by some 'Colleges' and 'Academies', where the main subject was Elocution. Their standards and staying power, however, varied greatly.

Dr Michael Sanderson, whose deeply-researched and important book on the 'social history of the acting profession, 1880–1983' has a full chapter on 'The training of the actor before 1914', and to which I am much indebted for the rest of this section, points out that 'Academies originally or primarily devoted to music also often taught drama and elocution. This training was valuable for singers, especially in opera, but was also useful for non-singing actors. The London Academy of Music was founded in 1861 and taught elocution from the 1860s.'[3] Some of the best training before the Edwardian era, as with that of Tree's Academy itself, was probably given with attachment to a working theatre company. One of these was run by a Sarah Thorne at Margate's Theatre Royal in 1885, where no less a name than George Arliss had been a student. Ben Greet (1857–1936, and knighted in 1929), another of the actor-manager breed who presented Shakespeare in the provinces and in Regent's Park, and himself a student of Sarah Thorne, opened his Academy of Acting in Bedford Street, the Strand, in 1896. Among his alumni were Sybil Thorndyke, Mrs Pat Campbell and H. B. Irving (one of Sir Henry's two sons). Yet another knighted actor-manager, Sir Frank Benson, who also toured the provinces with Shakespeare and later wrote a handbook on acting, formalized the training given with his company in 1901. Many subsequent young players were proud of the appellation 'Old Bensonian'.[4]

In the 1890s, 'the best known teacher of acting in England' – albeit American born – was Hermann Vezin. He had a studio by Waterloo Bridge where, up to 1914, rapid speech and clear enunciation were his hallmark. One of his students was Rosina Filippi, half-sister to Eleonora Duse, and called the 'foremost woman teacher of drama', among whose pupils in the early years of the century were Lewis Casson and Felix Aylmer. 'She preceded Lilian Baylis in experimenting with the bringing of Shakespeare to the people after Emma Cons' death in 1912.'[5] Two other well-regarded teachers of the period were Henry Neville, whose Dramatic Academy was founded in 1884; and Cairns James, whose Academy in Oxford Street, where Gerald du Maurier devised and adjudicated improvisation exercises, had a curriculum which included fencing lessons, singing, and instruction in scenes from plays.[6]

Tree's Academy of Dramatic Art was moved in 1905 to 62 Gower Street, after the 'sheer inconvenience' of having students cluttering up a working theatre like His Majesty's. Then in 1906, control of the Academy passed from Tree to a Council of distinguished theatre personalities: Bancroft, Hare, Alexander, Forbes-Robertson, Cyril Maude, Arthur Bourchier, Pinero, Barrie, as well as Tree himself – and later, in 1912, Shaw and Irene Vanbrugh. The latter's name is perpetuated in RADA's current theatre for public performances. The total number of students in 1908 was about fifty, which rose to a hundred by 1910. Girls outnumbered the men by four to one. The late Athene Seyler, who was there in the early 1900s, recalled her fellow students as being all of good education and manners. 'The essential purpose of the Academy was training for the stage' – but as with Drama in Education later in the century, those who did not prove capable of a stage career nevertheless 'derived social and personal benefit from the training'.[7] At the time, when higher education for women was so limited, the Academy 'broadened the experience of its mainly girl-student body'. It was, in fact, a kind of 'finishing school', and for many years afterwards this impression was a difficult one for the Academy, and indeed other schools, to quell in the public mind. Acting, to the English, was essentially a dilettante activity.

What was actually taught at Gower Street in those days? 'When interviewed on the eve of its opening, Tree said that the principal subjects would be voice production, elocution, blank verse, Shake-speare, dancing, fencing, acrobatics and mime, gesture appropri-ate to periods (minuets, the use of the fan) and the acting of plays.'[8] By 1906 the structure of the curriculum had taken clear shape. As is still mostly the case today, there were three eleven-week terms. The whole course was for four terms (about fifteen months) with the final term, as today, having an Annual Public Performance of graduates given at a West End theatre. Fees had begun at six guineas a term in 1905, but doubled from 1906 until 1914. The children of actors were admitted for half-fees – not a custom to have survived – although there were scholar-ships available after 1910, and twenty-two were given in the next four years. The Academy was not run for profit; and, in fact, Tree had to meet a deficit himself. Master-classes or rehearsals by distinguished actors and playwrights were an important part of the final term. Most ex-students got work in the West End (66.7 per cent men, 36.3 per cent women) or in provincial tours (24.1 per cent men, 52.2 per cent women).[9] The percentages re-flect the fact that men were in much shorter supply, and also that they found it easier to get work in the West End where, as is still the case today, more than twice the number of available parts were for men. Today, actresses are at last making strong objections not only to this, but also to the lack of parity in salaries.

The odd thing about Elsie Fogarty's creation of the Central School of Speech and Drama in 1906 was that she was said to have 'strongly disapproved of the stage', and her attitude to drama training mainly emphasized a scientific approach to speech and voice. Central's curriculum from 1908 to 1914 comprised Elocu-tion and Speech Training, Dancing, Fencing, Physical Training, Voice Production and Rehearsal. It will have been noted that Rehearsal and the Acting of Plays come last on both the Acad-emy's and Central's curriculums, whilst voice and speech are a very strong first. The microphone had not yet brought a laziness in regard to the importance of clear diction and a supported vo-cal instrument in large theatres (or even quite small ones!). In the 1990s, it is mostly only those actors who have survived the rig-ours of a classical repertoire with the RSC, the National, the English Shakespeare Company, or the Renaissance Theatre Com-pany and their like, who have developed a vocal focus and capacity

over several more years than the average training period to match
the kind of stage speech demanded as *de rigueur* by the actor-
managers of the Edwardian period, and by such dramatists as
Shaw, Granville-Barker, Galsworthy and Maugham.

At Central the fees were eleven guineas a term in 1908, rising
to thirty-six pounds a year for the first year and thirty pounds
for the second year from 1912. Again, it was mostly girl students
at Central, where for every hundred there were only fifteen men
students. The physiological aspects of speech, and particularly
the perception of rhythm, were developed at Central by Dr H.
H. Hulbert (father of Jack and Claude Hulbert). Fogarty herself
was responsible for developing a new consciousness about the
need for speech training in education at a national level, as well
as medical aspects concerning physique and stammering and other
hindrances. In view of her personal preferences about the nature
of her work, she must have found more satisfaction than she had
at Central when she started a speech clinic at St Thomas's Hospital in 1914.

While the two new vocational training schools in London were
getting established, three other significant and certainly more idealistic projects were struggling to be born abroad. Stanislavski's
first Studio was founded in 1905 on the Povarskaya 'where young
actors could experiment with new ideas and new methods'.[10] This
was followed by the First Studio at the Moscow Art in 1912,
and subsequently three more Studios up until 1921, together with
one for opera singers in 1924. Stanislavski first referred to his
'System' in 1909, but *An Actor Prepares* was not published in
English until 1936. His vital influence on twentieth-century acting will be discussed in Chapter 8. Meanwhile, in Italy and in
France, the other two schools were to be aborted with the outbreak of the First World War.

Edward Gordon Craig (1872–1966) published a sort of prospectus for his school at the Arena Goldoni in Florence in 1913.[11]
Lord Howard de Walden was to be the main provider of funds –
for a limited period of five years. The words 'actor' and 'acting'
are never once mentioned in any description of the school, and
the nearest we come to any performance is 'marionette designing, making and performing'. No female students seem to have
been envisaged, in fact altogether 'only one or two students will

be selected who satisfy the Director's requirements'. Copeau, who visited the Arena in 1915, and at several later times paid tribute to Craig as 'the great initiator', did not believe there were ever any paying students. 'He is not a theatre director. He is not trying to form a company of actors to fulfil the requirements of a repertoire. Theoretically, the actor does not interest him. . . . He has often said to me: "You believe in the actor. *I do not.*"'[12] Despite the Arena being 'big enough to hold 1500 spectators with a stage larger than those of the average English theatre', Craig never intended any performances there. The 'Aims and Objects' of the Gordon Craig School were expressly 'to discover and define once and for all the elemental forms and methods which are the bases and key-stones of the finest Theatre Art and to inspire a new Theatre into being'. Craig was never one to shrink from stating his concept of the ideal. The school's organization was to be in two separate bodies. The First Division to be 'of workers and teachers who are at the same time students of Mr Craig's methods, and who experiment under his direction. Among these are Musicians, Electricians, Wood-Carvers, Modellers, Designers, Photographers, Scene-painters, Carpenters, etc., each of whom teaches the others something of his own particular craft and who is himself taught something by the others. The Second Division to be composed of paying students who learn various crafts from the teachers and workers in the First Division. These students are expected to have a good general knowledge, and must be of proved capacity before they will be allowed to join the School.' No actors to be seen around, and yet in the subjects of study found listed under 'The Work of the School' by Ernest Marriott[13] there are such performance-orientated lessons as Voice Training, Gymnastics, Dancing, Fencing and Mimo-drama, 'all of which,' says Mr Marriott, 'are part and parcel of *Stage Managing*' (his italics). Copeau notes this contradiction but could not penetrate Craig's vagueness on the subject.

It was in the same year, 1913, that Copeau wrote his own manifesto, 'An Attempt at Dramatic Renovation', with which to open his own school attached to the Théâtre du Vieux Colombier on the Left Bank, not then a fashionable district of Paris. But for him also, history was to intervene.

7

The French Avant-Garde:
Copeau – 'The seed from which we have all grown'

Jacques Copeau (1879–1949) had a tremendous ideal: it was no less than 'the renewal of man in the theatre'.[1] This necessitated the development of a complete education for the actor, as opposed to a mere 'dramatic training'. It meant establishing a commune of actors whose collective life would support the integrity of their performances. Their mutual aim would be to prepare for the theatre of the future; and even allowing for the current achievements of a director-guru like Mnouchkine, the ideal still obtains. Copeau's concept was more than just a school attached to a theatre company, it was the vocation of Theatre itself as a School, being a community, an education *and* a training. 'I see no true transformation possible in theatre except through and by a social transformation. New dramatic forms will come from new ways of living, thinking and feeling.'[2]

Albert Camus, who owed his own urge and passion for the theatre to Copeau, said of him that 'In the history of the French theatre there are two periods: before Copeau and after Copeau.'[3] At the time of his death, Jean-Louis Barrault commented: 'Copeau was the *seed* from which we have all grown and it will remain alive as long as we live.'[4]

One of Copeau's major preoccupations was 'the continual search for appropriate means of renewing the relationship between training and performance, of practising for one's practice'. Even today, most actors are inclined to think that all they need to improve their craft is more parts to play, but Copeau 'wanted his actors to improve *for* their parts, not through them, and that improvement he saw as being of the whole person, not just an individual's technique'.[5] Copeau's own background was that of a critic and man of letters. He was a co-founder (with André Gide and Jean Schlumberger) of the influential *Nouvelle Revue Française* in 1909, when he was thirty. He did not become involved in the theatre until his adaptation for the stage of *The Brothers Karamazov* in 1911. He was neither an actor nor a theatre technician, but simply a man with a vision to pursue.

Copeau once wrote to Granville-Barker, with whom he was close in spirit, that 'the art of the theatre is the art of acting, first, last and all the time'.[6] In this, he was reacting against Craig's ideals, despite his respect for them, and against his symbolist predecessor, Lugné-Poë. The writer for this actors' theatre – the poet-dramatist on whom he pinned such hopes – failed to materialize. This was a failure for the French theatre during his time, except for the work of Paul Claudel and Jean Giraudoux, which Barrault and Jouvet respectively were to stage later. It was not until much later still, after his death in fact, that writers like Anouilh, Sartre, Genet and Beckett found international audiences. It was Copeau's belief – today, unfortunately, grown rather unfashionable – that the true content of the actors' theatre is the concern of the writer, or as he preferred to put it, the Poet; and he saw his own pioneering efforts as directed very much to this cause. The director was there for the selection and treatment of the repertoire. Rudlin comments that 'The purification, both physical and ideological, of the stage and the education of the actor as human being as well as technical exponent, were thus to be simply necessary preparations for the coming of the Poet, the new Aeschylus, the new Shakespeare, the new Molière.' What Copeau 'really lacked was someone to play Chekhov to his Stanislavsky' – a dramatist of greatness. He said as much himself in 1938 for an article published in Buenos Aires.[7]

As mentioned earlier, it was in 1913 that Copeau wrote his manifesto announcing the opening of the Vieux Colombier Theatre, which included the idea of Theatre as a School. He already knew of Stanislavski's First Studio school attached to the Moscow Art Theatre (1912) and must have seen in it a model for his own project. Copeau's new company opened in Paris in October 1913, and in the following year went on a one-week tour to England. Then with the outbreak of war it had to close. The school had not yet been given a chance of birth. Copeau had failed his medical for military service, so in 1915, in addition to visiting Craig in Florence, he went to Geneva where he met Appia, Dalcroze, Stravinsky and Pitoëff. He corresponded with Jouvet about plans for a new stage at the Vieux Colombier. Then, in his notebook for 21 January 1916, he was 'proposing to establish the Vieux Colombier School as a kind of *war-time relief organization*' (his italics) with a team comprising ten young pupils, ten adult pupils – five of them actors from the company and five future candidates – and five teachers, 'a total of 25 people to be supported – lodging, board, laundry – at the expense of the school'. Already a tentative start had been made with twelve children at the Club Gymnastique in the rue de Vaugirard during the previous November, with Suzanne Bing as his main helper. Despite the war, Copeau wanted '*something* to exist'. The student numbers soon increased to twenty-two children at the rue de Vaugirard, 'including one who had worked with Isadora Duncan', and in the 'big workshop that will become my office' at the Vieux Colombier, periodic sessions with some fifteen adults were also begun.[8]

After working in Geneva, Copeau went in 1917 on a six-month lecture tour of the USA. While there he was offered finance by Otto Kahn, a New York banker and generous patron of the arts, to bring his company to New York in November. The next year a second season was organized, which opened at the Garrick Theatre in October 1918 and lasted until the following April. During this time no less than twenty-five plays were presented, virtually one per week. In June, Copeau returned to Paris where the Vieux Colombier reopened in February 1920, followed by a summer tour of forty-two cities with his own translation and adaptation (with Suzanne Bing) of *The Winter's Tale*.

With all this work-load, it was not until the end of the following year, 1921, that the Vieux Colombier School truly reopened in new premises on the rue du Cherche-Midi, under the direction of Jules Romains (1885–1972). But it was the ubiquitous Suzanne Bing (1885–1967), a brilliant actress in her own right, whose work was central to the School's creation. Copeau said that 'without her, my plans would probably never have come to fruition. For more than ten years she took the heaviest share of a thankless task, and to a certain extent sacrificing her own career.'[9]

In his First Prospectus, for the year December 1921–July 1922, Copeau wrote: 'The Vieux Colombier School is a technical school. It proposes to give its students a professional introduction which is as methodical and complete as possible. The centre of its programme is theatrical technique, envisaged in all its aspects. It gives greatest importance to the formation of accomplished actors...'[10] Subjects under separate staff responsibility included: Prosody, versification/Poetic technique/Theory of the theatre, dramatic instinct/Reading, diction/Acting, mise-en-scène/French language, memory/Vieux Colombier Repertoire/Theatrical architecture/Music and song/Acrobatics/Hebert method of physical education (this was a system of exercises designed by a Lieut. Hebert and especially suitable for outdoor gymnastics)/Dance/Workshops in modelling, costume, décor and stage architecture.

That is quite a Prospectus, with a breadth of coverage that most of today's leading theatre schools would envy. It was probably too ambitious to be thorough; nevertheless, when the Second Year Prospectus was written (for 1922–3), there were still further additions, but with some of the old headings slightly amended. Copeau had now taken over as General Director, although at least one student of the time complained that after three and a half years at the School they received in all only sixty minutes of lessons from 'le patron'.[11] There were probably good reasons for this. Copeau was more the inspired initiator of the curriculum than an experienced performer and teacher himself. His was the overall view guiding the ideal; and, indeed, one of the new subjects he introduced for the second year was 'an overall view of the history of civilization', philosophical schools and communities, literary and artistic schools, daily life and 'how it is expressed in poetry, music and theatre'. The second year also saw the introduction of what was called the Apprenticeship Group, admission by 'examination and proper references' for twelve young people of both sexes, aged between fourteen and twenty. The minimum study period was three years, with classes from 9 to 12, and 2 to 5.30. The students worked and lived communally, and no performance work was undertaken until the third year of training. (This ideal remains as rare today as it was then.)

The teaching was based on education of the body/craft skills/
singing/exercises in dramatic expression, especially of mime and
physical games/improvisation/elocution, diction and declamation/
general education and dramatic theory. There were also courses
reserved for the company, for outside professionals, and for the
public.[12]

For the following year (1924), it was planned for the School
to present their interpretation of a Japanese Noh play as a 'first
contact with the general public'. This 'exhibition of talent' (one
of the meanings of 'Noh') never actually took place, owing to
one of the leading actors spraining his knee; but a dress rehearsal
in the presence of Granville-Barker moved and impressed that
master to enthusiastic comment. He told Copeau and the students
that 'up to now he had been full of doubt about the possibility
of a drama school, but today he was convinced that only on this
foundation could a work of dramatic art emerge, and that if
three years' work gave this result, in ten years we would be capable
of any kind of production'. Granville-Barker, who only two years
before had published his seminal book on *The Exemplary Theatre*,
wrote further to Copeau from his hotel, 'what I saw has life in it
– that's the first thing . . . The Moscow people have it as well –
that for second . . . and to the third . . . while the Noh was in
itself as complete and beautiful a thing of its kind as I have ever
seen (Oh! falling short of perfect execution of course, but *right*
always in intention), what stirred me was that I could see the
future in it.' He went on to hope that Copeau would now 'find
native things' for the students to do. There was a danger in the
strict artistic form of the Noh being so 'isolated from life as we
see and interpret it'. We need 'our own convention', but this
leads 'into deep waters'.[13]

For all Granville-Barker's praise of the Vieux Colombier School,
it was only two months later that Copeau announced its closure
(in May 1924). The company was transferred to Louis Jouvet,
and Copeau retired to Morteuil in Burgundy, taking with him
several pupils and a few company members to pursue his researches. The group became known as 'Les Copiaus', and the
following year they started giving local performances about the
wine-makers, and *L'Illusion*, after Corneille. The group then moved
on to another Burgundy village, Pernand-Vergelesses, where once

again a training curriculum was organized. This School lasted until 1929, but Copeau himself kept few records. There is an account of a visit made by one Jacques Prenat which reports Copeau as saying 'The problem of the actor is basically a corporeal one: the actor is standing on the stage. . . . Because the body, for the actor, starts out by being an obstacle. Afterwards, it becomes a terrible hurdle to link physical action with the text. In order to do it naturally, a prolonged effort is necessary.'[14] Any working actor will recognize the truth of this observation. Interestingly, it seems to anticipate what occupied Stanislavski in the early 1930s when he was working with a group of friends and young actors on what became known as the Method of Physical Action.[15] More of that in the next section. One of Copeau's most effective researches for training at Pernand was into the use of the mask, and in particular the expressionless or 'universal' mask. He used it to loosen up bodily inhibitions and extend the possibilities of purely physical expression. This is now standard practice in actor training.

In 1926, at a lecture given in Brussels, Copeau explained why he had given up his company and his theatre. It will come as no surprise to readers in the 1990s that financial difficulties were at the top of the list. The theatre was too small, and even full houses could not provide a living. 'It is impossible, especially under difficult material conditions, for the real work of dramatic creation to remain compatible with the overwhelming necessities of running a theatre.' *Plus ça change, plus c'est la même chose.* Other reasons were more idealistic. We have not yet produced a dramatic aesthetic, he complained, to express our age. 'It is the theatre's imperative objective to rediscover its functions and its natural vocation.' Moreover,

the theatre will not rediscover its grandeur until it ceases being an exploitation and becomes a ceremony . . . to save the theatre we must leave it . . . we are tired of keeping alive a cult whose deity is absent. It has been necessary to leave the big city where our austerity was only taken as an affectation, where bad influences were working to recapture us, and our ideas were being seized to popularize them and make money.

Then Copeau ringingly states the creed which nearly seventy years later still awaits its true accomplishment. His nephew, Michel Saint-Denis, took on the mantle and nearly succeeded, as we shall see, but market forces still obtain above all else. 'There will be no new theatre which does not start from a school, where everything must be absorbed, from first principles ... only there will be realized that unity of all the dramatic elements ... through the reconciliation of the creator with the director, and the identification of the author with the actor.'[16]

The ideal is of a new theatre 'purified and made worthy of our civilization'. Back in 1917, Copeau was already saying that 'No matter how we approach the problem of theatre, we come back to the problem of the actor as the instrument and perfect realizer of a dramatic idea.' For him, that actor did not exist in the modern theatre; he had to be educated, to be made. 'Give me real actors, and, on a platform of plain rough-hewn boards, I will promise to produce real comedy. ... The stage is the place for the drama, not the décor or the equipment. It belongs to the actors, not to the technicians or the scene-painters. It should always be ready for the actors and for action.'[17] Ironically, it is like the actor-despising Craig that Copeau also sees that stage, that theatre, as 'open to the air, the sun and the moon'[18] – a public celebration rather than a private seance. Theatre is a sacred business, it stems from solemnity as well as 'real comedy'. It 'rediscovers a little of its lost signification, it re-establishes its place in the city, its station in culture, its power and its nobility, each time it comes near to the primitive conditions which, in ancient Greece, at the time of the Great Dionysia, constituted a religious festival'.[19] This kind of theatre requires initiation, not only for the actors but also for the audience. It requires imagination and sincerity in both. It is at the centre of life and living.

Writing late in his life, in 1941, Copeau set down his vision for the future, the leitmotiv of his career. The prototypes of ancient Athens, the religious Mysteries of the Middle Ages, Shakespeare's and Molière's companies, these were 'the indispensable preface to all development of popular theatre'. It will find its *sense* and its *life* (his italics) defined in the poetic and in those lasting genres of human social intercourse, the tragic, the comic, the satirical and a wonder at our situation in the universe. To recall it into existence there is need for a large school, 'a centre of theatrical culture . . . generously subsidized by the state', where 'all forms are studied and practised, stimulated by a dominant spirit'.[20] That spirit could no longer be himself. Long since he had handed over the mantle to others to be the avant-garde in Paris, first to Louis Jouvet who took over the Vieux Colombier in 1924, and to Charles Dullin who had also worked with him there before a personality clash led to them parting ways in 1918; then later these two were joined by Georges Pitoëff and Gaston Baty. Together they dominated the French stage between the wars, forming a loose professional association which became known in 1927 as the Cartel des Quatre. Copeau's ideals were its shared artistic creed, although with different emphases.

The four pillars of the Cartel were born within two years of each other: Louis Jouvet (1887–1951), Charles Dullin (1885–1949), Georges Pitoëff (1887–1939), and Gaston Baty (1885–1952). They all gained an advantage from occupying their own specific theatres over long periods, thus building up a faithful public for their idiosyncratic work. They were all, of course, play directors; three of them were also star actors (Dullin, Jouvet and Pitoëff), and two of them were playwrights (Baty and Pitoëff). Baty, it may be seen, is the odd man out, more especially because he was the only one who had no working connection with Copeau. Nevertheless, his ideal of an 'integral theatre' was close to Copeau's vision, with all its elements in harmony, and despite its having no special regard for the text. The mise-en-scène was all in all, and Baty was a magician in conjuring it up. It was the three actor-directors who had a special interest in the primacy of the text and its performance. This, of course, was Copeau's fervent concern, and the three of them did much to consolidate it during their influential existence over more than two decades.

The Copeau tradition and that of the Cartel des Quatre continues in France unbroken to this day. It was transported over the Channel to England when Michel Saint-Denis brought it with him, briefly at first in 1931, then again more permanently from 1935. Meanwhile, in 1936, Copeau, Jouvet, Dullin and Baty were all made co-directors of the Comédie-Française. As so often happens, the avant-garde had become the establishment.

Two men who were students of Dullin, Artaud in 1921 and

Barrault in 1931, were growing to become dominant influences themselves during the 1930s. Their important contributions are considered in Chapter 10; and in Chapter 11, yet a third important student of Dullin's – Jean Vilar – takes up the tradition in reviving Gémier's dream of the Théâtre National Populaire. Meanwhile, first in Russia from before the turn of the century, and then in Germany during the 1920s, the making of the modern actor was being forged between the heat of 'emotional recall' and the steel of cerebral 'alienation'.

8

The Russian 'Revolution': Stanislavski's Studio Schools

With hindsight, it is quite remarkable how widely separated yet mutually significant events in a given sphere may be seen to have happened round about the same time. Even similar thinking and ideals may later be seen to have co-existed at the same time, without detailed knowledge of each other. Perhaps Rupert Sheldrake's 'morphic resonance' is an explanation. However that may be, it was in 1912, when Copeau, Jouvet and Dullin were planning in Paris, and Craig was preparing the Arena Goldoni in Florence, that Konstantin Stanislavski (1863–1938) in Moscow inaugurated the First Studio for teaching actors his newly-formed 'System'. Actually, it was not his first 'Studio' – as mentioned earlier, that had been unsuccessfully started with Meyerhold in charge in 1905 – but it was the first to bring his new method of working to the attention of the full company at the Moscow Art Theatre; and even this was not, strictly speaking, his idea but that of his co-founder and co-director, V. I. Nemirovich-Danchenko (1859–1943), who gave the order for the actors – willing or not – to attend the training whenever possible.

The man put in charge of the First Studio was not, once again, Stanislavski himself, but his close colleague and friend, Leopold Sulerjitski.[1] Stanislavski was very busy with his company work and had to content himself with visiting master-classes, à la 'Tortsov' in *An Actor Prepares*. Sulerjitski, described by Stanislavski as 'a remarkable man of exceptional talents', was the complete all-rounder whose 'whole life was a poetic fairy tale'. It was he who brought Stanislavski the news of Chekhov's death in 1904. After all kinds of extraordinary adventures and hardships, in 1906 this friend of Tolstoy with 'short legs and a fine singing voice', became attached to the Moscow Art Theatre, working at Stanislavski's side as his 'closest assistant'. He was never employed officially and was much resented by Nemirovich-Danchenko for, as he thought, coming between himself and Stanislavski. Indeed, Stanislavski complains in his journal, 6 November 1907: 'It's grotesque. I am paying Sulerjitski with my own money. He is working all out and still I have to beg permission from V.I. [Nemirovich-Danchenko] who does nothing, to have his help. When Suler heard about it he almost walked out of the theatre.'[2] It was Stanislavski's turn to nearly walk out of the company when, because of his illness, Sulerjitski had been in full charge for the first time of an early dress rehearsal of the suitably-named *The Drama of Life*, and Nemirovich-Danchenko, relishing new managerial powers, snubbed the occasion which he would normally have attented.[3] In September of the following year, 1908, after long rehearsals and great technical difficulties, Stanislavski had one of his greatest successes with a production of *The Blue Bird*. Its renown reached Paris where, two years later, it was Sulerjitski who was sent to reproduce it 'move for move for Réjane'.[4]

It would seem that Stanislavski felt closer, and owed more allegiance, to his friend Sulerjitski than he did at this time to his co-founder and director. It was with Sulerjitski that he shared the dream 'of creating a spiritual order of actors ... men and women of broad and uplifted views, of wide horizons and ideas, who knew the soul of man and aimed at noble artistic ideals, who could worship in the theatre as in a temple', and who could live together on an estate near the city to give their performances to an audience who would then stay the night.[5] Copeau would have liked that. In 1911, Sulerjitski and Stanislavski worked together with that other great idealist of the time, Gordon Craig, who had been brought to them by Isadora Duncan, to realize – or partly realize – an extraordinary, now historical not to say notorious production of *Hamlet*, employing Craig's revolutionary 'screens'. It was Sulerjitski who used what little English he had to help interpret for Craig (with bits of German thrown in) and, in general, to mediate between these two uncompromising artists, while at the same time warding off the increasingly worried Nemirovich-Danchenko.[6] At around this time, recalls Stanislavski, 'Sulerjitski went to a private dramatic school run by one of the actors of our Theatre and established a class according to my plans. After several years this class yielded results and many of its pupils were accepted in the Theatre. Among them was Yevgeny Vakhtangov . . .'[7] The company, including some of the older actors, seeing these results, requested a chance to develop for themselves also, but within the strictures of daily performance and rehearsal. A new production of Tolstoy's *The Living Corpse*, also in 1911, gave an opportunity for this to happen with so many small parts and walk-ons involved. Then, as we have noted, to everyone's surprise it was Nemirovich-Danchenko who insisted (possibly, with a politic use of his new powers, voted by the board of shareholders, to patch up his differences) that Stanislavski's new methods of work – the 'System' – should be studied and accepted by the company. Stanislavski was to give explanations before rehearsals commenced. Thus began the First Studio. But it was not located within the Moscow Art building. A large hall was hired on the top floor of the old premises of the Society of Art and Literature, coincidentally the scene of Stanislavski's frenzied amateur days. In addition to Vakhtangov, other members at the time were Michael Chekhov, Richard Boleslavski and Maria Ouspenskaya.[8] All three were later to make their mark in the USA during the 1920s and after, where their training activities were seminal to what became known as the 'Method' in that country. Stanislavski began to give 'a full course of study' at the First Studio but was soon forced to hand over much of the work to Sulerjitski.

Before looking in some detail at this work, let us glance back briefly to Stanislavski's first attempt at a Studio in 1905 – the Studio on Povarskaya. It was there that the basic studies in body movement, in voice, and especially emotions and the voice, took shape in his mind.[9] Although he did not call it as such until 1909, the 'System' was being born. It was at this time that he met again Vsevolod Meyerhold (1874–1940) who had been a member of the original Moscow Art Theatre company. Meyerhold had played Konstantin Treplev in their first production of *The Seagull* in 1898 (the previous Alexandrinski Theatre's production in 1896 had failed miserably), but he left in 1902 to start his own company in the provinces. Konstantin's line 'We must have new forms' would have come convincingly from his lips. The ultra-naturalism of Chekhov was not for him. He knew what he wanted but had no means to realize it. Stanislavski gave him the chance to do so, understanding that they had many ideas in common about actor training. They both felt the need for a 'laboratory' to investigate these ideas, and so the Theatrical Studio was set up by Stanislavski, with Meyerhold as its artistic director.[10] They made the mistake of renting 'a very fine house' and spent far too much money on decorating it. Stanislavski was left paying the debts for many years to come. A company of young actors had been gathered and rehearsed outside Moscow at Pushkino (as the early Moscow Art Theatre had done). But Stanislavski kept himself at a distance from the work, not wishing to have to deal with two theatre companies. Although some may have thought that the Theatrical Studio was subsidiary of the Art Theatre, this was never the case. As Meyerhold himself said, it 'functioned independently from first to last'.[11]

Despite the later popular reputation that Stanislavski has earned for realism in acting, 'the principle of the new Studio ... was that realism no longer interested the public. The time for the unreal on the stage had arrived.'[12] This sounds more Meyerhold than Stanislavski; nevertheless, it was Stanislavski who had noted how the painter, and musician, and poet were all applying 'impressionism' in their art; now, so must the theatre. Meyerhold knew how to inspire such a radical new approach in his pupils. Stanislavski on the other hand had personal misgivings. He saw no way of creating this impressionist counterpart, the delicate shades of human feeling, in the work of the actor. He feared violating 'the spiritual and creative apparatus of the actor. I thought that tens and hundreds of years and a whole new culture were necessary to make us actors pass the road that had already been passed by the other arts.' Moreover, it was unfair to expect inexperienced students to cope with new problems and hardships that would dismay 'masters of the art and its technique'.[13]

On top of these doubts, and just as the Theatrical Studio was about to show results with some public performance of its first summer of work, the First Revolution broke about them. There was no option but to shut the Studio down. But at least one record of the achievement of even that early work comes from poet and critic Valery Bryusov, who wrote at the time: 'I was one of the few fortunate enough to see the dress rehearsal of Maeterlinck's *Death of Tintagiles* at the Studio. It was altogether one of the most fascinating performances I have ever seen.'[14] Nevertheless, this opinion was not exactly shared by Stanislavski himself who saw through what was essentially the work of a clever young director exploiting a group of inadequate young actors.[15] Meyerhold is, perhaps, staying with his ego trip when he prefaced his own fairly detailed account of this time with the statement that

> although the Theatre-Studio never opened its doors to the public, it still played a most significant part in the history of the Russian theatre. There is no doubt that everything which our leading theatres began subsequently to produce with such nervous excitement and extreme haste derived from that one source; all the motives underlying their various new interpretations were interrelated and were familiar to anyone who had been concerned in the work of the Theatre-Studio.[16]

Yet for all these fine words, Meyerhold was actually glad that the Studio had to close its doors, and even grateful to it for showing him what *not* to be doing. He had to find his own way, and not to be yoked with Stanislavski's ideas. Early in 1906, he wrote in a letter that 'The collapse of the Studio was my salvation: it wasn't what I wanted, not what I wanted at all.'[17]

Back now to Stanislavski and the First Studio of 1912. This, as already described, evolved as a direct result of Nemirovich-Danchenko's politic decision in August 1911 to have the new 'System' made official and taught to all the Moscow Art company. Once again, it was not to be a school so much as a laboratory for experiment and research. Stanislavski would lay down its policy and projects and exercises, Sulerjitski would run it. Stanislavski's overriding idea was to develop *'the superconscious through the conscious'* in the work of the actor. 'That is the meaning of the thing to which I have devoted my life since the year 1906,' he said, and 'to which I will devote my life while there is life in me'.[18] He had asked the Art Theatre management committee for certain conditions under which he could work for the next three years. These were virtually granted, and with Nemirovich-Danchenko's blessing also, now that he had full managerial powers over the whole Art Theatre operation, including the First Studio and the teaching of the system, and could issue any 'correctives' he might think necessary.[19]

Stanislavski describes the place and work of the First Studio in *My Life in Art*, and for all the fact that it was never definitive and always developing and changing in emphasis, that early work largely set the pattern for the subsequent Studios and training groups which he ran. The large hall on the top floor which housed the First Studio gathered all the various activities under one roof – a small stage, not raised because of the low ceiling, the classes, the rehearsals, a scenic workroom, a sewing room, and the office. Many a famous school has started with as little, but none with a more determined and idealistic curriculum as its *raison d'être*: the Stanislavski System. Not all the students or company actors were equally gifted, but all were enthusiastic and given individual attention. Exercises were used for 'creative feeling', for 'analysis of the role', for 'orchestration of the role on the basis of consistency and the logic of emotion'. All the work was done under the most intimate circumstances. This included performances to the public given in an 'auditorium' more like a private apartment, yet having raked seating for well over a hundred persons. One of the first productions, 'rehearsed by Boleslavsky and produced by Sulerjitsky', was *The Wreck of 'The Hope'*, for which rehearsals were constantly being held up because some of the actors were away on call for rehearsing another production taking place simultaneously at the Theatre. Stanislavski was not going to allow his Studio to take second place, however, and he stated adamantly that the Studio performance 'must take place at any cost' being the thing upon which the future of the students would depend.[20]

The first Studio work continued for the stipulated three years, and even the dream that Stanislavski and Sulerjitski shared of an out-of-town company working and living together was actually achieved. The Studio actors, under Sulerjitski, went for two or three summers around 1913–15 to a large plot of land bought by Stanislavski on the shore of the Black Sea in the Crimea, a few miles from Eupatoria. There they 'lived the life of primeval men' – building their own communal accommodation, and even stables, barns and an ice-house. Sulerjitski repeated the methods he had used with the Dukhobors, a Caucasian peasant group whom he had led into Canadian exile years before at the behest of Tolstoy, which is to say that he established a very severe regime.[21] Back in Moscow, it was Sulerjitski's production of Dickens's *The Cricket on the Hearth*, given by the First Studio in the 1914–15 season, that Stanislavski felt for the first time sounded 'those deep and heartfelt notes of superconscious feeling in the measure and the form' of which he had dreamed, and which were still absent from the main theatre's work.[22] Nicolai Efros, too, the critic and chronicler of the Moscow Art Theatre, thought it the best production he had seen that year.[23]

Having achieved so much with the First Studio students, Stanislavski felt that he had to start all over again with the new generation, the second set of students, and so in 1916, the Second Studio was formed. But this was at a time when his energies were already vastly overstretched. Although he took rehearsals for the Second Studio's opening presentation of *The Golden Ring*, he was also playing no less than six leading roles in the company's repertoire, having difficulties with Aleksandr Blok, the symbolist poet, over his play *The Rose and the Cross* (eventually staged in Britain in 1941), having even more serious difficulties with Nemirovich-Danchenko over rehearsals for Dostoievski's *The Village of Stepanchikovo*, settling an industrial dispute at his factory and a walk-out of propsmen at the theatre, and on top of all that, his dear friend Sulerjitski became seriously ill and died on 17 December.[24] The year 1916 was an *annus horribilis* indeed.

In December 1918 he was invited to set up an Opera Studio by the Moscow Opera at the Bolshoi Theatre, which 'wanted to put the dramatic side of its performances on a higher footing'.[25] The artists of the Opera invited the Moscow Art Theatre actors to a lavish party, and a few days later Stanislavski started giving the singers lectures and demonstrations. But he met with some of the same resistance from the older established ones as he had experienced at first with the Moscow Art company. It was difficult for them to submit to being students again. However, sacri-

fices were made, and even the difficulties of concert and performance priorities keeping those potentially interested away, and the
still-dangerous post-Revolution streets, did not prevent the Opera
Studio establishing regular classes in the System.

In 1920 the Third Studio of the Moscow Art Theatre was set
up, which by now, with Sulerjitski dead, was more the work of
the 'beloved disciple' Yevgeny Vakhtangov (1883–1922) than
Stanislavski himself. Vakhtangov had, after all, joined the company way back in 1911, and had already been closely associated
with the work of the First Studio. In 1921, a Fourth Studio was
established, the last to be so numberd, although, of course, training in the System continued in other ways.

What was being taught that was so new and special? Can it be
summarized? Not really, because Stanislavski himself was always
changing his mind. Many people tried to persuade him to write a
definitive book about his System; but although he made considerable attempts from time to time, the result was ultimately unsatisfactory due to much editing, revision, new material, and perhaps
most significant of all for English readers, difficulties with translation. It was left until after his death in 1938, in fact until the
1950s and early 1960s, for his confused legacy to be sorted out.
In Russia, his Complete Works run to no less than twelve volumes (and still apparently rising; there were originally eight volumes in 1964, of which only four have so far been translated
into English). The publication details have been well documented
and summarized by Jean Benedetti in both his excellent *Introduction* and thoroughly researched biography (see Note 2).

In the USA, naturally, ever since the 1924 visit of the Moscow
Art company, there have been many attempts to describe the System,
the neatest and best-informed of which has probably been that
of Sonia Moore,[26] herself Russian and an attender at Vakhtangov's
Third Studio, who later moved to New York where she founded
her own Studio and also the American Center for Stanislavski
Theatre Art. Also influential has been Stella Adler (1901–92),
member of a renowned New York theatrical dynasty, and who
was herself closely connected with the origins of the System. At
the American Laboratory Theatre in the 1920s she had lessons
from Maria Ouspenskaya and Richard Boleslavski, both members of the First Studio, as we have noted. In the early 1930s, in

the Group Theatre (of which more later), she became disturbed by Lee Strasberg's 'excessive use of affective memory exercises' and went to Paris where she was fortunate enough to be introduced to Stanislavski by Harold Clurman. Stanislavski took her complaints with understanding, and for the next five weeks coached her daily in rectifying the difficulties she had experienced in playing a role for Strasberg. With a provenance like that she was able to return to the USA and the Group Theatre and give her own classes. Subsequently, she had a distinguished career as an actress, and in 1949 opened her own Acting Studio, later renamed the Stella Adler Conservatory of Acting. A second branch was opened in Los Angeles in 1986; and eventually, her long-awaited book *The Technique of Acting* – one of today's children of the System – was published in 1988.[27]

Several attempts have been made to put the System's headings into diagrammatic form, including a number by Stanislavski himself found in his archives, and now kept in the Moscow Art Theatre Museum. Benedetti reproduces one in his *Introduction*; but no such diagram can be more than a shorthand guide for the already-informed. So many of the 'labels' require detailed prior exposition, together with living interpretation where possible, to be clearly understood; and of course, no integrated performance is so hard-edged in its patterning. The mysterious theatrical experience is all and no diagram can be expected to dissect its components as a way of understanding how it was created. Semioticians make their academic attempts but in the final analysis they cannot succeed. Who can define the mental and spiritual state of the actor when the blood is throbbing and the mind is blown with inspiration?

Let us now return to the mid-1920s and see what was happening to actor training in Russia beyond the confines of the Moscow Art Theatre. The latter had been on a highly successful American tour during 1924, but when Stanislavski eventually returned in August he found a new and hostile scene. Most innovations suffer a period of opposition on the rebound, and this was now happening to the System. It will be remembered that Meyerhold had been invited to run the 1905 Studio for Stanislavski only to discover that it had taught him what he did *not* want to pursue. Likewise,

Vakhtangov began to break away from the System in 1920 with the Third Studio, wishing to extend and go beyond its basic adherence to 'natural laws'; and two other renowned Russian directors, also in revolt, were Alexander Tairov and Theodore Komisarjevski.

After the ill-fated 1905 Studio, Meyerhold's next directorial assignment, a year later, was with Theodore's sister, Vera Komisarjevskaya, at her theatre in St Petersburg, where he was given full scope for his ideas. The actors in his hands came close to realizing the Craigean ideal of the über-marionette; but his employer, a talented and renowned actress, could not stand being treated as a puppet in her own theatre, and he was dismissed. He was replaced by another original talent, less heard of today, Nicolai Evreinov (1879–1953), who was also opposed to Stanislavski's ideas.[28] Meyerhold went on to spend the next nine years from 1908 until 1917 working for the two Imperial Theatres in St Petersburg, the Alexandrinski (renamed the Pushkin in 1937) and the Marinski Opera. He was deliberately placed there by management as an *enfant terrible* to stir up the traditionalists. However, he was inclined to behave himself there for a while, consolidating his previous work. In 1910, at the Alexandrinski, he had a great success with *Don Juan,* introducing *commedia*-style improvisation which was a direct challenge to the more traditional and rigidly-structured work at the Moscow Art Theatre. At the time, long before Artaud, he was strongly influenced by the Oriental theatre with its purity of convention and imagery. Some of these ideas were developed in his own Studio, set up between 1914 and 1917. Then in February 1917 a monumental production of Lermontov's *Masquerade* was the culmination of his work in St Petersburg; but this 'richest theatrical spectacle of the decade' coincided with the first shots of the Revolution, and not surprisingly he was accused of profligacy and megalomaniac extravagance. Although the production was to have a long subsequent history, before the year was out Meyerhold 'had thrown in his lot with the Bolsheviks and pledged himself to the democratization of the new, Soviet theatre'.[29] However, political revolution is one thing, artistic revolution quite another. Like saints to the Church, Meyerhold was more of an embarrassment to the Party than an asset. Official policy cast him off and in 1920 he

began to develop his own training system known as Bio-mech-
anics. This made of the actor an athlete, an acrobat and a human
machine; its demands were stringent, and it anticipated much of
the early Grotowski and modern creative dance. In 1926, he staged
The Government Inspector in a totally original and controversial
manner. It was a climactic achievement and 'perhaps the clearest
and most coherent realization of the style which . . . he defined as
the "tragic grotesque"'.[30] Thereafter, throughout the 1930s, he
was frustrated by the mundane 'socialist realism' attitude to all
art which was mercilessly adopted and adhered to by the Stalin
regime.

A year or so before Stanislavski's death in 1938, the two frequently met again for discussions, and to some extent they revived the friendship they had at the beginning of the century.
Meyerhold was by now almost the sole survivor of any importance from those early idealistic days. Their ideas might still differ but there was a mutual professional respect. Stanislavski saw
him as a natural heir, not so much for the System perhaps as for
the future of Russian theatre. They worked together on Meyerhold's
project to stage Mozart's *Don Giovanni*, and it was Meyerhold
who completed Stanislavski's last production, Verdi's *Rigoletto*.
But in 1939 when Meyerhold was given a chance to publicly
recant his 'decadent ideas', he used the occasion to declare instead the right of the artist to experiment. His courage earned
him immediate arrest, and it is believed that he was eventually
shot in a Moscow prison on 2 February 1940.

Vakhtangov was not as technically minded as Meyerhold, but
he made wide use of new theatre forms, including that same 'grotesque' style. He employed it to great effect in a famous production of *The Dybbuk* in 1922, which virtually set the manner
of the Jewish Habima Theatre's work for many years afterwards.
As a director, he was a much-feared disciplinarian, and his main
ambition was to reconcile the best of both Stanislavski and
Meyerhold. He was told by Stanislavski, after a dress rehearsal of
Gozzi's *Turandot* the subsequent performance of which Stanislavski
did not live to see, that he had succeeded as none before in realizing the ideals of the Moscow Art Theatre. It may well have
been true, but at only thirty-nine he had burnt himself out.

Alexander Tairov (1885–1950), like Meyerhold, treated his actors

as puppets, and also found himself up against the Stalinist attitude to experiment. However, he behaved with more tact and
circumspection, not to say compromise, and at least managed to
keep fairly active until nearly the end of his life. Like Gaston
Baty, he believed in the idea of a 'total theatre' – all forms of
theatre and other arts, especially music, being rolled into one all-
embracing experience. He called his ideal 'the synthetic theatre',
and the building most associated with his work was the Kamerny,
'a chamber theatre for connoisseurs'.[31]

Theodore Komisarjevski (1882–1954) was a prolific director –
or regisseur as he preferred to be called – in Moscow between
1907–19 where he did some brilliant and well-received work.
Oddly, he was ignored by Stanislavski who only mentions him
once in passing in *My Life in Art*. In 1909, he worked with
Evreinov in St Petersburg, but in 1919, having seen the way Revolutionary Russia was likely to regard his work, he became an
itinerant exile, mostly in Europe, working for Hebertot in Paris
for a while in the 1920s and contributing some startling and
influential productions in London's West End and at Stratford-
upon-Avon in the 1930s. He was married for a short time to
Peggy Ashcroft, who appeared in many of his productions at that
period. In 1935 he published *The Theatre and a Changing Civilization* in which he made the ideological mistake of backing Fascism
and Nazism as the road for the future of a cultural humanity.
His theatrical dictums had more validity, but he is not often spoken of today. Of acting, he maintained that it was 'a result of
the processes of *creative assimilation* and not of ordinary *association* [his italics], which Stanislavski recommends to actors when
on the stage'. He goes on:

> The emotional content of a stage action cannot be expressed,
> as Stanislavski thinks, by the substitution of the actor's per-
> sonal psychic experiences for those of the characters. Only
> penetration into the *artistic form* of the play and of the part
> can make the actor's imagination work in the right direction
> and assist him in the embodiment of the character. In order
> to 'live his part', *an actor has to live with its form,* through
> which he discovers the *right* thoughts and feelings, and which
> stimulates his imagination. The content and the form cannot

be severed in a work of art without its destruction [all his italics].[32]

Tairov also thought that 'stage feelings were essentially imaginative creations' and he would have agreed with Komisarjevski's view of theatre as a 'synthesis of the arts'. Komisarjevski also aligns with Piscator in seeing theatre as having to do with actual life as well as aesthetics. But he has no respect for writers. Actors and regisseurs were the artists of theatre, and form was more important than content. In this, he was subscribing to an important attitude yet, I would suggest, a major fallacy in twentieth-century art. However, he wanted the theatre 'to *develop* people's minds and *not to stupefy* them' (his italics). After the relative failure of Barrie's *The Boy David,* which he directed in London in 1936, he went to the USA where he remained until his death, long after the end of the Second World War which saw the downfall of his political idols.

On 29 October 1928, at a gala performance celebrating the thirtieth anniversary of the Moscow Art Theatre, appearing as Vershinin in Act One of *Three Sisters,* Stanislavski, then aged sixty-five, had a severe heart-attack during the performance. He managed to finish the act and took two curtain calls before collapsing. It was to be his last performance as an actor. As his doctor drove him home he did not expect him to reach there alive. As it happened, he survived another ten years in constant ill-health and weakness. But even had he died in 1928, the roots of his enduring fame had already been planted – in the USA. Only the year before, he had said goodbye to Michael Chekhov who, having fallen out with the authorities, had left the Soviet Union for good and gone to join Ouspenskaya, Boleslavski, Sonia Moore, along with Adler, Clurman, Strasberg and the rest of the Theatre Guild and later Group Theatre and Actor's Studio luminaries in the USA. It is really to these, and to Elizabeth Reynolds Hapgood and her exclusive translation rights, and to the burgeoning cinema industry where the close-up camera strongly favoured the System for film rather than stage acting, that Stanislavski owes his renown as a teacher in the West.[33]

Despite firm instructions from his doctor to stop working, in 1935 Stanislavski set up a new Opera Dramatic Studio as a training academy for young artists. But it was not to be the usual sort of drama school. It was more a scientific laboratory, not geared to end-performances, but looking into the ways and means by which an actor approaches a character. This question of methodology was Stanislavski's lifetime quest, and now at last he felt he was getting near to some sort of answer with what he called 'the method of physical action'. Although a cogent summary of his teaching was actually given only a few weeks before his death in 1938, this final Studio work was still only to be considered as 'work in progress'.[34]

The Method of Physical Action was given demonstration in a major Art Theatre project to present *Tartuffe* which Stanislavski worked on from 1936 until his body finally gave up its struggle two years later. He never saw it produced, which did not interest him anyway, and he had not even run a single act with the actors, even after two years. But fortunately the rehearsals were recorded by V. O. Toporkov[35] and give us the nearest description of what Stanislavski was never to complete writing himself; that is, a re-drafting of his previously published tenets for actor training in the light of his latest thinking. After his death, his assistant Mikhail Kedrov continued the work on *Tartuffe* and prepared an unmounted run-through for the management and other members of the company in the Theatre's foyer. It was generally agreed that the technical concentration on precise physical action led to a behavioural truthfulness and, perhaps equally important, to a theatrical viability. The success of the run-through eventually led to a public performance in December 1939.

What does Stanislavski's work mean for actors today? What is his principal legacy to world theatre as the centenary of the Moscow Art Theatre approaches in just a few years' time? Some answers were given at a week-long Seminar on Stanislavski's work organized by the then Soviet Centre of the International Theatre Institute in Moscow during April 1981. It was attended by eighty-five delegates from twenty-six countries, and provided an extraordinary retrospective.

One of the first speakers was the actress Angelina Stepanova who recalled working with Stanislavski. 'He helped us all to live in art,' she said. 'He had a *total* attitude, and saw theatre as the best means for people to understand each other, rather than fighting.'

'He said that an actor should become pregnant with a role, alive inside with ideas about it.' 'He loved actors more than any, but was ruthless to all. One actor who refused to play in a crowd scene was fired for four years.' 'An example of detail: an actor looked for the switch when entering the character's own room – to which Stanislavski responded sharply, "You *know* where the switch is!"' 'On the actor's preparation before a performance, he said, "You must make up your soul as well as your face."' 'We live for this – to prepare ourselves to act. I see young actors today who seem to be saying "Take me anyhow, take me as I am" – but this is not Stanislavski's System.' When asked whether she had tried any other ways of acting than the System, just for fun, she answered, 'We don't need any other system, even for fun.'

Oleg Yefremov, Director of the Moscow Art Theatre, said that 'Russia argues about the heritage as much as anyone.' 'The motive for the System was to investigate the art of conveying feelings.' 'Stanislavski did not ask "*How* did the actors perform?" but "Was there a *living* character there?"' 'Actions are the material of our art, which means more than simple movement – sitting immobile could be a logical psycho-physical action.' 'The most important thing was to develop the System's notions of "the living man" – an actor's technique could be beautiful but it comes essentially from the warmth inside the man.' Yefremov quoted Nemirovich-Danchenko's dictum that 'the main enemy of progress in the theatre is the audience'.

Roman Szydlowski, Secretary of the ITI Study Committee, made the point that Stanislavski's main importance was in having brought a moral approach to the theatre, and a purity of intent. This was echoed by many others, among them Anatoly Efros. Efros trained as an actor at the Mossoviet Theatre but forgot acting as soon as possible to become a director. He told of how Stanislavski had turned the business-like world of Russian theatre into something holy. 'He never looked for special success. He was a poet where the rest of us were administrators. He was a cultured man, as intellectual as Chekhov, as wise as Tolstoy.' Efros spoke of how the work of the director was to encourage the actors to grasp their 'through-line', not just line by line, but with the movement of the whole scene, rejecting what was not important. He stood, he said, for an experimental theatre, for keeping a balance of styles and trying to be understood by everybody. He stood for art as a religion, but not a sect. With regard to the way of physical actions, and the possibilities of communication with no other means (like dialogue), he quoted Stanislavski as saying that 'if there is a glass wall between audience and stage through which you can hear nothing, the audience should still be able to understand everything'. (Watching a foreign film without subtitles, or one on TV with the sound turned down, might be a comparable example.)

The next day, the Seminar was given the opportunity to watch Efros rehearse Molière's *Don Juan*, and in the evening to see a performance of his much-praised production of Gogol's *Marriage*. You must eat and digest a style, he said, in order to be strong in re-creating it. 'But we all have our clichés!' 'The most wonderful style is to combine the serious and the comic because that is life.' He sometimes thought that just four plays would be enough for a lifetime's work – say, *Hamlet, Romeo and Juliet, Three Sisters* and *The Cherry Orchard* – giving five different productions of each depending on one's mood and one's age!

Many other directors and delegates addressed the Seminar, but it was Angelina Stepanova who spoke again to sum things up. 'To all actors struggling in rehearsal,' she said, 'remember Konstantin Stanislavski – he loved the art, now you love it. I shall die soon, and no one will remember what I say, but I see here now how Stanislavski's words and teaching have not died, nor will they do so.'[36] It was a moving valedictory statement with which to conclude a remarkable meeting, representing so many nations beyond Russia.

Stanislavski's contribution to the making of the twentieth-century actor was his recognition, beyond system and methodology, that the quality of an artist and their work is in direct proportion to their quality as a person. He himself, for all his strictness and occasional obtuseness, clearly gave and received much love. The 'life in art' draws its best inspiration from having created a valid mode for the art of living.

Copeau, of course, had understood this; and another seminal influence who recognized the necessity of 'real life' entering the life of the theatre and of actors was Erwin Piscator (1893–1966) in Germany.

9

The German Twenties:
Acting and Politics with Piscator and Brecht

Probably the most significant event to influence theories of acting in this century, though perhaps not acting itself, did not occur on a first night but in the German trenches at Ypres in 1915. A 22-year-old soldier was surrounded by exploding grenades and, frozen with fear, could not obey his commanding officer's order to get moving and go over the top. The officer demanded querulously what he had done before the war. Piscator's account of his feelings when replying is worth quoting at length:

> ... the word 'actor' which I had difficulty in uttering – this profession for which I had been fighting – my idea of the theatre, which had been for me the highest and most important goal I could strive for, seemed so stupid, so ridiculous, so false and inadequate to the situation I was in, that I was less afraid of the grenades coming towards me than I was ashamed of having chosen such a profession.
>
> It was a little episode, but ... from that time I wanted to rid myself of the feeling which I had experienced that art has nothing to do with reality and is not sturdy enough to help us face up to it. I have tried to find truth everywhere in order not to be ashamed of my profession. I have sought for it behind the fourth wall of the magical theatre of Max Reinhardt, behind the abstractions of the naturalists in the open fields of the expressionists, and in the romanticism of the literature of pity. I wanted to feel that art is able to deal

with every situation and every problem, and that we artists are able to grow through it to such stature that we can deal with life. I tried to create such a theatre and I found that it called for a new view on acting.'[1]

Mention of the flamboyant Austrian director Max Reinhardt (1873–1943), whose student Piscator had been, and of the fourth wall – that 'unintelligent' illusion which Piscator had always sought to break down – perhaps indicate contributing elements to that shame he had felt in the trenches. Nevertheless, Reinhardt was a worthy theatrical master to follow, and one whose own ambition had steadfastly aimed at bringing actor and spectator together – 'as close together as possible' – although his international reputation was as much for spectacle as for the successful intimacy of his 'chamber theatre', the Kammerspiele, set up in Berlin in 1906, seating only 292, and with no division of stage from audience. Reinhardt is a giant figure in the history of theatre for the first third or so of this century, with no less than 600 productions listed from 1900 in Berlin to 1943 in New York.[2] He was among the first to establish the importance of the director; he excelled at choreographing crowd scenes; and he introduced the concept of 'Epic' staging before either Piscator or Brecht became associated with that genre. He built the enormous thrust stage and arena of the Grosses Schauspielhaus in Berlin in 1919, seating 3000 (only the public mostly chose to stay away from its productions). Before that he had staged such worthy but difficult masterpieces as *Salome* in 1903, *Spring Awakening* in 1906, *Danton's Death* in 1916 and *A Dream Play* in 1921. In London, there was the extraordinary staging of *The Miracle* at Olympia in 1911, and of *Oedipus Rex* in 1912 at Covent Garden, with Sir John Martin-Harvey, and décor by Ernst Stern. But he did not care to theorize or write books, letting his work speak for itself, albeit ephemerally. The result has been that today he is less studied than Brecht, for example, who wrote a great deal; and alongside the countless studies of Brecht, J. L. Styan's 1982 monograph of Reinhardt was the first in English since 1924 – other, that is, than the memoir by Reinhardt's son Gottfried, published in New York in 1979. In the latter, with understandable touchiness but also with perspicacity, Gottfried dares to ask of Piscator and Brecht: 'Whenever did they perform for the working class as Reinhardt did?'[3]

Before 1900, Reinhardt had been an actor with Otto Brahm's Deutsches Theater in Berlin, but he gave up acting in 1903 for full-time production work, eventually taking over the Deutsches Theater in 1907 until 1915. Although he recognized the prime importance of the actor, he was not especially interested in the actor's ways and means, nor in analysis of the craft. He never set up a training school, being more concerned with the technical possibilities of staging, and of freeing the theatre from what he saw as the shackles of literature. It is to Piscator, and in particular to his close associate, Brecht, that we must look for the 'new view of acting'.

It was not solely that 1915 experience at Ypres that influenced Piscator's future. He was in and out of the Flanders trenches as an infantry unit signaller (semioticians please note) until the summer of 1917 when he was seconded to an army theatre unit. Immediately after the war, he spoke at the inaugural meeting of a revolutionary Soldier's Council before returning to Berlin and joining the newly-formed German Communist Party.[4] Theatre from now on was to have political relevance if it was to be worth anything. It was to be a theatre which appealed to the intellect as much as, or more than, the emotions; and the old conventions such as 'unity of time' and an inviolate text could be disregarded. On his return to Berlin he became involved with Marxist members of the Dada movement. He briefly moved to Kaliningrad (Königsberg) in the USSR where he staged a number of Expressionist works, and acted again himself in *The Ghost Sonata*. Then in October 1920, back in Berlin, he opened the Proletarisches Theater with a Communist Youth leader, mostly with amateur actors and touring workers' clubs, playing short pieces which became known as Agit-prop.[5] Piscator was one of the first directors to use film-strips and cartoons together with live actors, and pioneered the genre called 'Documentary Theatre'. As a communist he believed in the theatre as a tool for propaganda and social reform. When he wrote his book *Das Politische Theater* in 1929, he began it with the words: 'I date everything from August 4th, 1914...' and later he describes the style of acting which that initial impetus led him to develop in his productions as 'hard, unambiguous, unsentimental' and belonging 'to the intellectual structure of the theatre, to its pedagogy'.[6] In short, Epic Theatre demanded 'objective acting'.

Also in 1929, there came interesting tangential support for Piscator's view from an actor and director at the Mannheim Theater, Lorenz Kjerbühl-Petersen. It was in that year that he published *Die Schauspielkunst*, translated in 1935 by Sarah T. Barrows as *Psychology of Acting*, in which he criticizes the personal emotional identification in acting encouraged by Stanislavski. He suggests that the evolution of acting has been warped by the twentieth century's emphasis on the 'extreme individualism' of the actor's art. He warns that it 'leads ultimately to complete annihilation of the factors that are essential to acting', and that 'self-portrayal does not signify true art'. It is the spectator who should experience the emotion; and the actor himself often confuses the excitement of the performance with the emotions of the role.[7] A critical and detached attitude to the presentation of a role clearly adumbrates Brecht's *Verfremdung*, or 'alienation technique'. But in Brecht's theory, not only was the acting to be objective; the audience, too, was to be encouraged in taking an objective view of the subjective action in the drama. However, as Nemirovich-Danchenko had observed earlier, audiences are not so easy to train as actors.

Piscator's own description of 'objective acting' is given in the essay he wrote especially for Cole and Chinoy's *Actors on Acting* in 1949. In it, he disagrees with Brecht for romanticizing the concept of 'alienation' by basing it in the modes of oriental classical theatre.

> I agreed that the 'alienation' idea would make use of our intelligence and bring us into closer contact with the facts. I, however, wanted to get hold of the whole human being. I will only separate intelligence and emotion so that I can unite them again on a higher level. . . .We don't want the modern actor improvising his emotions behind the 'fourth wall', but we want him to give us commentaries on these emotions – playing not only a result but the thought which created the result. We want to see the roots and not the fruit alone, the seed and not the plant alone. To do this, the modern ac-

tor ... needs what I have called 'the new objectivity'.

Schopenhauer describes this objectivity very clearly: 'Nobody is ever able to look at his own picture in a mirror with the look of "alienation", which is the primary requirement of objectivity. The true objective look is, in the last analysis, possible only through the moral egoism of a deeply felt "non-I" making it possible to see all the shortcomings without any reservations, the picture as it is, really faithful and true.' ... You the actor become the mirror in which the audience can see themselves. It will be your duty to help them to come to the right conclusions and to destroy the untrue and flattering picture of the I. The audience as your mirror, my actor, and you as the mirror of the audience! The stage itself will be of help to you in creating this new objectivity.... All the modern scenic inventions which I used created a new dimension for the actor.

There are elements in all this which are a mere rearrangement of words to describe what has always happened in the theatrical event. It is not at all clear what Schopenhauer's 'moral egoism of a deeply felt "non-I"' might mean in an actor's actual performance of a role. Piscator anticipates such an objection by asking himself whether he means to do away with all the magic and illusion of theatre, and whether the actor is to 'give up his subjective life which makes him an integral emotional part of the events'.

No, by all means, no! The more objective he becomes, the more he succeeds in reaching the highest personal (subjective) form. The bold and beautiful architecture of a monologue adds to the text. Subjective and objective acting united produce the highest form of acting.

He goes on to mention Laurence Olivier, Jean-Louis Barrault and Louis Jouvet as examples of actors who instinctively play Epic Theatre, and to note in passing that they are also directors. He sees the Epic actor as a sort of narrator, no longer just copying a character but 'assuming human proportions, becoming three dimensional'.

They act with the knowledge that life is more important than the play – but that at the same time, it is understood that at the particular moment, there is no more dignified example of life than this particular slice of life in this particular play. It is the finiteness of the theatre versus the infiniteness of life ... Through the union of objective acting with the subjective action, [the actor] will be not merely an object in the hands of the playwright, but a creator. By objectivizing himself he becomes a subject – and being governed by both, he becomes alive.

Piscator seems to be struggling with words to say what he means, but the impetus given by his experience in the trenches is still clear enough. The Piscator Theatre, he tells us elsewhere, is not aiming at an aesthetic evaluation of the world but 'a conscious will to change it'. James Roose-Evans reminds us that Piscator called his new theatre 'a theatre of search'. Even at the end of his life he was still looking for 'hard, difficult plays, steeped in reality, plays that have never existed'.[8]

Piscator's preoccupation with 'reality' *vis-à-vis* theatre and film, and the search for a truthful way of showing that reality so that life might be changed to be more in tune with it, led to a difficult mixture for the audience's brain to unpick. On the one hand, there was two-dimensional film depicting real events; and on the other, a three-dimensional stage 'reality' depicting fiction. He was rejecting traditional staging because it 'emphasized surface illusion'; yet at the same time he was using theatrical 'magic' and artifice to paint a reality. In all this, the actor was to be integrated into the overall pattern of sound, colour and movement – sometimes to the point of oblivion. He was no longer the prime focus of attention, as in the 'old theatre', but just one facet of a production, reduced to a cartoon, a puppet, a cipher. From one aspect, this was a strange way of justifying the term 'actor', about which he had felt so ashamed. From another viewpoint, it anticipated the 'New Age' thinking of the 1980s in which the romantic, subjective ego of the artist is no longer relevant, but only the 'objectivity' of the artefact and what it says. As Lorenz Kjerbühl-Petersen had said: 'Self-portrayal does not signify true art.' It also anticipated the Canadian sociologist Marshall McLuhan, in the

1960s, with its understanding in theatrical terms that 'the medium is the message' rather than its separate facets and content. It was Piscator and not McLuhan who wrote: 'Technology has made the earth small, [and] the whole of humanity has gained a quality of instantaneity.'[9] The 'Global Village' was around the corner.

Piscator's big opportunity to start realizing his more ambitious aims came in 1924 when he was invited to direct at the Volksbühne, Berlin's most prestigious theatre, seating 1800, and having a large revolving stage, cyclorama, adjustable rostra and stage raking. His successful work there put him much in demand and he was responsible for no less than eleven productions over the next two to three years. But by 1927, the Volksbühne management were getting nervous about his uncompromising Marxism; and in any case, he was now looking for a theatre of his own. Plans had been under way for the Bauhaus architect, Walter Gropius, to design for him a 'Total-Theater' which would embrace all Piscator's technical demands, but this dream project was not to be realized, and for the usual reason: finance. As an interim measure in 1927–8 he formed his own company known as the 'Piscator-Bühne' at the fashionably-located Theater am Nollendorfplatz, where he staged revolutionary versions of Brecht, Tolstoy and Toller with some success. At this time he even established a Studio for small-scale productions, and was offering courses in acting in which the emphasis – à la Meyerhold – was on physical training.[10] But the new company and its subsidiary activities only lasted for some nine months before being forced into liquidation. John Allen comments that this could hardly be called an artistic failure because Piscator was not trying to create an art theatre but a political one; yet ironically, it was the artistic achievement that suffered criticism for its political content.[11]

During the Piscator-Bühne's first production, Ernst Toller's *Hoppla, wir leben!*, a great deal of time was spent by Piscator during rehearsals discussing with each actor the political significance of their roles, especially the class aspect. Brecht, who had joined the company at this time, commented later that he thought Piscator possibly failed to share the actors' problem over the new style, being more interested in ingenious scenic invention.[12] The brief attempt to set up training for the 'new actor' was not to be revived until twelve years later in New York.

In 1933, like so many others, Reinhardt and Brecht included, Piscator left Hitler's Germany and went abroad. First he stopped over in Moscow for a while to make a film, then having been warned not to return to Berlin he spent two totally unproductive years in France. Finally, in December 1938, he left for New York where he was to become director for the Dramatic Workshop of the School for Social Research, an organization which ran two off-Broadway theatres. In the 1940s, the Epic style was introduced to New York in productions of Sartre's *The Flies* and Robert Penn Warren's *All the King's Men*. After the war, he returned occasionally to Berlin where he staged *Danton's Death* and *Requiem for a Nun* at the Schiller Theater, and *Death of a Salesman* at the Theater am Kurfürstendamm, both in the then Western sector of the city. Whilst it was Caspar Neher, Brecht's close colleague, who had designed the production of *Danton's Death,* it is interesting to note that Piscator was not apparently invited to join Brecht's newly-formed Berliner Ensemble in the Communist sector, either at the Deutsches Theater in 1949, or after 1954 at the Theater am Schiffbauerdamm. Piscator explained in a later interview that 'Brecht is my brother but our views of totality differ. Brecht unveils significant details of human life whilst I attempt to give a conspectus of political matters as a whole.'[13] But no doubt the truth also included the fact that one 'boss' was thought enough; and that Brecht wished to distance himself from the early seminal influence, now that it was absorbed and he was his own man; or perhaps he considered that Piscator had collaborated too much with the capitalist ethos and audience to get those expensive Western sector productions mounted. Whatever the reason, in any case it was not so much Brecht who was Piscator's true heir in the revived German theatre but Peter Stein (of whom more later).

In 1962, Piscator's 1956 version of *War and Peace* was seen in a production by Val May at the Bristol Old Vic, and later in London. That same year, Piscator took over the Theater am Kurfürstendamm where he staged a magnificent single version of Hauptmann's four plays on *The House of Atreus*, with Japanese-style screens, symbolic orbs of red, black and gold, and a translucent stage lit from beneath. (The great classical story was given another impressive production by Ariane Mnouchkine thirty years later, as described in Chapter 12.) Piscator's last appointment was as Artistic Director of the new Freie Volksbühne in West Berlin where he directed, among other premières, Hochhuth's *The Representative* and Weiss's *The Investigation*, both strongly in the documentary tradition he had initiated in the 1920s. In the USA, where he spent thirteen years, his influence is marked in the work of Arthur Miller, Tennessee Williams and Julian Beck's Living Theatre; in England, his example can be seen not only in the obvious case of Joan Littlewood's Theatre Workshop, but also in the extraordinary creative explosion which has been seen in stage design during more recent years – for example, Bob Crowley's staggering setting for Richard Eyre's 1991 production at the Olivier Theatre of David Hare's *Murmuring Judges*.

Visual and scenic invention in production were, indeed, one of Piscator's major contributions to theatre in this century, as witness the exhibition in honour of his work mounted by the Arts Council at the Hayward Gallery in 1971; but his importance to the making of the professional actor in the century remains with that alignment with reality forged in the trenches at Ypres. That attitude was also expressed a few days before his death in March 1966, and is quoted by Braun from the catalogue to the Hayward exhibition. Piscator had noted the wonderful new theatre buildings in Germany, and also noted with disappointment that they were only presenting the same old types of plays. He goes on:

> Only now and then does theatre penetrate further, into the spiritual realm, beyond a mere interpretation of a work, to gain a far wider significance, to represent the spirit of a nation. The theatre as the home of the nation's conscience, the stage as the moral institution of the century; this should be the image of the theatre twenty years after [the Second World War].[14]

Despite their separate ways after that war, the name usually most closely associated with Piscator's political theatre, and whose plays have mostly illustrated that volte-face in acting style which does *not* require the audience to suspend its disbelief, was of course Bertolt Brecht (1898–1956). So much has been written about Brecht, and indeed, he wrote so much himself about his work, that the intention here must be to focus mainly on his views about acting and what these have meant in professional practice.

Nine days before his death on 14 August 1956, Brecht pinned his last message to the Berliner Ensemble on the notice-board of the Theater am Schiffbauerdamm. It read, in part:

> For our London season we need to bear two things in mind. First: we shall be offering most of the audience a pure pantomime, a kind of silent film on the stage for they know no German.[15] ... Second: there is in England a long-standing fear that German art (literature, painting, music) must be terribly heavy, slow, laborious and pedestrian. So our playing needs to be quick, light, strong. This is not a question of hurry, but of speed, not simply of quicker playing, but of quick thinking. We must keep the tempo of a run-through and infect it with quiet strength, with our own fun.[16]

The London season opened on 27 August, with Helene Weigel playing the title role in Brecht's production of his *Mother Courage*. The English acting profession attended with keen interest to have an authentic experience of the much-spoken-of 'alienation effect' in acting. Surely the company's leading lady and widow of the dramatist would be an exemplar? But what did they actually witness? Here was an actress at the peak of her powers, engaging us in exactly the same way as any other great performer; showing us a woman whose predicament and destiny we could identify with, whose story was indeed a comment on the barbarity of war, but which above all was a salute to the human spirit. Whatever this 'alienation technique' was, it did not seem to make much difference to the *acting* of a story. To the *production*: yes. There were the spot-bars in view, and the placards explaining the scenes, and the simple hints at location – all those Brechtian elements we had read about, and which undoubtedly influenced many a subsequent designer and director and playwright. But what was the traditional British actor to make of it all? At the time, the answer was 'very little'. Only now, in hindsight, can both the significance and the non-significance of Brecht's theory be seen more clearly for what it was, and is.

Brecht's early influence came through Reinhardt's productions,

Piscator's Epic style, Japanese Noh theatre and Shakespearian narrative. He was not interested in naturalism, 'nor psychological drama, nor poetic mystery, nor elusive fantasy'.[17] With Reinhardt, to whom he was briefly attached as a supernumerary 'dramaturg' together with Carl Zuckmayer in 1924, he was a pre-Osborne example of the 'angry young man' with an overweening ego, seldom turning up, and looking 'like a cross between a lorry driver and a Jesuit seminarist' in his flapping leather jacket (not to become *de rigueur* until fifty years later). Zuckmayer goes on to describe how what Brecht wanted was nothing less than 'complete control' over programming and staging, and to encourage smoking in the audience as it might dispose them to think! 'As this was refused him he confined himself to coming and drawing his pay.' Not surprisingly, this unethical attitude led to his contract being allowed to lapse the following year.[18]

Brecht's ruthless, uncompromising attitude, and his imperviousness to what he regarded as conventional criticism, involved his actors in similar castigation. In one of his most original early productions, the 1931 much-revised version of *Mann ist Mann* (variously translated as 'A Man's a Man' or 'Man Equals Man'), the actor Peter Lorre exasperated audiences with his manner of speaking in a disjointed and heavily-stressed way, as instructed by Brecht. But it was all part of the total concept: the scenery, too, was 'fragmentary, the costumes fantastic and Caspar Neher's projections enormous caricatures'.[19] Lorre, of course, was already an accomplished and well-known actor in Berlin, although his most famous role before his Hollywood career was to come the following year with the release in 1932 of Fritz Lang's film *M*. Lorre's acting in *Mann ist Mann* was defended by Brecht in his notes to the production published as 'The Question of Criteria for Judging Acting'.[20]

Those on the night who felt him to be lacking in 'carrying-power' or 'the gift of making his meaning clear' could have satisfied themselves about his gifts in this direction at the early rehearsals. If these hitherto accepted hallmarks of great acting faded away at the performance (only to be replaced, in my view, by other hallmarks, of a new style of acting) this was the result aimed at by the rehearsals.

Brecht then analyses these aims at some length:

> The impression intended was of a man simply reading a case
> for the defence prepared at some quite different period, without
> understanding what is meant as he did so. And this was
> indeed the impression left on any of the audience who knew
> how to make such observations.

> All the same, the epic theatre has profound reasons for in-
> sisting on such a reversal of criteria. Part of the social trans-
> formation of the theatre is that the spectator should not be
> worked on in the usual way. *The theatre is no longer the
> place where his interest is aroused but where he brings it to
> be satisfied.* [My italics]

This presupposes an audience which hungers for an 'interest to
be satisfied' – which precisely explains why Brecht appeals to the
intelligentsia rather than a popular audience.

> It may be that the epic theatre . . . will simply do away with
> the notion of the actor who 'carries the play'; for the play is
> no longer 'carried' by him in the old sense.

> It is a matter of establishing quite new rules for the art of
> acting (playing against the flow, letting one's characteristics
> be defined by one's fellow actors, etc.).

The bracketed comment here shows how confused Brecht's thinking
had become. 'Against the flow' can only mean 'against the text,
or written narrative' yet a sentence later he is justifying this as
'helping the playwright to make a point'; and as for a role being
defined by the attitude of other roles, this is nothing new, for it
happens whether the actor 'allows' it or not.

Again, Brecht states the obvious when he says 'the epic actor
lets his character grow before the spectator's eyes out of the way
in which he behaves'. Nothing new in that either; and interestingly, he quotes Chaplin as in many ways coming 'closer to the
epic than to the dramatic theatre's requirements'. It might be
deduced from this that he saw the patently comic model – as in

Leonard Rossiter's Hitlerian Arturo Ui, akin to Chaplin's Great Dictator – as more epic than the dramatic mode of, say, Olivier's Henry V or Diana Rigg's Medea. This is a strange dichotomy, and it twists the dictionary meaning of the word 'epic' from seriously pertaining to 'heroic achievements' to laughing at them. This, indeed, may give an 'alienated' or objective view of them. But the root of this theory was not so much to ridicule as to find what Brecht frequently referred to as the *gestus*.

The concept of *gestus* included at once gesture, attitude, gist of argument and point of expression, but it excluded the psychological and metaphysical aspects unless these could be given in definite physical terms.[21] *Gestus* preceded the notorious *Verfremdungseffekt*, or 'alienation effect', by some four years. Brecht's first use of *Verfremdung* was in 1935; and ultimately, he lived to regret the term. It would have been better translated, perhaps, to mean 'distancing'. Brecht used an improvization exercise in rehearsal wherein his actors had to 'deliver a monologue as reported speech, starting with: "He says that – "'.[22] This is one of the best explanations of what 'alienation technique' was supposed to do in the process of rehearsal and performance. Braun calls it 'using the characters to "illustrate" the narrative rather than "live" their roles'.[23] Brecht himself wrote of 'the realm of gest or *gestus*' as being 'the realm of attitudes adopted by the characters towards one another'. He goes on:

> The 'story' is the theatre's great operation, the complete fitting together of all the gestic incidents, embracing the communications and impulses that must now go to make up the audience's entertainment.
>
> Each single incident has its basic gest: Richard Gloster courts his victim's widow. The child's true mother is found by means of a chalk circle. God has a bet with the Devil for Dr Faustus's soul. Wozzeck buys a cheap knife in order to do his wife in, etc. The grouping of the characters on the stage and the movements of the groups must be such that the necessary beauty is attained above all by the elegance with which the material conveying that gest is set out and laid bare to the understanding of the audience.[24]

It would seem that Brecht's theoretical writing, like that of Stanislavski, has suffered at crucial points over the matter of translation. Not only do *gestus* and *Verfremdung* need careful annotation; so does the word *Wissenschaft*. Willett comments that it is really a broader term than the simple English 'science' and that 'Brecht certainly regarded it as embracing the Marxist view of history as well as the natural sciences.' In an early 'Dialogue about Acting', written in 1929, Brecht uses the term extensively to describe both the audience and the actor in his new theatre. The actor is to demonstrate his knowledge of human relations, behaviour and capacities in a conscious, suggestive and descriptive way (i.e. scientifically) for 'an audience of the scientific age'. The 'Dialogue' continues:

Are we to see science in the theatre then?
No. Theatre.
I see: scientific man is to have his theatre like everybody else.
Yes. Only the theatre has already got scientific man for its audience, even if it doesn't do anything to acknowledge the fact. For this audience hangs its brains up in the cloakroom along with its coat.[25]

The 'Dialogue' compares instructively with Piscator's view of acting as a 'dehumanized' activity for which, as we have noted, Piscator was much criticized. Brecht is careful to stress that the actor's knowledge is about being human and not merely a cipher. But in respect of also denying his actors the psychological and metaphysical dimensions of being human (except through physical terms, that is, denying the actor language for these), he is inclined to want to have his theoretical cake and to eat it.

What Brecht is really describing in his 'new technique of acting' is the *process* which all acting involves, whatever its style or nature; he is showing *how it works* whilst doing it, rather than creating anything new in the doing itself. He is interested in showing the *how* rather than the *what,* the demonstration rather than the performance, the 'scientific' analysis rather than the 'magic' of illusion. All the same, 'art' was to be legitimately used in this demonstration, so that it was not 'just like life' after all; it was a concoction; it was, in short, theatre. Harry Secombe in *The Goon*

Show once described himself as 'disappearing through little hole in middle of record'. Brecht is rather like that, and moreover, by now the record has worn rather thin. His circular argument is encapsulated in the following paragraph from 'Short Description of a New Technique of Acting which Produces an Alienation Effect':

> Once the idea of total transformation is abandoned the actor speaks his part not as if he were improvising it himself but like a quotation. At the same time he obviously has to render all the quotation's overtones, the remark's full human and concrete shape; similarly the gesture he makes must have the full substance of a human gesture even though it now represents a copy.[26]

What, you might ask, has changed? It is submitted that there is nothing 'new' here. It is merely describing what acting has always been and always will be – the representation of someone else. The context in which this is done may be acknowledged (with the collusion of the audience) to be either real or fictional, and it may engender either a subjective or an objective reaction. The actor, or surrogate person, may be either a high priest in a religious ritual, a political voice on a soap-box in the wilderness, or the 'all-licens'd fool' in popular entertainment. There, but for the grace of God, go we. To paraphrase Tom Stoppard, we are people – the opposite of actors. Alienation, or difference, is the natural name of the game. The sacred floor-space of the stage, whether in ancient Greece, the Globe's wooden O, the 'wilderness' of Drury Lane or the tight confines of a cellar in Soho, defines by inches or many yards the absolute separation of person from actor.

Richard Eyre, Director of the National Theatre, talks of intellect alone making the actor 'seem doltish, describing a performance rather than giving it'. This precisely echoes Brecht's attempts to define his new rules for acting. Eyre dubs it 'university acting' – 'all architecture and no heart, assembled by an intelligent mind conscious of meanings, of content, of style, of history, *over*conscious in short, and saddled with an implicit editorial commentary that runs parallel to the performance, telling the audience what to think about the character and his predicament – and that the actor is more important, or more intelligent, than the character he is playing. It's like music written by computer.'[27] Brecht's work sometimes gives the impression of theatre composed by computer.

Late in his life, in 1952, Brecht outlined the areas of common concern in theatre practice between himself and Stanislavski. These included 'the feeling for a play's poetry' rather than mere reportage, 'the sense of responsibility to society' or an ethical theatre, 'ensemble playing' the 'importance of the broad conception' along with 'a wealth of subtly elaborated detail', 'truthfulness as a duty' in the actor's work on himself and on his role, 'unity of naturalness and style', the 'representation of reality as full of contradictions'. But after those incontestable principles, Brecht ends by turning his last two points in his own direction: Stanislavski, he says, 'was a convinced humanist, and as such conducted his theatre along the road of socialism', and finally, 'he invented new artistic methods for every production' and others 'in turn developed their teacher's art further in complete freedom'. As Willett indicates in a footnote, the last point is 'clearly an appeal not to stick with Stanislavski'.

Brecht's most important theoretical statement was probably 'A Short Organum for the Theatre', written in 1948 with some subsequent appendices. He called it 'a description of a theatre of the scientific age'. We have already noted the broad sense of 'scientific' which he gave to *Wissenschaft*. The language and numbered division of the 'Short Organum' is portentous, not to say pretentious. He 'agrees' with Aristotle (almost surprising himself at being so old-fashioned) that 'narrative is the soul of drama'. He finds the 'noblest function that we have found for theatre . . . is to give pleasure'. Note the arrogance of that 'we have found' – as though audiences throughout the history of the drama had not already done so! Throughout the piece, it is Marxist dogma which castigates audiences and the acting profession alike for not being among those 'most impatient to make great alterations' in society. 'The theatre has to become geared to reality if it is to be in a position to turn out effective representations of reality, *and to be allowed to do so* [my italics].' Because good actors compound the crime of keeping audiences 'as if in a trance' he would 'like them to be as bad as possible'.[28] It is a strange way, to say the least, of getting 'geared into reality'.

When Brecht talks of the actor as appearing 'on the stage in a double role, as Laughton and as Galileo', he is merely describing that well-known genre of acting known as 'personality acting' in which the actor, usually a star-name, is more or less the same in whatever role he appears. Rex Harrison and Robert Morley used to be good examples; whereas Alec Guinness and Daniel Day-Lewis are probably better placed in the genre of 'character actor' in which there is a remarkable identification with the role played, erasing their own personality. Laughton, perhaps, spanned both genres in his remarkable career, but Brecht will have none of the 'character actor', seeing it as fundamentally dishonest or 'hiding behind a veil'. The actor's original function – that of being a 'hypocrite', a dissembler – is no longer permissible.

For Brecht, the class war took precedence over everything else: 'for art to be "unpolitical" means only to ally itself with the "ruling" group'. He does not say whether this would apply to a communist ruling group. Kenneth Tynan, writing in the year that the Berliner Ensemble first came to London, noted that behind every line of Brecht's work 'there beats a passionate desire to improve the human condition'. That is true, and it was a worthy desire; but like Shaw, he made the mistake of thinking that by *using* the theatre overtly for his own political purposes he could nevertheless avoid betraying it, albeit only in part, at its essential artistic heart. Shakespeare never did that, nor even Ibsen, and certainly not Chekhov, however much there was a political sub-text in all their plays. Brecht said that 'the exposition of the story and its communication by suitable means of alienation constitute the main business of theatre'. Had he only left out those two words 'of alienation', he would have been absolutely right. He got it right when he says a little later that 'if art reflects life it does so with special mirrors'. But, of course, that begs the question as to the nature of those 'special mirrors'.[29]

Brecht was undoubtedly a playwright of considerable power, but his ironic fate, as observed by Gottfried Reinhardt, was to be ignored by those whom he most wanted to serve and find himself fêted by those he most despised, the capitalist cultural élite. Academia found itself much more inclined to write theses on Brecht and his work than, for example, on Noël Coward or Terence Rattigan, or even the great Max Reinhardt. Moreover, he became a very convenient figure, especially to curriculum planners without much time, for the theoretical division of twentieth-century theatrical studies. All this may have over-stressed his actual importance, not only in popular theatre, but as representing an advance upon, or at least an equal counterpart to, Stanislavski's psychological theatre, and naturalism as a mode of acting. It is, perhaps, a significant pointer in the 1990s that each weekly issue of the professional newspaper *The Stage* has several training schools who indicate their allegiance to the Stanislavski approach, but none who specialize in the Brechtian style, however much it might be discussed. Even the Berliner Ensemble itself, adapting to the newly unified city, inclines to reject its founder and look to pastures new.

In an article in the *Independent*, 14 January 1993, Aaron Hicklin reported how, in the hands of five directors, the Ensemble had been privatized. The leading German playwright, the late Heiner Müller, was at the helm with a £10 million budget at his disposal. But Brecht's reputation had not survived along with this spring cleaning. 'Identified with a discredited regime which rewarded his loyalty with perks unimaginable to normal citizens, the great dramatist of the century has been dubbed a hypocrite by many in the German media.' The term 'hypocrite' is particularly ironic in view of Brecht's own dismissal of the dissembling actor. However, Müller's regard for Brecht was not in doubt even though his plays would no longer take pride of place and only be performed occasionally. 'The theatre is no longer committed to the dusty repertoire which saw the Ensemble decline from an artistic powerhouse into a theatrical waxworks.' Müller himself was not without his critics. A London review of his re-working of *Les Liaisons Dangereuses*, *Quartet*, at the Lilian Baylis Theatre, left Jeremy Kingston 'pointlessly puzzled'.[30] But in Berlin it was Brecht's daughter, no less, who castigated his plans. Barbara Brecht-Schall had fought a rearguard action for the Ensemble since the death of her mother, Helene Weigel, in 1971. But now that the tide of history had swept over all but the peaks of the company's past greatness, she said that 'As far as I am concerned there is no more Berliner Ensemble. That's definite, and I wish they would call it something else. Müller's Magic Show, or whatever.' For his part, Müller transformed everything in a bid to revive the name if not the style of the company to its former glory. He altered seating (and standing) arrangements, the assumptions about repertoire, a de-unionized membership, and envisaged joint ventures with other European theatres. Not that he gave up on the left-wing ideals, for which he was also criticized. His philosophy was an aggressive one for the 1990s:

> The age of pretending to know the truth on stage is over. What we are looking for on stage is conflict and confrontation.... There are so many illusions and lies now. We have to find a way to disturb the consensus, to disturb the peace, which is an illusionary thing in Germany. The fall of the Wall was a defeat, and the consequence is that we have to begin from the beginning.

Brecht would have liked that. Perhaps his spirit will live on in the new Berliner Ensemble after all. However, with the untimely death of Müller on 30 December 1995, the future of the company is once again an open question.

At the end of the twentieth century, Brecht takes his rightful place in theatrical history, but as a dramatist and a director more than a prime initiator of any significant change in the making of the professional actor.

10

The 'Turbulent Thirties': Saint-Denis, Guthrie, Clurman, Doone, Artaud and Barrault – The Seminal Initiators

When the critic J. C. Trewin detailed a decade of London theatre as 'The Turbulent Thirties',[1] he had no cause to mention Artaud, Barrault or Clurman (all of whom worked abroad), and only gave a single passing note on Doone's Group Theatre, three short references to Saint-Denis, and eight acknowledgements of Guthrie productions with never more than a sentence on each. Yet Trewin's record is a copious and accurate one. It is only in hindsight, some sixty years later, that the true underlying turbulence can be discerned in Western theatre. It had been stirred up by the avant-garde in Moscow, Paris, Berlin and New York, but very little in London. The English capital found its most serious theatre-going during the 1930s with the plays of J. B. Priestley, James Bridie, Emlyn Williams and Dodie Smith; there was still the ageing Shaw, mostly at Malvern, and a final theatrical fling from Maugham with *Sheppey*; also the Coward of *Private Lives* came up with *Cavalcade*, and even Eliot's *Murder in the Cathedral* reached the West End at the Duchess Theatre in 1936; round the corner, Ivor Novello held sway at Drury Lane, but at least over the Waterloo Bridge, Lilian Baylis was flying the flag of national culture at the Old Vic from her tiny office behind the prompt-side stage box, all for the greater glory of God (whom she knew well) and Shakespeare (less well).[2]

The names chosen to mark the 1930s here, of course, are re-nowned more for their artistic turbulence than a commercial or popular one, although there were times when some of them caused both to happen.

120

Michel Saint-Denis (1897–1971)

For all the major influence of Stanislavski's theoretical writings, Michel Saint-Denis was probably the most important practical teacher of acting from the 1930s to the 1960s in both Europe and later the USA. Peter Hall said of him that his whole life 'was a quest for truth in the theatre':

> He believed, of course, in craft, in technique, but only as *means*. Acting was not a trick to be learned and then performed; it was not imitation, but rather revelation of the whole human personality . . . the theatre was not a place to hide: it was a place to *be*.[3]

This was the inheritance from his uncle and mentor, Copeau, and an ongoing truth which is continually in danger of being lost, especially in increasingly materialistic times.

More than Piscator or Brecht – and despite having been in the front line in 1916 at the age of nineteen – Saint-Denis recognized the two kinds of reality for what they are: that of the man and that of the artist. In 1920, with Copeau at the Vieux Colombier, 'a new reality had been brought to the interpretation of the French classics, a reality that had style, animated by a human "realistic" truthfulness'.[4] Realistic has to be in inverted commas because it was not naturalism. 'A complete actor cannot take shape, a dramatist cannot grow out of photographic naturalism. True representation of reality requires transposition and style.'[5] What Saint-Denis meant by style will be examined in a moment. In 1922 he saw a performance of *The Cherry Orchard* when Stanislavski visited Paris with the Moscow Art Theatre. It was a seminal experience for him, and for the other students from Copeau's school who went 'ready to laugh . . . at those naturalistic people' but soon changed their tune. Reporting an interview in *The Guardian* for 5 December 1961, the opening night of Saint-Denis' own production of *The Cherry Orchard* for the Royal Shakespeare Company in Stratford, Gareth Lloyd Evans said, 'The words "naturalism", "realism" and "style" he uses like chess pieces in his persistent attempts to give pattern to his thinking . . . He encompasses the theatre of the world like a benevolent dictator;

in him the word "dedication" becomes flesh.'

In 1931 he started his own company at the Vieux Colombier, La Compagnie des Quinze, in direct succession to Les Copiaux. It was his first directorship, and the company was more fortunate than Copeau's in finding a dramatist of quality in André Obey. With Obey, the style was 'epic' before that term had really become known in Paris (though it was the same year as Brecht's *Mann ist Mann* in Berlin). Until 1935, Saint-Denis directed about ten plays for the Compagnie des Quinze, and acted in most of them. Annually, between 1931 and 1934, the company visited London for three-to-four week seasons which, in hindsight, proved a most important influence. But in 1934, with Parisian cultural life treating them as little more than a curiosity, a discouraged and somewhat decimated company left the capital to try and re-establish itself near Aix-en-Provence at a rather exotic location called 'Beau Manoir'. The venture lasted only six months, partly for lack of money and partly because of the usual difficulties attendant upon communal life.

However, because the London theatrical profession seemed to appreciate their work so enthusiastically (more than such critics as J. C. Trewin), a theatre studio in the English capital was decided upon, with the necessary financial help being generously offered by half-a-dozen leading actors of the time, together with Guthrie and the designers 'Motley'. Marius Goring, who had been with Saint-Denis at Aix-en-Provence, introduced him to George Devine and Glen Byam Shaw, thus establishing a long and fruitful partnership. With them, in 1935–6, Saint-Denis set up the London Theatre Studio (LTS). His wish was to extend the creative basis of the training with the Compagnie des Quinze:

> Our purpose was to enlarge the actor's field of expression and to equip him in such a way that he could put each technique that he learned to the service of his acting without falling into the trap of specialization in any of them . . . We were not interested in quick results, we were interested in the gradual growth of each individual talent.[6]

It has been said that Saint-Denis was sometimes cruel in his teaching; but that might be reported of most great teachers who have a persistence, an obstinacy, a passion to see something 'real' happen on stage. His approach to this 'reality' was clear from the start. 'Theatre is not life, theatre is theatre ... and I might add that theatre is a revelation: a concrete, intellectual, emotional and sensual revelation of life by means of this art which is called the art of the stage.'[7] Improvisation was the most important part of the work at the LTS (something with which Guthrie never agreed). An unused chapel in Islington, north London, was converted and became the Studio's home. One of its most exciting productions was *A Midsummer Night's Dream*, directed by Marius Goring, which 'opened doors to new ways of vocal expression'.[8] The LTS remained in business until 1939. Apart from Saint-Denis' own accounts, a full description of the work at the LTS is given by Irving Wardle in his excellent *The Theatres of George Devine*, Cape, 1978, pp. 51–88.

John Gielgud was once asked what was meant by 'style'. He replied that it was 'knowing what kind of play you are in'. Saint-Denis had a lot to say about it in the only book he published during his lifetime, *Theatre: The Rediscovery of Style*. It is never easy to define, but Saint-Denis made several attempts:

> ... good manners, proper training, elegance, a sense of period, and revelation of the personality – all these things are inherent in style ... Style is like wine: better as it grows older. It also becomes more evident with time. Hence the confusion between style and period ... Style has its own reality: it is made up of a choice of words, of shape, of rhythm and emphasis. It cannot be separated from meaning, nor can it be separated from form ... Style does not lie. It is the expression of real understanding.[9]

In considering Stanislavski's system, Saint-Denis thought that when applied literally it merely led to 'realism' (meaning, I think, in this context, 'naturalism') but that given selection and discrimination it could achieve its aim of being 'the grammar of all styles'. Style liberates artistry from the mud of naturalism. It deserves our love and respect, but we must never confuse it with that awful thing 'stylisation'. Saint-Denis saw Expressionism as having contributed to that false use of the word.

One of the main problems to be solved in structuring the training of actors (and indeed, in directing actors) is to find the right balance between telling them what to do and giving space to the actor's own invention. Saint-Denis never claimed to have solved the conundrum, but he thought Jean Vilar came close to doing so at the Théâtre National Populaire. Vilar favoured word rehearsals for a third of the rehearsal period before any detailed fixing of the stage action. He did not want the actor moving, or being pre-set, too early; and when he did get on the stage his own sensitivities would determine the nature of his physical reactions.

Theatre schools, noted Saint-Denis, seem to provoke many theatre people to hostility; but of the half dozen he initiated during his life, he felt that the Old Vic School (1946–52) was 'the most complete'. There, he limited the number of students as much as possible, and albeit partly experimental, the 'chief practical purpose was wholly and above all to serve interpretation'.[10] Three years was considered the minimum course time (although in postwar England, the state would only support two years, whereas in France it was three, and in Russia four). The ideals for training which Saint-Denis laid down at the Old Vic School remain enshrined, but of course, practical details and conditions have been much changed or modified since then, as was noted in the Introduction. In the very first term there was a three-week rehearsal period of a Shakespeare play under the Principal. This 'rather nasty operation' was called 'the test' and enabled all the rest of the staff to assess each student's level of ability. Students and the complete staff then met for a critical 'post-mortem' on the work shown. In less draconian fashion, ongoing assessment with internal performance work is a continuing tradition, though not necessarily so early in a course. 'Theories of acting' were not taught, but each phase of tuition was allowed to illuminate slowly what these might incur. The training had three main parts: cultural, technical, and acting interpretation with improvisation. The last of these was considered the most important training tool, although as we have noted (*pace* Guthrie), its place in professional rehearsals is less primal (in most cases), if only because all experienced actors employ it anyway in the true rehearsal process. A similarly important training tool was the use of the mask. Saint-

Denis' experience with Les Copiaux in Burgundy (1924–9) had been a re-creation of the improvisational ideals and practice of the *commedia dell'arte*. It was a particularly French tradition, despite its Italian origin, moving through Molière and Debureau to the Vieux Colombier. It explains much of both Copeau's and Saint-Denis' devotion to the mask, especially as a training device, and to improvisation as the most creative means of rehearsal.

In her Introduction to the posthumous publication of *Training for the Theatre*, Suria Saint-Denis quotes one of her husband's letters to a friend: 'Everything, as you know, depends on the doing, on how things are *understood* and *done*. How is one to make this concrete?' The Old Vic School was his effort to make concrete his understanding of theatre and acting through 'the thing done' (the Greek *dromenon*, which gives us the very word, drama). 'To him,' says Suria Saint-Denis, 'a school was not only a place to learn from the past; he felt it should also be a place to try out new ideas and to experiment in ways not possible in the commercial theatre.'[11] The school which has most followed this philosophy in England is Drama Centre London, founded in 1963 when John Blatchley (himself an ex-student of Saint-Denis), Yat Malmgren and Christopher Fettes (the current Principal), broke away from the more conventional Central School to adopt a more Stanislavskian emphasis. Simon Callow's book, *Being an Actor* (1984), describes what it was like being a student there in the early 1970s. *Training for the Theatre* extends the basic ideas and principles of training expressed in *Theatre: The Rediscovery of Style*, and puts flesh on the bare bones of a schedule for teaching. It speaks with authority for itself, is available, and needs no repetition here. Detailed charts for each term of a four-year course codify the Saint-Denis teaching practice (pages 88–99).

The five post-war years, 1947–52, which saw the all-too-short existence of the Old Vic Theatre School and the Young Vic Company, were of seminal importance to actor training in Britain. During this time, Saint-Denis, Devine and Byam Shaw set the guidelines adopted by most leading drama schools during the following forty years, and which are still important. Moreover, not only in this country but in Strasbourg (1952–7), in Montreal (1960), in New York (1968 onwards), and again in England at the Stratford Studio of the RSC from 1962 for a brief period,[12] the schools set up by Saint-Denis have represented an ideal for progressive training schedules to emulate, whether in French or in English. Saint-Denis saw a school as 'a place to re-invent theatre'. It is doubtful whether such a statement could be found in the prospectuses of today's leading drama schools, for all that they have tried to follow in his footsteps. But in the heady days of new planning for theatre (as for everything else) after the Second World War, such an idea was exciting and possible. It led to the creation of the Old Vic Theatre Centre in 1947, which included not only the School and the Young Vic touring company, but an experimental group run by the three joint directors, although unfortunately the latter never got off the drawing-board. The liaison with the Old Vic Company and its wide-ranging repertoire was an essential ingredient 'to the existence of a *total* school' (his italics). Irving Wardle devotes four chapters to an extended account of the work of the Old Vic Centre in his book on George Devine. Just as it had really started, the whole operation was brought rudely to a halt by the Arts Council, who refused funding to pay the Company's debts. The Governors of the Old Vic appear to have been woefully inadequate in exercising their responsibilities; and by an ironic cross-current, it was Tyrone Guthrie who, like Brutus, put in the final dagger. Olivier described the demise with some spleen as 'unimaginatively misguided' and a 'crass mistake' which would 'no doubt be passed off with the customary apologetic smirk'.[13]

In the USA, Saint-Denis found so-called actor training at the university Drama departments 'a little bit too abstract, too intellectual. This sort of discussion makes a young actor much too conscious of the problems of acting instead of inducing him to *experience* acting with spontaneity. I often had the feeling that teachers were training other teachers rather than the actors.'[14] It is a criticism not without foundation in our own university Drama departments and academia in general. Following a stroke in the spring of 1969, Saint-Denis was unable to attend the opening of the Juilliard School of New York's Lincoln Center in September. He did not live to see the achievement of this school, the last on which he set the seal of his inspiration and philosophy.

Tyrone Guthrie (1900–71)

With Rupert Doone, Tyrone Guthrie is the only other English-man (Anglo-Irishman, actually) among the six names chosen for this chapter, a ratio which may speak for itself. There were some good British directors in the 1930s – Harcourt Williams at the Old Vic, Norman Marshall at the Gate, Basil Dean, and, of course, John Gielgud and Emlyn Williams who often directed the pieces in which they starred – but Guthrie stood tallest (both culturally and literally) among them. C. B. Cochrane was probably the most famous theatrical name of the period, but like Hugh Beaumont at H. M. Tennent Ltd, he was an impresario rather than a director or actor. 'Cockie' and 'Binkie' were showmen looking on.

Why Guthrie is still called an 'actor' as well as 'director' in Dictionaries and Companions to the Theatre is hard to understand. According to his own account[15] he never got past a few walk-ons in his first and only job as a professional actor with J. B. Fagan's company at Oxford in 1924. Thereafter, it was directing all the way, and creating companies and theatres. He started at the Cambridge Festival Theatre, then came to London with one of the Cambridge productions in 1931 – James Bridie's *The Anatomist*. In 1933, he started the first of many seasons at the Old Vic where most of his Shakespearian work was done. George Rowell notes that the Annual Report for 1933–4 affirmed that Guthrie 'had been instrumental in bringing into the theatre many of the younger generation, particularly the definitely artistic section, which might otherwise have never entered it'.[16] But he was not then kept on by Lilian Baylis. The next two years at the Old Vic were run by Henry Cass – unsuccessfully – so Baylis brought Guthrie back for the 1936–7 season, and he stayed on for another ten years. Baylis herself died in November 1937 of a heart attack, aged sixty-three; just before the delayed opening of an ill-fated *Macbeth* with Olivier, directed by Saint-Denis. By 1939 Guthrie was appointed Administrator of both the Old Vic and Sadler's Wells, a job which lasted until 1945. He was brought back again for the troubled period 1951–2 on a temporary basis to clear up after the Old Vic Centre débâcle. He then freelanced for a few years at the Edinburgh Festival and abroad. He set up the Shakespearian Festival Theatre, Stratford, Ontario, in 1953, staying until 1957. In 1963, the Guthrie Theatre at Minneapolis opened (originally called the Minnesota Theatre Company until 1971).

At his best, Guthrie was a creative and experimental director, and his importance to the actor in our context is that he had a high regard for 'sound professional workmanship' with, as he might well have added, no nonsense. The strength of the British acting profession out of the 1930s, and for some twenty years after the Second World War, owes much to his unwavering standards and leadership. Yet he was always very humble about them. Unlike Brecht, he thought it 'impudence to set about uplifting and ennobling your fellow citizens. It implies that you know not only what is good for you, but also what is good for them.' Moreover, after forty years of mastering 'a limited repertory of the tricks of the trade', he confessed to 'a certainty that I do not know very well what is good and not at all what will be popular'.[17] He was knighted for services to the theatre in 1961.

Guthrie wrote several books, some radio plays and one play for the stage, *Top of the Ladder*, plus many articles and talks. He wrote an autobiography, *A Life in the Theatre* (1960), and *In Various Directions: A View of Theatre* (1965); and after his death there was an 'Authorized Biography' by James Forsyth in 1976. The blurb for the latter calls him 'one of the greatest figures in the development of the National Theatre'. But it was abroad that his achievements have been more obvious in the later years of his life, both at Stratford, Ontario, and Minneapolis:

> He created not simply theatre, but complete theatrical communities wherever he went: self-reliant, anti-metropolitan, and above all, theatre as a profound ritual, with a direct spiritual and social significance even, and especially, for the most unsophisticated. But never for an instant, joyless, pulpit theatre. The hallmark of his work was a sense of rampant, fire-cracker celebration.

In our context, his most pertinent book is *Tyrone Guthrie on Acting*, published by Studio Vista, London, in the year of his death, 1971. Unfortunately, it has been long out of print.

Nearly forty years earlier he had written a rather strange book called *Theatre Prospect*. In it the young Guthrie sees 'the relation between the stage and the audience as constituting the essence of "Theatre"'. The book deals with the 'organization' of theatre for its survival in the face of rising competition from the cinema, radio, and even the gramophone (television was not yet publicly around). The 'break with naturalism' is a key point, and with it 'a revival of romance, with poets again discovering intimations of immortality, and seeing in the material world around them the symbols of a universe more real, though unseen'.[18] That is a prophetic thought for 1932, with Eliot and Fry yet to write their verse plays (not to mention Auden, Isherwood, Spender and the rest), but it may also speak for a more distant future – the future of a ritual theatre in the twenty-first century. Also in *Theatre Prospect*, Guthrie was already thinking of the ideal of 'a school attached to the theatre' with the students being offered engagements in the regular company. He had Copeau's example in mind, whose work at the Vieux Colombier and 'Burgundian rustication' he had admired from a distance; but the work of the Compagnie des Quinze he had experienced with its 'technical excellence'. It is all the more strange, therefore, that he denied Michel Saint-Denis his Old Vic School attached to the company just when that school was getting established in 1951, apparently telling him that 'he didn't believe in training for actors'.[19] Yet in 1935 he had put up £1300 of his own money to help Saint-Denis start the London Theatre Studio. It did not make much sense; Guthrie himself would not explain it; in today's terms, it was probable that as a pragmatic Administrator he was forced to obey market-forces above any other criteria.

Lord Esher, Chairman of the Vic Governors, 'could never understand Saint-Denis' broken English, and dismissed him accordingly as a foreigner whose proper place was somewhere else'.[20] In May 1951, Saint-Denis had been demoted from overall control of the Old Vic Centre to Director of the School. Everyone at the Centre resigned, and Llewellyn Rees, then Administrator, was forced out. Only Hugh Hunt remained. Guthrie was persuaded to return as Administrator 'leaving Hugh Hunt awkwardly designated Administrative Director'. Guthrie disbanded the Experimental Theatre Centre and Young Vic Company at once, and allowed the School merely to honour its obligation to the current students until their course finished in the summer of 1952.

Nevertheless, it was natural that Guthrie should address the question of training in *Tyrone Guthrie on Acting*. Unlike today's directors, he believed in the rehearsed readings of plays as being more useful than improvisation exercises; and in the voice as being by far the most important instrument which the actor must command. In the very first term, he wanted to see phonetic symbols mastered, and by the end of the first year the student must pass an exam in the anatomy of the vocal mechanism, breath control and enunciation, and sight reading a vocal line of music. 'If he fails, I should sling him out . . . The general level of student achievement' is more important than losing someone who may *look* like star material, but will never sound like it.[21] The NCDT might usefully take such an exam on board before granting Accreditation to the rest of a school's training. It was Guthrie's contention, in an interesting variation on both Stanislavski and Brecht, that the actor should 'go through the *ritual* [his italics] of a performance in such a manner as to make the fiction acceptable – not as fact, but as an interesting and pleasurable experience'. The actor has 'to translate imagination into practice' which involves 'not only *what* is to be expressed and *why*, but also *how*'. In most gifted practice, the imagination and the technique go together. Guthrie was ruthless about this: 'If a student has very little imagination, he ought not, in my view, to be encouraged towards the stage.'[22] For beginners he had a few definitive statements such as: 'Learning to breathe is the basis of all acting' . . . 'the meaningless pause is the deadliest sin of bad acting . . . fidgeting is the next most deadly' . . . 'how you REACT is frequently more important than what you yourself have to say or do'.[23] A well-trained actor's voice 'should be able to manage, at moderate speed and sufficiently loudly to carry in a large theatre, SEVEN lines of blank verse' . . . also 'easily cover a range of two and a half octaves. In normal conversation we rarely use more than one.'[24] He believed that the student actor should spend at least sixty per cent of his first year on the study of the voice. Not surprisingly, he noted that this never happened, as far as he knew; and indeed, it is no longer the case in the 1990s, perhaps even less so.

Likewise on the matter of improvisation, his training-wisdom is virtually heretical: 'I cannot see what use this is to an actor.' Perhaps, he says, a professional company may find an 'elusive meaning by improvising an analogous situation' – although 'this is a literary rather than a histrionic exercise' – but 'I cannot see why improvisation should be considered a valuable part of elementary training'.[25] He goes on to suggest, with some justification, that the stress on 'impro' may be because of economic convenience and ease of class involvement and arrangement ... no texts to buy, no scenery, props or learning of lines. Similarly, he comments, it is economically convenient to treat drama as literature, and to think that it can be adequately studied as part of a literary curriculum. It is not 'literature', nor can it be taught as such. To believe that it can be so taught is like believing you can teach surgery by taking a general course in biology. Educationalists please note.

Guthrie concludes his book on acting with this comment:

> Fewer and fewer actors regard the theatre as either the economic or artistic focus of their professional lives ... I am convinced that film and television are neither organized to encourage skilled, as opposed to marketable, actors, nor to develop in actors a serious and responsible attitude to their profession ... Acting as a calling somewhere between factory-work and prostitution is in demand as never before. Acting as a serious profession is in grave danger of extinction.[26]

That may be putting it a bit roughly, and perhaps unfairly, but the idealist speaks loud and clear. Today he would probably have commented on the media reducing acting to the occupation of 'luvvies'. Guthrie was the most *practical* of theatre men, and he more than most recognized that the root of 'drama' is 'the thing done'. He helped give the British theatre of the mid-century its enviably solid base for good acting; a base which now towards the end of the century is indeed in that 'grave danger' he foresaw, not because the actors are not serious, but because those who hold the purse-strings for subsidy and training are not serious.

Harold Clurman (1901–80)

In Paris in the early 1920s, his own age within a year of the calendar, Clurman 'wrote a thesis at the Sorbonne on the French

drama from 1890 to 1914, went regularly to the theatre, saw the
Moscow Art Theatre before they left for New York, and attended
lectures at Copeau's school at the Théâtre du Vieux Colombier
as well as all the Copeau productions'.[27] It was from this rich
European soil that Clurman's theatrical roots drew their suste-
nance. When he returned to New York in June 1924 to look for
a job, he knew it had to be in the theatre. However, with no job
forthcoming at first,

> between July and October . . . I read all the practical and
> theoretical books on the modern theatre. I read Gordon Craig,
> but . . . I understood him poorly. There was something there,
> but I couldn't make it out. I had too little experience. The
> experience began with the new firm of Macgowan–Jones–
> O'Neill at the Greenwich Village Theatre and the Provincetown
> Playhouse.[28]

He got work with them as an extra for ten dollars a week, attending all rehearsals with Robert Edmond Jones and Stark Young
and Richard Boleslavski directing. It was an auspicious début,
but he was not with them for long. Next, he tried several times
to join the Theatre Guild, eventually succeeding in getting a stage
manager's job. At the Guild he first met Lee Strasberg. By the
summer of 1926 he was engaged to play a few small parts in
Franz Werfel's *Juarez and Maximilian*, directed by Philip Moeller,
and which had a magnificent cast including Alfred Lunt, Edward
G. Robinson, Henry Travers and Morris Carnovsky. The assistant stage manager was 'a sturdy girl from Akron, Ohio' and
they discussed the play's artistic failure together at length. Her
name was Cheryl Crawford.

Many factors then began to come together for Clurman. He
watched Strasberg using new methods of rehearsal with amateurs;
methods he had learnt at the American Laboratory Theatre. Clurman
himself enrolled at the Laboratory to take a course in directing
with Boleslavski. At the Laboratory he met Stella Adler, his future wife, and 'youngest daughter of my childhood hero, Jacob
Adler'. The Theatre Guild had started a school 'hoping to develop some fresh acting talent' and his friend Sanford Meisner
had enrolled but was not satisfied with the training. Clurman put

Meisner in touch with Strasberg. That same year, 1926, Copeau accepted an invitation to direct his dramatization of *The Brothers Karamazov* at the Theatre Guild. Clurman wrote a publicity article on Copeau, and was engaged for the production, helping Copeau when his English failed him. 'Copeau's presence in New York acted as a catalytic agent in bringing Strasberg and myself together with the thought of forming a theatre of our own.' The thought itself had been brewing between them for at least two years. Copeau's influence further exercised itself when he gave lectures the following year at both the Guild and the Laboratory.

It was between November 1930 and May 1931, in various small rooms in New York City, at 11.30 p.m. once a week, that a number of actors and other artists met at Clurman's passionate instigation. That was to be the start of the American Group Theatre.[29] After spending the summer in Connecticut, working themselves into a company, some twenty-eight actors and three directors returned to New York in September 1931 to open as 'The Group Theatre (under the Auspices of the Theatre Guild)' at the Martin Beck Theatre in Paul Green's *The House of Connelly*. It was a truly American experiment, but stemming from French and Russian ideals. The direction was by Lee Strasberg and Cheryl Crawford who, together with Clurman, composed the Group's triumvirate at the time; and in the cast were such names as Morris Carnovsky, Stella Adler, Ruth Nelson and Franchot Tone. Later, Tone was to leave for Hollywood, but the Group was joined by other names since entered into the hall of film fame: John Garfield, Lee Cobb, Martin Ritt, Frances Farmer, J. Edward Bromberg and Sanford Meisner. Tone himself returned for the 1938–9 season to play in *The Gentle People* by Irwin Shaw.

By 1932 Strasberg was initiating classes and exercises to stimulate the Group actors' imagination and resourcefulness. Clurman took them over when Strasberg was busy directing, developing various improvisational projects.[30] The Group went on a second summer camp which was described by one of them as 'a training ground for citizenship'. Indeed, echoing the experience of both Stanislavski and Copeau, Clurman comments that 'From an experiment in the theatre we were in some way impelled to an experiment in living.'[31] But as with his predecessors, the experiment did not quite work out. Nevertheless, the actors still kept looking for a fresh technique of playing 'founded on life values'. They wanted to convey through theatre their interest in the life of their times. It was this, perhaps more than anything else, which became the group's 'distinguishing mark' and, at once, its greatest strength and greatest weakness.

The nadir of their fortunes came in 1933. Clurman and the writer Clifford Odets wandered together round the dejected, Depression-ridden street corners, byways and cheap burlesque houses of New York City. The unemployment, the hunger and the destitution of those days etched themselves into Odets' creative unconscious, to rise again two years later in his play about the taxi-drivers' union strike, *Waiting for Lefty* (written, incidentally, in three feverish nights, a not-unusual syndrome for a good play whose pregnant condition has often been much longer). 'The taxi strike of February 1934,' says Clurman, 'had been a minor incident in the labor crisis of this period.' But the Group Theatre's production of the play in 1935 touched a much deeper chord in audience response. When they are called upon at the end of the play to join in the urgent demand to 'Strike! Strike!' – this was 'something more than a tribute to the play's effectiveness, more even than a testimony of the audience's hunger for constructive social action – it was the birth cry of the Thirties. Our youth had found its voice.' 'Strike' was *Lefty*'s lyric message 'for greater dignity . . . for a bolder humanity . . . for the full stature of man'.[32] The tremendous success of the play saw the consummation (in Clurman's word) of the Group's ideals. To it was added a 'favourable but not sensational newspaper reception' for *Awake and Sing*, another play written out of the distress of the Depression 'and Odets' whole youth'. Although, by the time it was revived in 1939, the same reviewer, Brooks Atkinson of the *New York Times*, found it 'could not be praised too highly'.[33] *Waiting for Lefty* being only one hour long, Odets supplied a companion piece, *Till the Day I Die*, an anti-Nazi short story, which for 1935 was one of the earliest of the genre. At one time, thirty-two cities were seeing the double-bill simultaneously.

The American Group Theatre had strong socialist affiliations, more so than the London Group Theatre, although as we shall see, that, too, had its left-wing aspects. (The red flag was more truly raised in 1936 London by the Unity Theatre at King's Cross.)

But the American public in particular shunned labels such as 'Left theatre', fearing it for its political subversion. Nevertheless, the American Group Theatre was striving for a much wider appeal, looking for support from the best elements of society 'regardless of political sympathies'.

The Group's troubles were less political than artistic. Even in 1931, Clurman was having some difficulties with Strasberg, although 'touchiness' was admitted on both sides. It was really a sort of power game they were playing. Clurman was the somewhat lax yet nevertheless presiding director at most sessions of the company, whereas the strictly disciplinarian Strasberg would ask him 'to please not speak to my actors' – a phrase he later apologized for using. It was sometimes asserted in the Group's later years that it 'attracted the unbalanced' and 'induced neurosis in normal people' – Stella Adler's experience with Strasberg in 1934 is perhaps relevant here – but as Clurman pointed out, quoting Thoreau, 'If a man does not keep step with his companions, it is perhaps because he hears a different drummer.'[34]

In 1935, Stella Adler led a number of the Group actors to take lessons from Michael Chekhov. 'The actors felt that they had achieved some measure of honesty and truth in their work, but Chekhov's gift for combining these with sharply expressive and yet very free color, rhythm and design was something in which they knew themselves to be deficient, and which they therefore envied.'[35] A couple of years later, when their fortunes had looked up with the success of *Golden Boy*, the Group began to think about starting their own training classes. Robert Lewis set up a small Group Theatre school which offered some scholarships supported by twenty paying pupils over a ten-week term. Some of the company actors taught, with specialist instructors in fencing, movement and speech brought in; but with so much touring by the Group, the school only lasted a season. Nevertheless, private classes or classes in other schools in New York continued, so that an indirect Group training took root and had its more lasting influence.

Around 1936, Clurman felt that the group's 'main problem was continuity of activity or the means to provide our company with work and livelihood'. It was the year in which he finally took over as Managing Director of the Group, but the old strained

relations with Strasberg continued, and now included Cheryl
Crawford as well. The Group was on the verge of dissolution
when the Actors' Committee drafted a long document analyzing
the problems encountered and suggesting ways forward in order
to save the company. The three founding directors were individually analysed for their successes and their failures in giving the
company guidance. The actors, with 'one tattered bond left
between them – a passionate concern for the Group idea', then
concluded with three key suggestions as to what had to be done.
First, an assurance of 'regular, predictable sustaining income' for
Group actors; second, 'sufficient artistic exercise' for them (meaning,
more than just one good part in a year); and finally, a theatre of
their own, with at least 'forty weeks' full production and
performance'.[36]

The document, which had been encouraged by Clurman, was
read to the assembled actors in the absence of the directors. Meeting
on their own, and despite Clurman's initial encouragement, the
three directors decided to resign as a body. This 'both pleased
and startled' the actors, who took up the challenge by inviting
everyone – directors and actors – to draft 'an outline of future
plans'. However, the breakdown was real, if only temporary. In
August of the following year, 1937, the Group was re-assembled,
and a production of Odets' new play *Golden Boy* was staged at
the Belasco Theatre. 'By money standards,' as Clurman is careful
to express it, 'it was the greatest success in the Group's history.'
They lived to fight another day – or to be precise, four more
years.

The very successful *Golden Boy*, after 248 performances in New
York and the film rights sold to Hollywood, came to London for
a further triumphant season in 1938. James Agate wrote that
'The acting attains a level which is something we know nothing
at all about.' In 1938–9, the Group had a final flowering with
Odets' *Rocket to the Moon*, Irwin Shaw's *The Gentle People*,
William Saroyan's *My Heart's in the Highlands* and Robert Ardrey's
Thunder Rock (which was much more successful in war-torn London
the following year, 1940, than it was in New York). Yet for all
these successes, the Group never found a physical base in New
York. 'At the zenith of our efforts,' wrote Clurman, 'we were as
far from being a truly established rooted organization as we had

been as unknown beginners in 1928.' The Group struggled on until 1941 and finally closed, hardly noticed, with the failure of a play by Irwin Shaw called *Retreat to Pleasure*.

Looking back with hindsight, Clurman had some sage and significant things to say arising from the Group experiment. 'The boy in *Awake and Sing* explains "We don't want life printed on dollar bills." Nearly all the Group plays may be said to stem from this sentiment. Nearly the whole impulse of the Thirties – whatever its more limited aspects – was fed on that fire.' He goes on to point out that one of the misfortunes of history is that the artist and the man of action are rarely combined in one person, or for that matter one group, one company, one institution. Our follies, he suggested, were less important than what brought us together; only we had to discover that 'we cannot do good "in general". To be true collectivists, we must be more deeply individual.'[37]

Rupert Doone (1903–66)

The London Group Theatre was set up in 1932 without having any knowledge of its American counterpart. In its first two years, influenced to some extent by the companies of Copeau and Saint-Denis, there was an 'experimental reading' of *Peer Gynt* and the first modern revival of a Tudor Interlude, *Fulgens and Lucrece*, later repeated on several occasions. In 1934 came Auden's *Dance of Death*, giving a Leftist label to the Group, and in 1937, their most famous success, the Auden–Isherwood *The Ascent of F. 6*. T. S. Eliot was associated with the Group from 1934, although his only dramatic contribution was *Sweeney Agonistes*, a minor work which prefigured *Murder in the Cathedral*, which was not destined to be staged by the Group. There was also an earlier Auden–Isherwood collaboration with *The Dog Beneath the Skin*. These were avant-garde pieces of note, but unfortunately the Group earned with them a reputation for rather careless presentation. Two other leading poets wrote for the Group in 1937 – Louis MacNeice with *Out of the Picture* and Stephen Spender with *Trial of a Judge* (a title rather too self-consciously in the footsteps of Eliot's successful *Murder in the Cathedral*). A final collaboration of Auden and Isherwood, *On the Frontier*, had a theme which was overtaken by events; not to mention the authors crossing their own frontier and emigrating to the USA before the play, which had opened in Cambridge in November 1938, finally reached its planned Shaftesbury Avenue destination for a single Sunday performance in February 1939. This was virtually the end of the London Group Theatre.

There was an attempted revival of the Group after the war, from 1950 until 1954, during which time it staged Sartre's *The Flies* (1951) and *Homage to Dylan Thomas* (1954); but it was finally wound up in 1956, the very year in which the English Stage Company was launched at the Royal Court, and for which it was something of a precursor. For most of its life the London Group Theatre was based at Anmer Hall's Westminster Theatre, which had re-opened in 1931 with Guthrie's first London production – Bridie's *The Anatomist* (with Henry Ainley, Flora Robson, Robert Eddison and Joan White in the cast). The young Guthrie, who for a short time looked like taking over the Group (and what a difference *that* might have made), became involved from 1933, stylishly choreographing song sequences, and in February 1934 co-directing *The Dance of Death*. But there was no doubt that the presiding central figure of the Group Theatre was Rupert Doone.

Doone's background was that of a dancer, with extensive cosmopolitan contacts which included Reinhardt, Cocteau, Diaghilev, Kurt Joos and Rudolph Laban. From this experience, like Saint-Denis, he brought a European influence to English theatre, and also the strict disciplines of classical ballet to the business of acting. Strangely allied to this was an obsession with Music Hall, a form then far from dead, which had the virtue of real contact with an audience without superficial naturalism. He had also worked in the mid-1920s with Basil Dean, Nigel Playfair, Noël Coward and C. B. Cochrane, albeit in a minor way. To those who worked with him he was obviously both 'infuriating, incoherent, tyrannical', and yet at the same time 'inventive, imaginative, productive and convincing'. He engendered an excitement among his company of young actors which had no counterpart in the commercial theatre of the times.

But for all Doone's leadership, the record shows clearly that the Group Theatre in London would never have got off the ground and survived for as long as it did if it had not been for 'the ambition and energy' and 'early spade-work' of a remarkable man who has received little official credit: John Ormerod Greenwood (1907–89). The 24-year-old Greenwood was the Organizing Secretary and inspirer of the Group before Doone even joined it. Greenwood also acted in most of the Group's productions until in 1937 he was summarily dismissed by Doone in a totally ruthless and insensitive way for one who had been so long a trusted colleague.

An early member of the company has said that the Group 'through the vision of Rupert Doone was the only one among "alternative" theatres of the time which saw the necessity of forming a permanent company on the basis of an intensive training of the actor'.[38] How much Doone was influenced by the visits to London of the Compagnie des Quinze is uncertain. He helped establish the Group Theatre without previous experience as actor or director, although John Allen says that 'In some respects he was a more original teacher than Michel Saint-Denis.' Yet the irony was 'that in 1936, when the Group was faltering, Saint-Denis ... established the London Theatre Studio, the very kind of school that Rupert had envisaged'.[39] The long-term objective of the original eight members (soon to be thirteen) of the Group 'was to train together and create an ensemble based on sound artistic principles'.

Where the American Group Theatre had Odets, and later Irwin Shaw and Saroyan, the London Group Theatre had the 'Faber poets' – Auden, Eliot, Spender and MacNeice. Both Group Theatres, as we have seen, had Leftish tendencies, but neither, essentially, were political theatres in the way that Piscator's or Brecht's theatres were, nor in the way that America's Federal Theatre Project or London's Unity Theatre were. Both Group Theatres were first and foremost aesthetic in their idealism, albeit with a strong socialist input from their writers. Most of their actors, like actors anywhere, were primarily concerned with 'having a good part' on which to work, escaping the shallowness of the commercial system, with perhaps the added bonus of a socially-significant context. In any case, along with the modern poets, the London Group Theatre included a number of classical pieces in its programming which apart from those already mentioned included

Vanbrugh's *The Provok'd Wife* (the Group's very first offering, given at the Everyman Theatre, Hampstead, on 3 April 1932), Shakespeare's *Timon of Athens* (in November 1935, staged by Nugent Monck, with music by Benjamin Britten, décor by Robert Medley and choreography by Doone), Goldoni's *Impresario from Smyrna* (staged by John Fernald in December 1935), and Aeschylus' *Agamemnon* (in November 1936, translated by MacNeice, again music by Britten, directed and choreographed by Doone).

Following precedents with Stanislavski, Copeau, Saint-Denis, and although they didn't know it, with their American contemporaries, Clurman, Strasberg and Crawford, the London Group Theatre had a two-week 'Summer Study' in Suffolk, in 1932. Doone was 'a demanding instructor'. In October, the classes continued in town. By April 1933, the Group's first brochure lists nearly 200 members, many of them well known, either then or later, as artists, poets, dancers, writers and, of course, actors. Sidnell provides cast lists for all the productions from 1932 to 1939, and also lists the hundreds of names who were paid-up subscribers to the Group Theatre between 1933 and 1935.[40]

Two of the longest-serving actors of the company took its ideals further and more lastingly into the acting profession when they became Principals of well-known Theatre Schools. John Allen, after a spell at the BBC and being HMI of Drama for the old ILEA, became Principal of the Central School of Speech and Drama. He has written extensively about the theatre, and has been on many influential panels concerning education and training. John Moody (1906–93) became head of the Old Vic Theatre School in 1940 for two years, which was mostly operated in evacuation to Warwickshire in those early war years. Moody took with him the very talented young tenor and operatic librettist, Geoffrey Dunn, who had taught voice in the early Group Theatre classes in London, and who had worked with the Group composer, Herbert Murrill, notable on a brilliant short opera, *Man in Cage*. Subsequently, Moody directed at the Old Vic and Birmingham Rep.; became Director of Sadler's Wells Opera Company for four years; was appointed Drama Director at the Arts Council; was a Director of the Bristol Old Vic; and in 1960 became Director of Productions at the Welsh National Opera, a company with which he was connected for many years.

As may be seen, both John Allen and John Moody led many-faceted careers, perhaps somewhat out of the public eye, but contributing much to the British theatre over more than fifty years. Ormerod Greenwood, incidentally, also went on to teach at the RADA for many years, and in later life became renowned for his writings on Quaker history and affairs. But in hindsight it was Rupert Doone who, as Michael Sidnell says, had the vision of a 'total theatre', combining dance, music and drama in a fresh and modern way. He was a complex personality and he left no books to make his case, but his contribution through his direction of the London Group Theatre 'was a rare and valuable one'.

Antonin Artaud (1896–1948)

Of the six seminal influences discussed in this chapter, Artaud has the least body of practical work to show for his importance. As an actor and a director he was active until 1935 but, apart from one or two incandescent moments, he was not particularly successful. He was principally a writer and a poet with a fiery and baroque nature; and although he wrote very little *for* the theatre, he wrote a great deal *about* it, and the place of the actor in it. 'The actor,' he said, in a memorable phrase, 'is an athlete of the heart... What the athlete depends upon in running is what the actor depends upon in shouting a passionate curse, but the actor's course is altogether interior.'[41] Artaud was original, radical, innovative, bringing an important understanding of oriental theatre to Western practice; but in his search 'to break through language in order to touch life', he was often crazy and irrational – a victim burning at the stake, 'signalling through the flames'.

Barrault called him 'the metaphysician of theatre', yet more than philosophy, it was his life that spoke and was his essential artefact. In his poverty and suffering and opium addiction and madness, he became an icon of the dilemma of the artist who tries to identify the truth of experience in their work; and wider even than that, he became a symbol for the neuroses of the twentieth century. Even at the age of twenty-nine he was writing that 'where others aspire to create works of art I do not want anything apart from showing my spirit... I cannot conceive of a work of art as distinct from life.' This attitude and ambition, taken to its logical and tragic extreme, made Artaud, in Martin Esslin's words, 'one of the archetypal, mythical heroes – or sacrificial victims – of our age'.[42] It also places him, as we have seen, in the direct tradition of Copeau, Stanislavski and Piscator as one who sought to bring 'reality' on to the stage, or at least to try and close the gap between art and life.

It was Lugné-Poë who offered Artaud his first acting role – a small non-speaking part in February 1921 at the Théâtre de l'Oeuvre; and then in the same year, Fermin Gémier recommended him to train with Charles Dullin at the Atelier. The following year he was designing the scenery and costumes for Calderón's *Life is a Dream*, and playing Basilio, the King of Poland, in it. Still with Dullin's Atelier, he played Tiresias in Cocteau's *Antigone*, with sets by Picasso, costumes by Coco Chanel and music by Honegger. In 1923–4 he was with Pitoëff's company for a while at the Comédie des Champs-Elysées, playing a robot in Capek's *R.U.R.*, directed by Theodore Komisarjevski. He joined the Surrealist movement; was starting to get involved in the film industry; and in May 1925, directed and played in *Au pied du mur* by Aragon at the Vieux Colombier. In 1926 he founded the Théâtre Alfred Jarry with Roger Vitrac and Robert Aron, whose manifesto was published in the *Nouvelle Revue Française*. In 1927, he was having his first psychoanalytic treatment and was also seen in two famous film roles: Marat in Abel Gance's *Napoléon*, and the young monk in Dreyer's *La Passion de Jeanne d'Arc* who accompanies Joan to the stake. Dreyer's achievement was to persuade Artaud to *do* nothing, just *look*, shooting him in close-ups which show an intense romantic image. Anaïs Nin, with whom he later fell in love, wrote in her diary for March 1933 of his eyes 'blue with languor, black with pain . . . he is all nerves . . . beautiful in love with Joan of Arc . . . the deep-set eyes of the mystic, as if shining from caverns . . . shadowy, mysterious'.[43]

In 1930 he went to Berlin to work in Pabst's film of Brecht's *Threepenny Opera*; and in the following year, back in Paris, he had the strongly-felt experience of witnessing the non-verbal, magical theatre of Balinese dancers. He worked as assistant to Jouvet for just one production in 1932, but he and Jouvet were chalk and cheese. At some stage, Lugné-Poë, Dullin, Pitoëff, Jouvet and Barrault all had to 'let go' of Artaud working with them. The theatre is a severely pragmatic business, and Artaud's ideas and actions were frequently impossible to contain (he was once thrown out of his rented room for causing a flood trying to drown a mouse!).[44] Most of 1933 he was writing, and in 1934, film acting took over again with the need for money, including a 'memorable' Savonarola in another of Gance's historical pieces, *Lucrèce Borgia*. The virtual climax of his practical theatre work was in 1935, when he directed and played the lead in *The Cenci* at the Théâtre des Folies Wagram, a great barn of a place, quite unsuitable, and later renamed the Théâtre de l'Etoile. It was a brave effort, but not surprisingly, it failed.

Thereafter, via Antwerp and Havana, he travelled to Mexico, Belgium and the west of Ireland before, in September 1937, he was deported from Dublin to Le Havre, being restrained in a strait-jacket whilst on board ship. Eventually, he was transferred to various asylums between December 1937 and March 1946. Ironically, it was in 1938 that *The Theatre and its Double* was published (mostly written five or six years earlier), which was the fullest and most influential statement of his ideas. Returning to the Parisian cultural scene as a ravaged myth of a man, he read some of his poetry at the Vieux Colombier in January 1947, memorably described later by André Gide:

> Of his material existence nothing remained except what was expressive... his face consumed by inner fire... his hands twisting in anguish... openly signalling abominable human distress, a sort of unreprievable damnation ... Certainly the marvellous actor this artist could become was rediscovered, but it was his own personality he was offering to the audience with a sort of shameless barn storming that did not conceal a total authenticity.[45]

Artaud once told Barrault that 'tragedy on the stage is not enough for me, I'll transfer it into my own life'. And so he did, becoming in the event 'the true existential hero' of our agonized times.

In this penultimate year of his life, he had an exhibition of his drawings at the famous Galerie Pierre and published two more books, one of them a brilliant essay in defence of a kindred spirit,

Vincent Van Gogh; and for what was to prove a final performance, he recorded a poem for four voices, xylophone and percussion for Radiodiffusion Française. It was called 'To Have Done
with God's Judgement' and was banned as being blasphemous
and obscene, although copies of the tape, surreptitiously preserved,
have survived. Martin Esslin, in his lucid monograph, describes
listening to Artaud's voice 'as he recites his weird and violent
words and utters his wild, piercing, inarticulate cries – outbursts
of such a deep intensity of anguish beyond speech that they freeze
the blood: it is as though all human suffering, mankind's sum-
total of damned-up, frustrated rage, torment and pain had been
compressed into these tortured, primal shrieks'.[46] This was his
last attempt to fulfil his concept of the 'Theatre of Cruelty', and
to show language taken through and beyond its uttermost limits.
On 4 March 1948, at the age of fifty-one, he was found dead in
his room at the mental hospital at Ivry on the outskirts of Paris,
where he had gone as a voluntary patient two years before. The
cause of death was an inoperable intestinal cancer. He was buried
four days later at Ivry, without religious rites.

The seminal importance of Artaud's writings, and in particular
The Theatre and its Double, may be seen in much subsequent
work done in this century in many countries. In France, of course,
there is the direct transmission through Barrault, Blin, Adamov,
Beckett, Genet, Mnouchkine and Savary; in England, through Brook
and Marowitz, Berkoff and the Canadian Robert Lepage; in the
USA through Malina and Beck, Chaikin, Schechner, Peter Schumann,
Anna Halprin, Richard Foreman and Robert Wilson; in Poland
through Grotowski and Kantor; in Italy through Alessandro Fersen
and Luca Ronconi; in Germany through Peter Handke and Heiner
Müller; in Scandinavia, Eugenio Barba; the list could be extended
throughout the field of experimental theatre. Artaud explained
the title of *The Theatre and its Double* to his editor at the NRF
by saying that 'if the theatre is a double of life, life is a double of
true theatre ... The double of the theatre is the *reality* which
today's mankind leaves unused.'[47] Artaud rejected suggestions to
replace the phrase 'The Theatre of Cruelty' with such alterna-
tives as 'The Alchemical Theatre', 'Theatre of the Absolute' or
'The Metaphysical Theatre'. Concerning the actor and acting, the
echoes of Craig's über-marionettes and Piscator's 'objective act-

ing' are evident in Artaud's requirement for a predetermination of sign, gesture and expression to convey a complex theatrical language with great technical skill.

Artaud was very aware, like many other twentieth-century philosophers, of the limits of the spoken word. It was the non-verbal element of consciousness which was important, for it was there that the poetic emotions lay, in a direct sense rather than the indirect sense of word-symbols 'standing in' for the actual experience. Artaud's importance to theatre in this century is defined by his passionate belief in its 'revolutionary potential and redemptive force' to change people and society. It was much more than just a place for entertainment. It was the Ritual Hall of mystery and enlightenment, the Holy Place where 'metanoia' took place, that is, the turning of minds and the assumption of spiritual life. He spoke of the theatre as incarnating the energy of myths which are no longer embodied in our lives. In sharing this communal experience, and indeed representing and guiding it, the actor became a priest once again; he reassumed the role of the shaman in society. It may not have happened quite yet, but it will happen. Hamlet gives the cue: the readiness is all.

In his manifesto for the Théâtre Alfred Jarry in 1926, the young Artaud was strongly influenced by Dullin's ideal of a theatre for spiritual enrichment: 'It is not to the mind or the senses of our audience that we address ourselves, but to their whole existence. Theirs and ours.' He goes on later to say that 'We see the theatre as a *truly magical* enterprise' where there is 'a certain *psychological* emotion [his italics again] in which the most secret recesses of the heart will be brought into the open'.[48] It is unusual for him to stress 'psychological', which habitually he identified with conventional and word-ridden theatre; but then it was part of Artaud's genius not to be consistent or over-structured in any way. From his youth he had observed that 'There are those who go to the theatre as if they were going to a brothel . . . for furtive pleasure, momentary excitement.' This is probably more true of cinema audiences today; but in a sophisticated sense rather than a puritan one, the moral stricture remains. There is a tabloid mentality in the theatre as well as in newspapers. Artaud's later response to this brothel-going attitude was the concept of a 'Theatre of Cruelty' which he explained in a letter to his editor, Jean Paulhan, as essentially meaning 'strictures, diligence, and impeccable resolution, irreversible and absolute determination'. The 'Theatre of Cruelty' was one in which there was a clear consciousness that the very act of living is hard, rigorous, inevitable, submitting to necessity. It might involve some 'sadism or bloodshed' but 'not exclusively'. As a phrase attached to Artaud's name, it is akin to the albatross for the Ancient Mariner, as the 'alienation effect' became for Brecht. In a later letter, Artaud explains 'cruelty' as referring to 'the whirlwind of the life that eats up darkness'.

Artaud's principal influence on the art of acting in this century has been to emphasize the 'impotence of language' and present a passionate case for non-verbal, physical acting in which movement, cries, signs and gesture, together with costume, colour, lighting and music, take precedence over text; a shamanistic theatre in which the action is a communal event, involving the actor and the spectator in the *same* experience, and not in a *separate* presentation of it. It was this which defined his attitude to 'theatre space' in which he anticipated Grotowski, Mnouchkine and Ronconi, among several others. 'The spectator,' he said, 'placed in the middle of the action is enveloped and covered by it.' His Sorbonne lecture on 'Theatre and the Plague' in April 1933 turned from describing something to the audience into an actual acting out of the dreadful suffering of a plague victim. Most of the audience couldn't take it and left in noisy protest. Instead of receiving something intellectually *from* the lecture, they were being asked to *share* and actually *give* of their own emotional empathy to the subject of the lecture. It was an experience which was at once atavistic and ahead of its time. Its proper place might be said to have been in a theatre and not a lecture hall, but Artaud was not one to be deflected by such a nicety. Artaud's cries today are distantly heard in the iconoclastic, irrational outbursts of Howard Barker, another voice crying in the wilderness. As Michel Foucault, a leading French philosopher who – like Artaud – sought to realize his ideas in life 'beyond good and evil', used to indicate: the rest of us have to measure our assumed sanity against these excesses.

In the late summer of 1946, Artaud wrote a collection of poems, published the following year as *Le Retour d'Artaud, le Mômo*. Le Mômo is the idiot, or holy fool, and in Esslin's words, he became 'a touchstone of our civilization'.[49] He touches it as prophet, priest, alchemist, oracle, gnostic, madman; but above all as the actor in his own drama, the existentialist anti-hero, doomed to magnificent failure.

Jean-Louis Barrault (1910–94)

Just as Artaud, in 1935, reached what turned out to be the climax of his efforts to embody his theories in practice with the production of *The Cenci*, Jean-Louis Barrault, aged twenty-five, was just beginning to create his own mark in a career which also owed much to the influence of Dullin, as well as that of the mime Etienne Decroux, from the Théâtre Alfred Jarry, and of course, to Artaud himself. Barrault suggested they should work together after *The Cenci*, but Artaud rejected the idea of collaboration. There could not be two absolute *auteurs*; and in any case, added Artaud in a letter, 'highly though I esteem you, I think you are fallible'.[50] Barrault's answer to this typically arrogant criticism is not known, but the brilliant mime more than got his own back when asked by his friend whom he saw 'almost every day' to imitate him. 'I did and he shouted "I've been r-r-robbed of my p-p-personality!"' (Artaud was prone to stuttering.) Barrault's respect for Artaud's genius remained undiminished: 'Through him the metaphysics of theatre had got right inside me.'[51]

Barrault had made his début on his twenty-first birthday at the Atelier as one of Volpone's servants. He had no money, but Dullin had recognized the potential talent and took him on without charging the usual school fees. Barrault felt he was 'being born for the second time', and remembering Gide's definition of sin as 'the one thing one cannot not do' he declared that he 'desired the theatre like a sin'.[52] At Dullin's school the subjects were improvisation, gymnastics, some work on the classics and on Claudel, and exercises in precise observation from a disciple of Stanislavski named Sokoloff. The purity of Dullin's approach to theatre drew its inspiration not only from Stanislavski but also from Craig and Copeau. His teaching 'was based on the essential importance of *living a situation sincerely*' (Barrault's italics).[53] Also at the school, as was mentioned above, Barrault came under the important influence of Etienne Decroux and his work on codifying mime and the art of gesture. The penniless young student could not afford any digs, so he slept onstage – in Volpone's bed – 'in love at the source of my art' and with the 'vibrating silence' of the empty theatre to accompany his dreams.

Four years later, in 1935, he was working with Jouvet, performing his own adaptation of Faulkner's novel *As I Lay Dying*. It was his entry into the theatrical life of Paris, declaring that 'world of poetry that was to impose itself on me for life ... I would be its slave, it would require of me servitude and the total gift of myself'.[54] He began working out for himself the Five Basic Rules of Acting. These were: (1) An actor must make himself heard and understood; (2) He must know how to observe and how to imitate; (3) He must answer three vital questions – 'Where have I come from, where am I going, and in what state am I?'; (4) concerning his environment, he must ask 'What am I doing here?'; and (5) concerns control within the different meanings of sincerity and exactness. For this last rule, the actor has to ask himself 'In spite of my sincerity is my character truly sincere?'[55] Or to put it the other way round: the acting will be right if the character is constantly sincere, but not if only the actor is sincere. The actor can 'never identify himself absolutely with the character he is playing' because in the theatre 'life is re-created through art'. This is a common observation, dramatically used by Maugham in his novel *Theatre*, that however 'good' and 'sincere' an actor may feel playing a role it can still be a bad performance as far as the character (and the audience) is concerned.

After these five main rules for the basic training of the actor, there are one or two other important practical considerations. One is the difficult art of pacing a performance, especially for a long and complex role, so that the final run to the curtain has the necessary reserves of energy and strength. Another is that sometimes, 'guided by inspiration, one discovers a way of doing things which, although it does not at first sight rest on truth, contains nevertheless aspects which are the very essence of truth. That is truly poetic interpretation.' Ultimately, 'the foundation of the whole discipline of acting ... is concentration and control of the will'. The rest is silence, and causing that silence to vibrate.[56]

The best-known international image of Barrault remains his

remarkable performance as the mime Deburau in Carné's film *Les Enfants du paradis* – the children of the 'Gods' at the Théâtre des Funambules on the Boulevard du Temple. Deburau's stage name was Baptiste, and around 1811 he had transformed the Harlequinade character of Pierrot into a melancholy but hopeful lover. Barrault's re-creation of this loose-robed, white-faced poet unable to speak his emotions employed all his best talents. The scenario was, indeed, his idea, although Jacques Prévert wrote it. Later, in his memoirs, Barrault wrote: 'To my joy, mime, theatre and cinema were brought together. This happened in the same year as Claudel's *Le Soulier de satin* at the Comédie-Française: 1943. Annus mirabilis: a real synthesis of one's life. And all this under the German Occupation!'[57] However, after the war, after six years as a Sociétaire, Barrault left the Comédie-Française in 1945 when the government decided to 're-form' it on stricter lines to which he felt he could not commit himself 'for life' – as is required of a Sociétaire. A year later he was invited to return as Administrateur, no less, but he also turned that down, having by then successfully established his own company at the Marigny Theatre.

In January 1954, the Compagnie Renaud-Barrault opened 'Le Petit Marigny' in the large façade of the Marigny itself. The small house had 250 seats, and the idea was to provide a welcome venue for new writing. But the owner-manager, Simone Volterra, could not stand the Marigny becoming the Renaud-Barrault theatre. They would have to leave; and so it was that in the prime of their careers they were obliged to become strolling players and go on an extended world tour. This happened in 1956, and their final production of *The Cherry Orchard* suitably spoke their tearful farewells. Three years later they were offered an even grander 'home' of their own, and were to stay there for nine years.

The Théâtre de France at the Odéon, or as it became known more tactfully for the sake of the Comédie-Française, the Odéon-Théâtre de France, was set up by André Malraux, the Minister for Culture in de Gaulle's government, specifically as a base for the Compagnie Renaud-Barrault. This official backing made it a kind of national theatre in itself; but it became even more dogged with financial and other problems than the 'private' Marigny had ever been. Finance and Culture Ministries hardly ever see eye to eye. Indeed, when Barrault visited a courteous official at the Ministry of Finance, he was told, memorably, 'To tell you the truth, I don't see the reason for your visit. For me you are only a *project* of Monsieur Malraux's, who is himself only a project of Monsieur de Gaulle.'[58] There speaks the eternal Civil Servant. Today in Britain, it might be Philip Hedley visiting a Senior Secretary at the Treasury and being told, 'For me you are only a project of the Arts Council Director, and in turn the Heritage Secretary, and themselves in turn again only projects of the Prime Minister.' The artist at the cutting-edge has little if any priority in the political game of devolving responsibility. Nevertheless, at this period in France the theatrical artists and politics were becoming dangerously mixed. Barrault staged Genet's *The Screens* in April 1966, and after an initial twelve peaceful performances, thereafter there was fighting in the theatre on nearly every occasion. Introducing the production in the theatre's 'house magazine', Barrault wrote: 'In the theatre there is a feeling even more sacred than the feeling for liberty, and this is Respect for the human being.' Later he goes on to comment that 'Art exists because we must never stop putting ourselves in question. We must kill ourselves every evening to be born afresh every morning. Art either is revolutionary or is not. A people's level of civilization is gauged by the proportion of liberty its government allows to the fine arts, to the spirit of tolerance.'[59] It would be encouraging to see those words carved over the portal of the Ministry for National Heritage, not to mention its underling, the Arts Council.

Within two more years, the flashpoint of revolution occurred in Paris with the Barraults right in the middle of it. The events of May 1968, at the Odéon and beyond it, proved to be yet another conclusion in their professional lives: there had been the Marigny period, then the tours, and now the Odéon-Théâtre de France period. 'For whom? For what?' he asks, not without despair. But true friends remained faithful, especially Roger Blin.[60] Blin was an actor and director who had worked with both Artaud and Barrault, and whose fame was mainly connected with the genre of plays under the label of Theatre of the Absurd. In 1953 he was much praised for his direction of *En attendant Godot*, in which he also played Pozzo. He died in 1984.

The end for the Barraults at the Odéon swiftly became a new

beginning. Dismissed by Malraux on 28 August, only one week later, on 5 September, Barrault came to an agreement with the Elysée-Montmartre and re-formed his company. They started rehearsals of *Rabelais* on 1 October. This was the fourth version of the script which Barrault had adapted as 'A dramatic game in two parts taken from the five books of François Rabelais'. It exploited the resources of modern theatre with brilliance. Paris saw it in December 1968, and the following September the company were invited to London to show it at the National Theatre, then at the Old Vic. It provided the elements for a new Barrault manifesto. It was:

> Theatre in the state of being born, through language as well as through bodily expression. The style of the strolling player. Close relations between actors and spectators. The joy of the body and the joy of the spirit. The carnal faculty of touching the mysteries of life. *Breaking out of one's own circle* [his italics] by an exaltation and enlargement of soul.[61]

Finally, a few words about mime, of which Barrault was such a consummate master. He asks why pantomime is such a popular art? 'Because the average human being is not vocal . . . Gestures often reveal the secrets which lurk behind them.' Of course, Artaud thought that too: no wonder they sometimes gave a rose to each other when they met. Mime can be 'as rich as spoken language', for the body 'axled on the spine, fed and strengthened through the respiratory bellows' contains 'a natural means of expression' through 'the attitude, the gesture and the indication'.[62]

From silent theatrical language, this survey now moves back to England in the 1950s, and to an extreme example of literary theatre in which words that had never been spoken in this way on a stage before created a watershed of style. The actor had never used this sort of language before although most of his audience knew it well. His craft was expanded, the theatre was taking a new direction, and at the same time it was returning the actor once again to be nearer the people.

11

A Note on the Fifties' Watershed at Sloane Square and Stratford East: Actors Link the 'Class Divide'

The Royal Court Theatre in Sloane Square has been essentially a writers' theatre during the tenure of the English Stage Company, but following what was only their third production, *Look Back in Anger*, in May 1956, during its peak years it contributed two most important factors to the development of the professional actor. Osborne's Jimmy Porter was one of the first of a line of working-class anti-heroes to extend the range of roles permissible to leading players; and when the same author's Archie Rice (coming less than a year later) was taken on by a leading classical actor, the courageous Laurence Olivier, that too crossed a 'divide' which had hitherto been almost sacrosanct. No longer were actors, and their public reputations, closeted in a particular genre. Whether they were classical actors, matinée idols, high or low comedians, farceurs or usually in musical comedy; whether they were upper-, middle- or lower-class 'types'; whether their fame was through stage, television or film – now at last, the actor was an artist who simply played human beings in whatever mode or place. Only the 'Spotlight' classifications remained to define the professional actor: leading, character or juvenile-character.

A similar watershed had achieved a fixed location three years earlier when Joan Littlewood's Theatre Workshop moved into the Theatre Royal, Stratford, in the East End of London in 1953. Its original aim had been to serve the local working-class community with an imaginative and truthful 'total' theatre, unsullied by the strictures of tradition and class division. In this ambition it failed (as did Arnold Wesker's Centre 42 ideal at the Round-house some seven years later), for whilst its rich programme of classics and new plays made the name Theatre Workshop inter-nationally famous, the name of Joan Littlewood – as John Elsom pointed out – was unheard of in a pub half a mile from the theatre.[1] Ironically, Theatre Workshop was the victim of its own ultimate commercial success. It started with the 1956 production of Brendan Behan's *The Quare Fellow*, followed in 1958 with Shelagh Delaney's *A Taste of Honey* and a further Behan play reportedly composed by most of the company, *The Hostage*. Both the latter pieces transferred to the West End in the following year, followed by two successful musicals, Frank Norman's *Fings Aint Wot They Used T' Be*, and Wolf Mankowitz's *Make Me an Offer*. The climax of Theatre Workshop's fortunes, and as it was later seen, its death sentence, came in 1963–4 with the company's creation of *Oh What a Lovely War!* At the Royal Court during those same years there were productions of Arnold Wesker's *Chips with Everything* and Osborne's *Inadmissible Evidence*, alongside classic revivals of Shaw, Shakespeare, Pirandello, Wedekind, Chekhov, and Brecht, with new work from Ionesco and Beckett. That is some programming, and it all contributed to the explo-sion of new theatrical life inaugurated largely in Stratford East and Sloane Square in the late 1950s and early 1960s.

For the actor, it was an enormously exciting period of release. George Devine's attitude to actors and acting was based on his experience with Michel Saint-Denis and Glen Byam Shaw at the London Theatre Studio and the Old Vic Centre. It was stylish, text-orientated, traditional in tone yet open to innovation, admit-ting the Copeau tradition and disciplines of improvisation and mask-work. Joan Littlewood and her associates, on the other hand, were anarchic, anti-traditional, not interested in élitist style or 'taste', but having enormous energies to devote to honesty and truth on stage, and ready at all times to engage in the 'class war' and have a bash at any forms of privilege and shallow cultural restrictions. Devine was primarily interested in plays of ideas. He once told John Osborne in 1956: 'I am very much more interested in content that in form. I do not think any play is really worth producing if it's not a play of ideas. Literally, the play's the thing.'[2] Littlewood's inclinations were almost exactly the opposite. The company work and the form rather than the content were the thing. She was 'anti-intellectual by disposition' and 'anti-literary' from upbringing.[3]

A word or two here about Jean Vilar (1912–71), as in many ways he and his theatres represent the French equivalent of the English Theatre Workshop, and the European continuity of our theme. He was most active, with the revived Théâtre National Populaire, in almost the same period as Theatre Workshop's main successes, 1951–63; and he espoused very similar ideals. He was in the tradition of Copeau and the Cartel, having trained with Dullin in the early 1930s, but whilst admiring them he did not think of himself as merely emulating them. His great ambition, and to some extent his achievement, was to advance the cause of popular theatre. 'More than a director, he was an outstanding *animateur*: a man motivated by an overall artistic policy in which moral and social as well as aesthetic considerations are intertwined.'[4] That might well have been written of Joan Littlewood also. Michel Saint-Denis thought highly of Vilar, having read the latter's book *De la Tradition Théâtrale* when it first came out in 1955. Saint-Denis quotes approvingly when Vilar says that 'one should not only give confidence to the actor but have confidence in him' and that 'there is no ready-made impersonation, there is no good acting without characterisation' and that 'the director's art is one of suggestion, not imposition'.[5] Like the early Theatre Workshop, Vilar had visited small towns and villages where theatre was almost non-existent as an acting-member of La Roulotte, a small touring company which operated during the Occupation in 1940–42; then in 1943 he returned to Paris to form his own Compagnie des Sept, 'a small art theatre in the tradition of the Vieux Colombier and the Atelier to which it was inevitably compared'.[6] It lasted for two years, with the first French production of Eliot's *Murder in the Cathedral* in 1945 as its final and, as it happened, most successful production. Around this time, Vilar was identifying the 'theatre workers' primary task as being to bring theatre to the materially disadvantaged and culturally deprived sections of society',[7] so when the chance came to create a theatrical festival at Avignon in 1947 he used it to do what was almost impossible in Paris; that is, to have a large, open arena stage (another *tréteau nu*) upon which to put in the simplest technical way drama of high quality for a broad-based and largely unsophisticated audience. Its success was immediate, so that even sceptical critics from the capital had to admit that it was 'one of the most exciting and innovative stages anywhere in France'.[8] After this, Vilar became the obvious name to lead a revival of the old Théâtre National Populaire in 1951. This he did for twelve years, before quarrels over the repertoire and over subsidy led him to resign. Nevertheless, millions of ordinary French people had come to regard it as 'their theatre', which had brought the type of theatrical pleasure to them that previously only an élitely-educated class had enjoyed.

Vilar's attitude to actors as noted by Saint-Denis was precisely echoed by Joan Littlewood. In a radio interview in 1959 she said: 'I believe very much in a theatre of actor-artists, and I think the trust that comes out of team work on what is often a new script, cleaning up points in production, or contact between actors, is essential to the development of the craft of acting and playwrighting.'

When he retired in 1964, George Devine claimed that in eight years he had brought no less than 126 new English plays to light, quite apart from many classic revivals and the training of twenty assistant directors, together with developing a new spirit of 'dedication to the essence of a work, and creative eccentricity'.[9] But for all the apparent success in his statistical claim, Devine's dream of finding new writers and of encouraging established ones to write more for the theatre, failed to materialize in any fecund way. In 1973, Hayman was reporting that from about 900 scripts submitted to the ESC each year, 'it seems very odd that so few interesting writers were found'.[10] Only two of those introduced through the Theatre Upstairs – E. A. Whitehead and Howard Barker – went on to make reputations, and even they are far from 'household names' to the average theatregoer. Another of Devine's ideals that had to be abandoned as early as the first year was having a 'true repertory'. It was tried again in 1965 by William Gaskill, but again it had to be abandoned. The truth was that with a theatre seating only about 400 persons, commercial viability depended upon enormous subsidy, or else and probably in addition, upon successful transfers, royalties, tours and film rights.

Nevertheless, the importance of the ESC in the late 1950s and early 1960s cannot be denied. Both Irving Wardle and Richard Findlater have described its history in detail, and its part in the extraordinary artistic renaissance of those years (see Notes). It was 'a major factor in the development of the National Theatre and also in the evolution of the alternative stage ... and through its graduates its influence percolated into television, opera and films'. It built 'bridges between theatre and other contemporary arts' and was 'a champion of theatrical freedom, playing a decisive role in the abolition of censorship'. Almost to Devine's surprise, the Court became identified from its earliest years with dissent and rebellion. 'It was the time of Suez, Hungary, and CND,' says Findlater, 'when a surge of feeling against the political and cultural Establishment ... swept a flock of brilliant, oddly assorted malcontents into his embrace.'[11] Beckett was in the West End with *Waiting for Godot*, also the Berliner Ensemble, and although Beckett and Brecht are poles apart, there was a 'bifocal loyalty' to them both at the Court. For the actor as well as the writer, it was 'a special place ... unpredictable ... [and having] a nucleus of promising young people'. That was Joan Plowright speaking, who found her own fame at the Court with Wesker's dream of a role for young actresses, Beatie Bryant in *Roots*, a character which 'spoke to and for our own generation and who had never before been seen on an English stage'.[12]

Devine was a member of the Building Committee for the National Theatre on the South Bank. He influenced the choice of architect, Denys Lasdun, who said later that time and again Devine would put the vision and 'abstract directives' of the theatre people into terms he could understand as an architect.[13] Yet he remains difficult to 'pin down' as a theatrical innovator, perhaps because he was more interested in content than form, and in other people's ideas rather than his own. He was a superb facilitator and enabler with little pride of his own. After his heart attack (on stage in early August 1965), Devine started dictating an autobiography, a project previously commissioned by Faber which he had put off. In it he offers advice to a godson wishing to enter the theatre. It rings out as his personal creed:

I was not strictly after a popular theatre à la Joan Littlewood–

Roger Planchon, but a theatre that would be part of the intellectual life of the country. In this respect, I consider I utterly failed... You should choose your theatre like you choose a religion. Make sure you don't get into the wrong temple. For me, the theatre is really a religion or way of life. You must decide what you feel the world is about and what you want to say about it, so that everything in the theatre you work in is saying the same thing... For me theatre is a temple of ideas, and ideas so well expressed it may be called art ... And if you can't find one you like, start one of your own.[14]

That is a very suitable 'final word' for one whom Irving Wardle described as 'the most important figure in our theatre since Lilian Baylis'.

Devine and Littlewood were both actors as well as directors and administrators. They were not in agreement over their methods or ideals, but they respected each other's aims, and certainly Devine fought for Theatre Workshop to be recognized by the Arts Council. Their joint influence, and the inheritance of the companies with which they were associated has affected, and continues to affect, the lives of all actors in Britain, and possibly beyond. Both Devine and Littlewood wanted to change the attitude of the public towards the theatre. In this they both may have failed. But they certainly changed – each in their own way – the attitude of playwrights and actors towards the profession.

12

The European Gurus:
Actors on a String with Brook, Kantor, Grotowski, Strehler, Stein, Planchon, and Mnouchkine

Each of the great European directors in this chapter deserves a book to themselves; and, indeed, with most of them this is already the case, and often more than one. The intention here is not to try and do each of them justice by covering the body of their life's work, but to take a brief overall view and select an example or two with quotations to illustrate their particular vision of theatre; also to indicate how their individual conceptual approaches affect the actors in their productions. What do they demand of the actor? How do those demands mould the actor's response in trying to satisfy them? All of them, incidentally, have at some time been described as 'magicians' and 'spell-binders', 'enchanters' and purveyors of 'theatrical wizardry'. But it has been their actors, together with their technical crew, who have actually had to make the vision and the magic work, whether by spinning plates, walking on stilts or hanging by trapeze, whilst still delivering the text.

Peter Brook

The latter examples, of course, come from Peter Brook's very influential RSC production of *A Midsummer Night's Dream* in 1970. That was the very year he left England (to the country's great cultural loss) in order to found the International Centre for Theatre Research in the only place he could find to do it: Paris.

158

Approaching the age of seventy, he still behaves – and looks – like the *enfant terrible* of the world's theatre, for no one country where he works can now lay claim to his genius for experimentation and innovation. Nevertheless, more recently he has returned to Britain from time to time – mainly in Scotland – with performances of his latest work, *The Mahabharata, Carmen, La Tempête, Impressions of Pelléas*; and in 1994 there was talk of a two-year project with Richard Eyre at the National Theatre to present *Signals Through the Flames*, drawn, of course, from Artaud whose 'Theatre of Cruelty' Brook had investigated with Charles Marowitz in 1964, but also looking at the work of Brecht and Stanislavski. In other words, Brook may be returning home to create an apotheosis of twentieth-century Western theatre practice, not only at the rightful 'headquarters' of his own theatrical roots but also as the mature statement of a lifetime's searching for a global theatrical form, involving more than one culture and more than one set of spiritual values as well. On this project he will be working together with the dramatist Nick Dear to produce a final text. Brook describes it as 'an exploration of a basic question: what theatre itself is, just that'.[1]

Brook's latest work, at the time of writing, is *L'Homme Qui*, which is based on some casebook studies of the psychologist Oliver Sacks, published as *The Man Who Mistook His Wife for a Hat*. (Sacks is probably best known for the film made of his book *Awakenings*, with Robin Williams and Robert de Niro.) Michael Billington reported on this production which he saw in Paris in March 1993:

> It is a series of stories about neurological disorders told with a lucid compassion that makes us keenly aware of our common humanity and that graphically extends the possibilities of theatre . . .
>
> Four of Brook's regular actors . . . who spent a year researching . . . alternate as doctors and patients. An onstage musician provides tactful, stringed accompaniment to moments of piercing sadness and occasional joy.

That is reminiscent of Shakespeare's frequently employed theatrical stratagem.

The power of theatre is that it gives us, however momentarily, a patient's eye-view of the world's mystifying strangeness.

There is, perhaps, a danger that this sort of thing could border on the voyeuristic and exploitative, but Billington points out that the result is more to create 'a strange kinship' with the victims, as in Pinter's *A Kind of Alaska* or Pomerance's *The Elephant Man*. In some way, it seems that Brook is becoming 'as much a philosopher as a director' but there can be no doubt that a piece like *L'Homme Qui* sends its audience away 'marvelling at the power of theatre to tell stories and feeling more at one with the human race'.[2]

One of the four actors in *L'Homme Qui*, Yoshi Oida, has been with Brook for twenty-five years, from the beginning of the International Centre, and he has written of the actor's role as essentially that of a storyteller. He has a very firm view, from his Eastern and Buddhist experience, of what he calls 'invisible theatre', that is, one which operates beyond the world of objects and material phenomena.

To achieve this universal level, the actors and the audience have to work co-operatively together ... When people leave the theatre, they should be different to when they arrived ... Ideal acting is the expression of the metaphysical world through physical acts: ideal theatre is the creation of an invisible world through visual presentation.

This is not to be described as religious theatre, but it certainly touches a spiritual dimension, a universal energy, which, in Oida's words again, 'goes beyond any particular culture' and in which 'the actor must spin an invisible thread between his own sense of the sacred and that of the audience'.[3]

For a major philosopher of the theatre, Brook has published very little himself, although much has been written about him and his work. His four Granada Northern lectures, given to university audiences as 'The Empty Space: The Theatre Today', were published in 1968 and taken over by Pelican Books in 1972. As far as I know, *The Empty Space* has never been out of print since that time, having grown in importance with the director's career. Its four headings of the 'Deadly', the 'Holy', the 'Rough' and the 'Immediate' Theatre have become part of theatrical parlance for academics and the profession alike. Twenty years later, in 1988, Methuen published *The Shifting Point*, his longest book, described in its subtitle as 'Forty Years of Theatrical Exploration: 1946–1987'. In late 1993 he offered the fruits of maturity in a short but profound adaptation from a two-day Paris workshop given in 1991, and from two lectures given in Kyoto the same year. The book is called *There Are No Secrets*, with the subtitle 'Thoughts on Acting and Theatre', and I shall restrict myself here to noting some of its central points for actors.

Out of the axiom that theatre is a concentrated form of life, Brook notes that there is 'a fundamental difference between what leads to an intensity of life and that which is merely commonplace'. It is that difference, ignored by the purveyors of 'Happenings' in the late 1950s and early 1960s, which reached their *reductio ad absurdum* when actors simply 'lived' onstage, as they might at home, only with an audience invited to watch. No text, no form, no concentration – and very boring. 'Happenings' found their more rightful place in the visual area called 'Performance Art' and the current genre defined as 'crossing all the boundaries of performance' – Live Art. Concerning the observation of 'actual life', some makers of television programmes have made a similar mistake in thinking that cameras observing a family in their daily life would be 'more real' and therefore more interesting than scripted 'soaps', despite the obvious necessity for much selective editing. Brook points out that 'For an actor's intentions to be perfectly clear, with intellectual alertness, true feeling and a balanced and tuned body, the three elements – thought, emotion, body – must be in perfect harmony. Only then can he fulfill the requirement to be more intense, within a short space of time than when he is at home.'[4] Behaviourist or 'natural' acting is precisely this 'art which conceals art' and is as difficult as the more obvious 'classical' forms. Professional critics understand this, but journalists and the lay-public see it as being 'as easy as falling off a log' – as with modern art, 'any child could do it as well' – and the 'luvvies' (now the accepted term for abuse of the acting profession) are resented for getting good money for a 'con-job'. Well, of course, it *is* a con-job, but one requiring discipline, experience and high artistry as its largely unrecognized and unrespected ingredient.

Whilst on the subject of acting and natural behaviour, Brook has some salutary things to say about improvisation. They are all the more important for coming from a director who is renowned for his belief in, and extensive use of, 'impro'. 'The first step,' he says, 'is important, but it is not sufficient. One must be very conscious of the many traps that are in what we call theatre games and exercises.' Many directors and teachers continue to fall into these traps, too inclined to accept that the tyranny of 'form' is somehow less 'true' than its absence.

> Often theatre groups who improvise regularly apply the principle of never interrupting an improvisation that is under way. If you really want to know what boredom is, watch an improvisation where two or three actors get going and 'do their thing' without being stopped. They inevitably find themselves very rapidly repeating clichés, often with a deadly slowness that lowers the vitality of everyone watching.[5]

Now that has the ring of truthful experience about it, and is a very necessary antidote to those who would quote Brook's belief in delaying any final form until the last moment of rehearsal to justify their own lack of rigour. 'Sometimes the most challenging improvisation need only last a matter of seconds,' he concludes. That, of course, is what has always happened in any case when an actor in rehearsal (and excitingly, sometimes in performance, too) has his energies of attention and imagination working at peak level. It is that actual 'first time' which is thereafter technically repeated 'as if for the first time'.

> In the hands of the true artist, everything can seem natural, even if its outward form is so artificial that it has no equivalent in nature . . . Natural means that the moment something happens there is no analysis, no comment, it just rings true.[6]

Brook's attitude to 'form' in the theatre is that it is deadly. Traditional forms are apt to freeze into an 'obsolete automatism'. 'There is no form, beginning with ourselves, that is not subject to the fundamental law of the universe: that of disappearance. All religion, all understanding, all tradition, all wisdom accepts birth and death.'[7] The process, in fact, is all. This philosophical and eminently Buddhist attitude (cf. the Heart Sutra) is much in keeping with post-Christian contemporary thinking. All forms arise from Chaos and return to it. For the artist, attempting to capture in an artefact the fleeting moment of truth, it is a hard lesson. The perfect performance can only be a perfect improvisation, one which as we have just noted is not only 'as if for the first time' but is literally 'for the only time'. That is the essential excitement of theatre: the uniqueness of every occasion, even in a long run. 'We are touching here,' says Brook, 'on a question of dynamics which will never end.'[8]

Tadeusz Kantor

If Peter Brook's great contribution has been the elusive search for a global authenticity in the theatrical event, using for the first time a cross-cultural company of actors from around the world, Tadeusz Kantor (1915–92) took the matter directly into his own hands, getting onstage with his actors during performance, part of the artefact he was creating. He was reinvesting the job of the director with its primitive religious function, the participating priest-actor conducting a ritual. There was no theatrical 'covering-up', but rather, in Brechtian terms, the 'making' of the occasion was there for all to see. In a sense, this was the apotheosis of the 'Happening' and almost indistinguishable from what is now called 'Live Art'. Kantor's approach to theatre, first established through his work for the Stary Theatre in Cracow during the decade 1945–55, and later developed with his own experimental company, Cricot 2, was echoed during the 1970s in the work of the American avant-garde directors Richard Foreman and Robert Wilson. An heir of this anarchic and usually borderline theatre work in the 1990s is probably the Canadian Robert Lepage.

Like Brook, Kantor's attitude to form in the theatre resolved itself into believing in the living process as the way forward. 'The development of Art,' he said, 'is not only of a formal nature, it is above all a permanent movement of change in thoughts and ideas.'

It is not for the first time that the contemporary theatre has experienced a great longing for a return to its beginnings and sources. It seeks new, far-back derivations from the original ceremonies, rituals, magic practices, feasts, festivals, games, parades and processions, mass theatre, street theatre, political and agitative theatre. Everywhere, Art is not a product of consumption but constitutes an integral element of life. There is no need to add that this is at the same time an escape from the dying theatre – an enterprise overburdened with bureaucracy.[9]

Unfortunately, Kantor (or his translator) has not been always as clear as this. The rest of the booklet from which the above is quoted is clogged with a careless use of language leading to indecipherable meanings. It was, perhaps, Kantor's misfortune that, unlike his countryman Jerzy Grotowski, he never had a book translated into readable English (with a Preface by Peter Brook) to commend his work to the wider cultural fields of western Europe and America.

Kantor's principal importance in our context is that with him, probably above all the other gurus, the actor is reduced to being a puppet on strings. Indeed, in *Dead Class* in 1975, and in other works, he literally replaced actors with life-size puppets. In this, his work has revealed how arid and without 'soul' Craig's ideal of the über-marionette might have become. (It required the greater genius of Pirandello in *The Mountain Giants* to use puppets as a means of showing the different possible layers of theatrical 'reality'.) Kantor saw acting as 'neither a reproduction nor reality itself' but as something 'in between' – more like 'a game of chess or cards'. The latter is 'a pure activity' whilst still retaining some 'substitutional' aspects. It puts all 'passions, conflicts, activities of life' at one remove 'from often dirty consequences'. The 'model of a new actor' is to be a player in a 'purified' game in which there are no spectators but only fellow-players. There are to be no 'onlookers' but only participants. This is the new Ritual; and the priest-actor-director controls the pieces on the gaming-board, or in other words, the holy area, or stage. 'It rejects actors and their rights, throws them beyond its sphere in an absolute manner. Their attempts and endeavours (often deceitful) to "smuggle" their artistic behaviour, are subjected to practical reality, reduced to their own deforming category.'[10]

In 'directing' his actors from onstage, or in view at the side of the stage, with gestures or nods of the head, Kantor was not so much influencing a prior-rehearsed performance as taking part in the manner of a priest who controls the rhythm of a completely-known ritual; or perhaps, one might use the orchestral analogy whereby the conductor is only underlining his own requirements previously indicated in rehearsal. This shows the artefact for what it is: a prepared piece. There is no dishonesty, no attempt to persuade of the illusion that this is happening without preparation. There is no 'as if for the first time'. There is simply the ritual performance, the 'game' of theatre.

But what about the 'game' itself, the performance, the text; for Kantor's theatre is not simply mime and movement? Kantor considers 'that a literary text contains a high degree of dynamics and condensation, it has enormous value for me and it may be utilised in the theatre'.[11] The text, in other words, does not determine what happens onstage, but is only one of the factors to 'be utilised'. Borowski explains further that

> During the phase of the 'Theatre of Nothing', at the performance of *The Madman and the Nun* in 1963, there occurred what Kantor defines as 'the separation of the dramatic text and the events accompanying it'. The actors merely utter the text of the play, without representation or interpretation. They comment on it, discuss it, leave off the subject and take it up again, repeat things many times.[12]

Kantor seems to have thought that this 'protected' the text from 'illusionary' content; but it might be imagined that even Brecht would have blanched at actors doing this to his written words.

Jerzy Grotowski

Where for Kantor theatre *was* his religion, with all its ephemeral nature and manipulation of truth requiring exposure in ritual actuality, his better-known countryman, Grotowski, became ultimately more interested in the religious activity for itself rather than in its theatrical expression, either for or in collaboration with an audience. As has been pointed out,[13] there is an element of 'histrionic genius' in the national character of Poland, and that country's post-war activity in the arts, particularly in its visual aspects, has had a widely disseminated influence. Grotowski was only twenty-six when he took over the Teatr 13 Rzedow in Opole in 1959; and perhaps because he was only one among so many talents at work in the country during the 1960s, the young theatrical guru was rather less heeded at home than he was abroad. He had previously trained at the Cracow Theatre School, and apparently visited Moscow to study the Stanislavski 'System'; and it was just two years after Kantor had left the Stary Theatre in Cracow that Grotowski joined it in 1957, directing plays by Chekhov and Ionesco among others. At the time, he also went back to his old school to teach student actors there. Then in 1965, the work and research at Opole having acquired the title of Theatre Laboratory, it transferred to Wroclaw with the added status of being called the Institute for Research into Acting.

It was only a year later, in 1966, that Peter Brook invited Grotowski to take a three-week workshop with the RSC actors working on *US*;[14] and early in 1969, the Theatre Laboratory company paid a fleeting visit to London, without, as it happened, creating much of a stir. If anything, the Polish guru was inclined to be mocked by the profession for having feet of theatrical clay. However, his international reputation grew impressively. He filled a particular need during the renaissance of the 1960s and early 1970s, and undoubtedly influenced the ideology and practice behind Brook's initial work in Paris from 1970; and also reinforced the established work of Julian Beck and Judith Malina's Living Theatre group in New York, which had started in 1947 but reached its main period at the time. In hindsight, it may be seen that his most serious contribution to changing traditional ways was less in the area of acting (where strenuous physical and vocal exercises, together with encounter techniques, were already well advanced) than in what was once called by Richard Southern 'the line of contact'. This referred to the spatial relationship between actors and audience, and how it has shifted in history and between different cultures. Since Restoration times in England, theatre architecture has dictated this relationship in a very rigid way. Grotowski's experiments in juggling around with both acting and audience areas found a sympathetic parallel with the new freedom of format experienced by dramatists writing film and television scenarios. However, after the experiments with *Acropolis* (1962 and later revised), Grotowski himself had commented that 'physicallly mingling actors and spectators under the banner of "direct participation" frequently only aroused psychological barriers, while "experience proves that by putting a distance between the actors and the spectators in space, one often rediscovers a (psychic) proximity"'.[15]

It was at a conference in New York, in December 1970, that Grotowski revealed – more as a personal confession than a theatrical credo – just where his concepts of 'Poor Theatre' and 'Theatre of Sources' and (shades of Piscator) 'Objective Drama' had led him:

> I am not interested in theatre anymore, only in what I can do leaving theatre behind ... Am I talking about a way of life, a kind of existence, rather than about theatre? Without a doubt. I think that at this point we are faced with a choice ... The quest for what is most essential in life.[16]

Grotowski's quest took him into a realm which he then called *paratheatre* which related 'to an activity which has its roots in drama, but which specifically does not result in a theatrical presentation before an audience'. Acting became 'only a minor part' of his group's activities, now comprising some seven actors. It had become no more than 'a pretext' for making 'that perilous leap from the safety of art into the unknown'.[17] In July 1975, at the Théâtre des Nations Festival held in Warsaw, Grotowski organized a 'University of Research'. Anyone could join in – 'Acting ambition is not required' – but there were to be no observers. In the progression from theatre to paratheatre, the actor/audience relationship had been lost in the business of a shared and living ritual. The Laboratory Theatre's past work and Grotowski's concept of 'Poor Theatre' (defined as the basic essential encounter of actor and spectator) are left behind, merely recorded in his book *Towards a Poor Theatre*, still in print but now largely shelved in academia rather than being a springboard for future theatre that it was meant at first to be; although it is true that some of the exercises described in it have a lasting value for group and individual work. The climax of the Laboratory's truly theatrical phase is generally acknowledged to be Grotowski's scenario and direction of *The Constant Prince* (1965–8), adapted by J. Slowacki from Calderón's text, and employing the exceptional talents of Ryszard Cieslak.

In the Laboratory's 'final' work at Wroclaw, *Apocalypsis cum Figuris* – if 'final' is the word for a project which lasted from 1968 until as late as 1980 at various times and venues – Grotowski went as far as was theatrically possible in putting actors and audience on an equal footing and without pretence; and even then, the spectator-participants were limited to thirty or less. There was no original text, with all the action and speech being improvised, but including an anthology of passages personally selected by the actors and mostly drawn from well-known classical literature or poetry.

In the years before leaving his experimental theatre practices behind him, Grotowski was described – not surprisingly – as a 'child of Stanislavski' who was desperately trying to rid himself of his theatrical father-figure. In a similar fashion he sought to distance himself from Artaud, with whose 'Theatre of Cruelty' and oriental interests there were obvious affinities.[18] But his way for the actor was in the genuine tradition of the *via negativa* – the restricted palette – or how much could be eliminated from the 'tricks' of acting technique. The kind of actor he attempted to train he called the 'archetypal actor'; but this actor had to start like any other actor with a basic training in body, voice and imagination. Physical exercises aimed to explore and exploit each bodily movement as a means of expression. The hands and the fingers were especially important, also types of walking, and simultaneous activity with different parts of the body, each at a different rhythm, together with the relaxation of muscles not engaged in motion. There was reference to the work of Laban, Delsarte, Dalcroze, and to other forms of 'creative movement' including Hatha-Yoga. Breath-control is fundamental for the voice as well as the body. Grotowski's voice studies included exercises for carrying-power, opening of the larynx, the voice base, placing the voice, vocal imagination, diction, pronunciation and pauses. A useful vocal limber imitates the mewing of a cat in trying to make a communication, employing the widest range of intonation, nuances and pitch. He placed great importance on developing a conscious use of resonators, of which eight principal ones may be located. Imagination is pursued through the study of mime, and of the facial mask, both natural and artificial. Last comes the imaginative interpretation of text, for with Grotowski the body came first, and then vocal expression. Do not think of the vocal instrument itself, he said, or of the words – but react, react with the body. This requires considerable discipline, but such disciplines, or any organized forms, are not to be forced on the body: 'theatre requires organic movements – not symmetrical ones'.[19]

Whilst it is true that actions mostly precede words, Grotowski appears to have underrated the value of the written text and spoken word for making a more exact and sophisticated expression than can be achieved through images of the body alone. Let me be clear about this. During World AIDS Day in November 1993, a television critic, in praising a drama about AIDS, said that 'it spoke louder than any words could utter'. He said this having just praised the writer for his screenplay and dialogue. What he might have said, meaning the same, was that the written story and dialogue, with its camera-treatment, direction, and acting, spoke more than a mere homily of words about AIDS could have done. The mystical overtones of body movements can undoubtedly be subtle, but they also tend to be vague without an exact context, and tend to lack the precise cutting-edge which only finely-tuned language can give. An argument is better developed through dialogue, humour and wit also (not a strong point with Grotowski), than through mime and gesture alone. There appears to have been no one around to take issue with Grotowski in the 1960s over the fact that in the Beginning was the Word, the Logos, the Creative Principle; and that from it comes Dialogos, or the exchange of reasoning minds. Artaud, it is true, sought 'freedom from the dictatorship of the author', as did Joan Littlewood; but the fact of the matter is likely to remain that the future of theatre as an art-form, distinct from social or individual therapy alone, will rely on fresh creative writing more than on the improvisation of actors and directors, however brilliant.

In 1969 Grotowski began to shift to a more professional attitude in the control of his material. 'There can be no confession
without control; confession implies clarity, lucidity and structure.
Plasma and chaos are a confession only of dilettantism.'[20] He
went on to say that unless you train to acquire 'a technique that
allows for the search for a creative act' then you are only after a
quick and easy success. No one could accuse Grotowski of that:
but it was too late. The circle that had begun in trying to get rid
of 'technique' had closed with finding the necessity for it; only
now he was no longer interested.

The *via negativa* led naturally to the idea that the actor should
express himself simply by 'being', which in turn required a 'total
surrender' of self. With this, Grotowski came to the borderline
between reality and illusion, between actual experience and imagined experience, between being and acting, in fact, between life
and the theatre. The error he had fallen into as a theatrical guru
was to make the assumption, in his disciple Eugenio Barba's words,
that 'everything which is art is artificial',[21] and in trying to follow this resentment to its extreme conclusion he let out the baby
of theatre with the bathwater of his theory about reality in performance. The undeniable fact is that theatre *is* a trade of artifice
and illusion, however strongly it may focus on the experience of
reality in its story-telling. But far from being less real because of
this, the artifice, by virtue of its condensation of experience, may
be said to be *more real* than life. It is usually more intensely true
than life itself because it is not 'diluted' in time and space in the
manner of our real lives. Grotowski seems to have found this
impossible to accept. Rejecting artifice, he crosses the boundary
between illusion and reality to that of reality alone. Only the
cultivation of religious expression was left to him.

In more recent years, he has been investigating ritual perfor-
mative techniques, trying to rediscover 'art as a way of knowledge where ritual and artistic expression were seamless'.[22] Among
those he has invited to work with him at the School of Fine Arts,
University of California, at Irvine, are 'Sufi dancers, Buddhist
incantation teachers, Haitians specializing in sun rhythms, and a
dervish'. But actors – no.

Since about 1986 Grotowski has been working in Italy, where
he runs a 'Workcentre' at Pontedera. The latest soundbite-sum-

mary for his researches there (coined by Peter Brook) is 'Art as vehicle'. The 'child of Stanislavski' continues to pursue the 'method of physical actions' which is where his mentor was forced to draw a halt in 1938. For the most recent detailed report on Grotowski's activities, see Thomas Richard's *At Work with Grotowski on Physical Actions* (Routledge, 1995). Grotowski himself contributes an essay to the book called 'From the Theatre Company to Art as Vehicle'; and this title encapsulates the polarity of two extremes which point to what he calls his 'final' position, his 'point of arrival' via Art as Presentation, Paratheatre and Theatre of Sources. His long journey is from the theatre we mostly recognize, the theatre of performance for an audience, to Art as Vehicle, in which what is created is for its own sake, a montage or Action by 'artists who do'. It would not be fair to call them actors any longer, because they do not seek perception of their work by an audience. The 'work' is on themselves: it is a kind of 'objective ritual' in which 'the elements of the Action are the instruments to work *on the body, the heart and the head of the doers*' (Grotowski's italics). We reach a somewhat similar scenario at the end of this book which I will not anticipate here. Suffice it to note that, even now, Grotowski cannot quite let go of his initial ideal at Opole of a performing theatre company: the extremes, he says, 'should remain in contact'.

Giorgio Strehler

Strehler was born in 1921 and is now in his mid-seventies. Together with actor-director Paolo Grassi, he founded the Piccolo Theatre of Milan in 1947. Their ideal was 'to create a public or community theatre subsidized by funds from the community (*collettività*) in the same way that citizens pay taxes to the state and municipality (*comune*), in proportion to their income, for the supporting of important institutions like hospitals and schools and for public administration and justice'. The idea was to create an art theatre not dependent on the market-forces of the box office, and within the means of every class to visit. 'Grassi and Strehler believed in theatre . . . as a kind of school for adults, a place where the public could become familiar with the texts of the great dramatic poets, and probe the problems of society, history, morals and thought.'[23] Since 1973, Strehler has run the Piccolo on his own. It has been renowned for a wide range of productions, including Gorki, Goldoni and Brecht, and it has toured internationally. In 1983, Strehler set up the Théâtre de l'Europe at the Paris Odéon where he staged notable productions which included 'an unforgettable *Tempest*', Corneille's *The Theatrical Illusion* and Strindberg's chamber-play *The Storm*. Herbert Blau comments on Strehler's work as 'something of a last will and testament to the illusory power of theater or its power *as illusion*' (his italics). With the productions mentioned above, and Eduardo de Filippo's *The Great Magician,* Strehler puts 'illusion as a matter of consciousness in the unmoored center of the stage' (Blau, *To All Appearances*, Routledge, 1992, p. 171).

Writing in May 1990, Michael Billington called Strehler 'the master-magician of modern European theatre';[24] and indeed, he is reminiscent of his compatriot Pirandello's character of Cotrone in *The Mountain Giants* (1929), known simply as the magician. At one point Cotrone says: 'Do you have to have people believe in you to believe in yourself?' and later, talking of his household of spirits (for the play takes place 'on the borderland of fantasy and reality'), he comments: 'For us it's enough to imagine something for the thing to materialize.'[25] Strehler would be typecasting for Cotrone, and like Pirandello himself towards the end of his life (he died in 1936), Strehler finds himself strung between the ideology of his art and the ineptness of Italian politics; not to mention Italy's version of England's cultural short-sightedness: starvation of arts subsidy. Between 1947 and 1966, Strehler staged no less than four separate productions of *The Mountain Giants* (at the Piccolo, 1947; Zurich, 1949; Düsseldorf, 1958; and back in Milan at the Teatro Lirico in 1966). Clearly he has been fascinated by the play's statement on the manifold nature and degrees of artistic form.

Pirandello himself described how he descended into 'the very depths of despair with this work which will be my greatest' and how it expressed 'the triumph of the imagination . . . the triumph of poetry – but it is tragedy too, the tragedy of poetry amidst the brutality of the world as it is today'.[26] In his 1947 production, and indeed, twenty or so years later, Strehler blended 'the real with the cosmic with unparalleled felicity, creating a spirit of innocence and guileless sensibility which delights in the enchant-ment of false lightning, apparitions and coloured lights... He drew from the text the very life-blood of poetry.' Carlo Terron reported in *Il Corriere di Milano,* 17 October 1947, that 'Giorgio Strehler's direction, while suffering from lack of space and strain-ing rather too far in the direction of the metaphysical and the tormented, extracted every delectable morsel from the text and avoided its more insidious pitfalls; he managed to suffuse the entire performance with an atmosphere of magic and enchantment.' Strehler's 1966 version was the legendary one, with a finale de-scribed as 'one of the few great spectacles in the history of the theatre which will never be forgotten'. In 1947, Strehler had a gauze curtain descend on the actors; in 1966, 'the iron safety-curtain came crashing down to smash the actor's cart'. The pro-duction stressed the three levels of theatre as they interweave in the story: the *scalognati,* or spirits of the house, with Cotrone as priest-magician, exist only in imagination alone, a kind of self-sufficient theatre company (like the Six Characters) but with all the stage machinery and devices of theatre at their disposal – puppets, costumes, props, the lot; then there is the troupe of ordinary professional actors with Cromo their character-actor and Ilse as their tragic leading lady, trying to get the message of the poet's play about hope and faith and compassion across to an uncaring world, ruled by the Giants of politics and technology, but the troupe is regarded as useless and futile, and falls apart like the contemporary theatre itself; and finally, there is the third level of theatrical existence 'when the actors perform their mime and theatre becomes ritual' with the company sacrificing itself at the hands of a popular audience to the ideals of purity in their work. But when the iron curtain falls, it smashes all three modes with the actors' cart, and any 'hope for a different future'. Strehler's conclusion was even more pessimistic than Pirandello's, which at least left some hope for dialogue between the factions when the Major-domo enters to apologize for the rude behaviour of the servants of the Giants. The director's aim, suggests Bisicchia, 'was to rescue the life-blood of art and draw it away from the theatre-as-machine'. The finale seemed to act as a kind of postscript to *Six Characters,* and be a final triumphant word in the battle between poetry and the political Giants, between the servants of market-force technology and the power of the individual imagination.

Ironically, Strehler is now the 'magician accused of making money vanish' rather than his country's leading theatre director. Accused of fraud, but protesting his innocence, he opts for self-imposed exile in Switzerland; whilst some in Italy call for the exile to be official on account of his production of *Faust*.[27] Part One of *Faust* was staged in the Piccolo Studio in May 1990, with Strehler starring, directing and having supervised the translation. He had been working on the project since 1982; the performance took around five hours; partly an internal drama and philosophical poem, partly 'dazzling spectacle . . . with Archangels rotating in upstage clouds and Mephistopheles talking to God while swimming in a sunken, fiery pit, leaving no doubt who is boss'.[28] Michael Billington goes on to describe how Faust being saved from suicide by the Easter revellers 'has the breathtaking beauty of Breughel's Peasant Wedding with red-plumed soldiers and gaily-apparelled citizens etched in dancing silhouette in the distant upstage area'. It is one of Strehler's trademarks to have full light upstage and shadow downstage. No quandary for him in addressing that old problem of the lighting director – whether to give the actors or the set priority. There is mystery and magic in having figures appear in half-light, and it was particularly appropriate with Faust 'constantly yearning for illumination'; not that photographs show anything but a full spot on his own performance. However, for the director, petty attempts at naturalism are not to be allowed to get in the way of Goethe's great dramatic metaphor of earthbound, sensual man striving for spiritual purity; and for all the consummate theatricality of Strehler's staging, the musicality and profundity of the language was to be given its full value. 'The most sensational coup comes when Mephistopheles offers to show Faust the whole world from on high: a vast globe-shaped black balloon ascends from the pit and the two travellers climb into its carriage to take off into the empyrean.'[29]

Neil Wallace (of Glasgow's Tramway Theatre) points out that 'it is ironic that the allegations Strehler faces are linked to one of his ambitious European ideas: international training for actors'. The irony is in the fact that it has been European Community funds, to the equivalent sum of some £300,000 over a number of years, which the Piccolo's administrators seem to have misused or misspent, some of it 'diverted' to help pay for *Faust*. Nevertheless, Strehler's previous productions have been described as 'some of the most memorable ever seen on the European stage'. With a reputation like that preceding him, it is perhaps not surprising that when his company visited the National's Lyttleton stage in 1992 with Goldoni's *Le Baruffe Chiozzotte* (The Chioggian Quarrels), 'critical disappointment was intense'.[30] Nevertheless, whilst still complaining of inadequate lighting on the actors' faces and too many pauses between the scenes, at least one critic, Robert Tanitch, praised how 'the quarrels, vocally and physically, were brilliantly orchestrated and choreographed by Strehler, [with] the volatile ensemble acting matching Goldoni's spontaneity, humanity and comic melancholy'.[31]

Strehler had twice before visited Britain with Goldoni productions: first at the Edinburgh Festival in 1956, and again in 1958 with *The Servant of Two Masters* at the Sadler's Wells Theatre. But it is now the *Faust* project for which he is most famous, not to say notorious; and as he said himself in June 1988, it 'is for me the ideal endpoint of all my work for the theatre'. In the *New Theatre Quarterly* for August 1993, Christopher Balme addressed its near-completion:

> In the ten years between 1982, when Strehler announced his intention to stage both parts of Goethe's *Faust* over six evenings, and the eventual two-evening performance amidst a 'Faust Festival' in 1992, the Faust project underwent a series of modifications and manifestations, in parallel with the struggle to create the Teatro Grande in Milan as a new house for the Piccolo.[32]

After the 'Goldoni Year' of 1992–3, the *Faust* project was planned to recommence in 1994, but Strehler's 'most recent pronouncements suggest that he no longer aims to present *Faust* in its entirety but seeks to stage approximately 9000 of its 12,000 verses'. He sees it as 'a pre-eminently theatrical text' at the same time as rejecting the idea of a unifying concept for the whole in favour of adapting 'diverse interpretive keys for different sections of the text'. Many scenes, at least initially, were simply read from lecterns.

There is an element of hubris with delusions of grandeur in Strehler's 1992 statement that his was 'the European project par excellence' and that it 'embraces the whole European humanistic culture ... a synthesis of all that is beautiful, elevated, immeasurable (the good and the bad) that "homo europeus" has given the world'.[33]

Nevertheless, some of this hyperbole is attributable to Goethe's own great aims in the work, who as Strehler comments was 'defining for us his concept of immortality' and how it is 'only through the mutation of life and its cyclical structure' that there is 'infinite regeneration of new life'. The theme is majestic, and it is not surprising that at least one Italian critic commented that 'When theatre can suggest so much it is at its highest level, it reconnects with its origins, with its philosophical-poetic-religious matrix.'[34] The uncompleted Grande Teatro is planned as a 1200-seat flexible building. The Studio seats only 500. But by 1989, Strehler was already beginning to realize that the Studio might have to suffice for staging both Parts if he was to achieve the production in his lifetime. The unusual and significant point about this great project is Strehler's identification with playing the character of Faust as well as directing the project as a whole. 'Now at seventy I sensed I had the need to rediscover the central importance of the actor after a lifetime as a director; perhaps I understood that I could play Faust now or never.'[35]

The Faust Festival in Milan (13 January–1 March 1992) coincided with official recognition by the Italian government in November 1991 of the Piccolo as a 'Teatro d'Europe'. But whether the economic and political climate in Italy during the late 1990s will allow its realization in the new Grande Teatro remains to be seen.

Peter Stein

If Strehler is Italy's leading theatre director, then it is Peter Stein who carries the label for Germany. Fritz Kortner called him 'the greatest hope for the German theatre', but Stein himself sees his problem as one of having to be German whilst seeking acceptance in a European context. In August 1993 he was telling Simon Reade at the Edinburgh Festival: 'My base is my language and I need it. I am best at reading and transmitting texts into my language and translating plays of my language into scene work and activities of actors . . . The thing that interests me is to analyse and read texts as though they are always new.'[36]

Stein virtually started his career in Munich in 1967 with a production of Edward Bond's *Saved,* adapted by Martin Sperr into German dialect. He followed it with productions of Schiller's *Intrigue and Love* and Brecht's *In the Jungle of the Cities.* He is a natural heir of Brecht in Germany, as witness his own summary of his approach to *Saved*: 'Economy was the main requirement in the design and in the acting. Composure and clarity, the invitation to criticize determined the realization of the whole play.' Michael Patterson, who quotes that passage, comments that it could refer to all Stein's later work.[37] That later work moves between Goethe and O'Casey, Ibsen and Handke, Shakespeare and Gorki, Aeschylus and O'Neill; even between Eugene Labiche and Botho Strauss, or the two combined (Strauss translated Labiche's *The Piggy Bank* in 1973). The theatre in which Stein made his name during the decade of 1970–80 was the old Schaubühne in West Berlin as it then was. He staged a nine-hour version of *The Oresteia* there in 1981. The New Schaubühne opened in September 1981, designed by Jürgen Sawade on the site of an early cinema built in 1927 by the renowned Erich Mendelsohn, and situated in the heart of Berlin's 'West End' on the Kurfürstendamm. It cost something like £25 million, but before it was even moved into by Stein's company in 1982, it had been branded as 'fossilized' and 'absorbed into the establishment, sold out to bribes'.[38]

Before this happened, two of Stein's renowned productions at the old Schaubühne had been Gorki's *Summerfolk* (1974–5, and later seen at London's National Theatre) and Shakespeare's *As You Like It* in 1977. For both there was a considerable period of research including visits by the company to both Russia and 'Elizabethan' England. *As You Like It* (sometimes compared in seminal importance to Brook's *Dream*) was staged in enormous film studios on the outskirts of Berlin which Stein used like the Great Hall of Tudor times. A full description of the production has been given by Patterson;[39] and Roose-Evans also describes how Stein staged the first part of the play with 'all the early court scenes together and had them dove-tailed, often overlapping or even played simultaneously, so that information was telescoped dramatically'.[40] This was done much in the manner of Mnouchkine's previous and much-acclaimed 1970–71 production of *1789* (of which more anon), in which the audience stood or promenaded in the centre around the various small stages on the perimeter of the studio area. These court scenes were given a stilted, wooden delivery and acting; then after them, the audience were led, almost one by one, down a corridor to another part of the vast studios where Arden had been created with real trees, and the acting became 'free' and natural. The characters were already 'living' there – Audrey churning her butter, the Lords ordering their butterfly collections, hunters shooting, and so on. The 'Seven Ages' speech was given by Jaques as a known 'party-piece' (and in English!). Phoebe admired her own reflection, Narcissus-like, in a 'real' pool. But 'psychological naturalism' was not attempted. Duke Frederick replaces Shakespeare's Epilogue, his armour discarded at the foot of a tree, declaiming instead 'the Cycle of the Seasons' – a prose poem by the French writer Francis Ponge, which summarizes Stein's view of Arden. The 'freedom' of nature is an illusion (with its own inflexible laws); we have to restructure the way forward with what we have, and not try to escape into an impossible world. Message for a then-divided Germany.

In 1990 Stein brought his extraordinary 1987 production of Eugene O'Neill's *The Hairy Ape* (1923) to London's National Theatre, where despite initial technical problems caused by the scale of the scenery, it created a memorable experience during its limited run. In 1992 his production of Debussy's *Pelléas and Mélisande* for the Welsh National Opera (conductor, Pierre Boulez) won the International Classical Music Award for Opera of the Year, and was also seen on television.

It was also in 1992 that Stein was appointed to direct the theatre programme at the Salzburg Festival; and already his in-fluence there has made it a major fixture in the theatrical as well as the musical calendar. Earlier, Stein had become estranged from the Schaubühne when they refused to stage his enormous year-long *Faust* project. Whether Strehler's similar and financially-crippling operation in Milan at more or less the same time influ-enced the Berlin decision is not known, but it seems likely. Stein's response was to plan an even bigger and more ambitious project at Salzburg. He bought the Felsenreitschule, with the intention of staging a three-year cycle of Shakespeare's Roman plays in it between 1992 and 1994. It is a spectacular, and some say, unduly troublesome arena, some forty to forty-five metres wide, open air but with a detachable sliding roof, and for a back-drop having three tiers of arches carved out of the rock of Salzburg's great Monchsberg cliff. A former seventeenth-century riding-school, it is no surprise to read that Max Reinhardt used it in 1933 to stage – yet again – *Faust*. Stein's production of *Julius Caesar* opened the cycle in 1992, only it was badly received by the German critics who complained that the actors were inaudible.[41] However, when it was brought to Edinburgh's Royal Highland Exhibition Hall in 1993, Michael Billington judged it 'a downright, unforgettable masterpiece'.[42]

Billington had hailed the production the previous year at Salzburg as having a vitality which reached the political heart of the play. With a cast of 37 boosted with 200 local amateurs and students, the crowd scenes in particular, so much a part of the story, had more than their usual impact where inadequacy of numbers so often strains credulity. Moreover, they were directed as a crowd in true Reinhardt fashion where, for comparison, David Thacker's modern-dress promenade version at Stratford's Other Place in 1993 attempted to use a very briefly instructed audience who mostly got inadvertently in the way of the action, and whose reactions were often more interesting than those of the actors. Stein actually combined togas and boiler-suits to point the timeless message about the power of oratory and inflammatory rhetoric: 'One of the production's most thrilling sights,' said Billington, 'is seeing this throng of individuals turned into a collective force who weave and sway around the orators and then tear their temporary trestle-stage to pieces.'[43] When he reviewed the production a year later at Edinburgh, Billington extended his description and judgement saying how he had never before 'been so aware of the sense of characters in the grip of some invisible destiny: something Stein enhances through the use of visual echoes . . . Caesar constantly casts prophetic glances at Cassius . . . Calpurnia, aware of the danger in the Capitol, hurls herself against a wall in naked desperation . . .' and so on. Stein, he says, 'does not lock the play into a rigid concept. His greatness lies in his minute exploration of the text (his own adaptation of the Schlegel translation), his ability to make every moment live theatrically and his uncanny gift of suggesting that a play is an act of collective memory.'[44]

Stein's three-year Roman cycle at Salzburg continued with Deborah Warner's *Coriolanus* in 1993, and concluded with his production of *Antony and Cleopatra* in 1994.

Meanwhile, at the Edinburgh Festival in 1994 Stein returned to the *Oresteia* of Aeschylus that he had previously tackled in Berlin in 1980–81, only now with greater power and poetry. There was seven and a half hours of it this time, performed in an arena the size of an ice-rink (the Murrayfield Ice Rink, to be precise), and what is more, in Russian with subtitles. For all these apparent handicaps, Michael Billington reported that he had never seen the huge arc of the trilogy – even from Hall, Mnouchkine or Ronconi – 'so clearly and vividly presented' (*Guardian*, 27 August 1994). Unusually, fellow-critic Michael Coveney found himself in agreement, noting how this 'momentous production moves inexorably from the violence of revenge to the uneasy establishment of a new democracy' (*Observer*, 18 August 1994). The staging, both agreed, was masterly in Moidele Bickel's simple spatial design with the audience on three sides. As to its length, Coveney comments interestingly that 'Theatre should take us into different time zones, and impose its own temporal rules. Stein does this brilliantly.' Billington notes that 'this great, life-enhancing production ... gives each moment a fierce emotional reality while conveying the sense of dynamism within the trilogy', and further, that with the 'suggestion that democratic freedom is at last a possibility', this concept of Stein's offers 'an overwhelming political and humanist experience'. Clearly, it was a theatrical privilege of high order for those fortunate enough – and selective enough – to have seen it.

Roger Planchon

If Stein was the natural heir to Brecht in Germany, then Roger Planchon (b. 1931) might well lay claim to the title for France. Planchon is a modern Renaissance figure, being at once a director, an actor, a writer for both theatre and cinema, and a film editor. He is renowned (though for some of his critics, this should read notorious) for transferring the focus of French theatre from Paris to the provinces, and of rejecting 'classical' for what he would term 'popular' theatre (but which nevertheless includes classical plays). As a young man of twenty from a rural peasant background in the Ardèche, with a Jesuit education and decorated for running messages for the Resistance at the age of twelve, he opened a small semi-amateur theatre with no fixed base, the Théâtre de la Comédie, in Lyon in 1950. Within two years the company found a base, turned professional, and stayed in Lyon for a further five years. They started with farces – both a good attraction and a good training; and some four of Planchon's actors from those early days stayed with him for the distinguished years that followed. It was in the 1950s that Planchon became extremely influenced by Brecht's theories and practice.

In 1957, his company moved to the nearby communist municipality of Villeurbanne, which dislikes being referred to as a suburb of the greater city, having plenty of its own cultural history. The company was renamed Théâtre de la Cité de Villeurbanne. It was in 1959 that the newly-formed Ministry of Cultural Affairs under André Malraux decided to do something about over-centralization of the theatre in France by giving more support to provincial groups and theatres. There were three distinct grades created, rising in status and subsidy: a *troupe permanente* (like the British Repertory company), a *centre dramatique* (for regional touring), and a *maison de la culture* (being an area's cultural centre).[45] The Théâtre de la Cité rose through them all with Planchon at the helm. He sought out his working-class audience at Villeurbanne, and this grass-roots contact between company and patrons was 'an education for both'. He used the working-class familiarity with cinema-going to develop and integrate that interest with his 'stage language', and of course, he had the admired Brecht's use of film as a tried format. 'Of course one explains and comments in a production,' he says,

> but I've never believed in making a theatre to attract 'the masses' with comprehensible plays or acceptable stories. What you have to do is put into a performance something of the

way people outside culture see things. There's no intermedi-
ate step, no easy way in – you have to turn the whole thing
round at once.[46]

Such was Planchon's fame and success at Villeurbanne that by
1972 his company was given further national recognition with
the revived title of Théâtre National Populaire (TNP). From Gémier's
dream in 1920, and Vilar's twelve exciting years from 1951 to
1963, the TNP in Paris had declined in popularity during the
following nine years under Georges Wilson, and eventually closed.
This was less Wilson's fault than that of the new Ministry policy
mentioned above. Planchon revived the national ideal by touring
provincial France on a regular basis with the TNP. The English
media now dub Planchon 'the artistic director of France's
National Theatre' but some Parisians especially might question
that label, and Planchon himself is wary of both the words 'National' and 'Populaire' in his company's title. His ideal of a truly
working-class theatre is as far from being achieved as were the
similar ideals of Brecht, Littlewood and Arnold Wesker's Centre
42 in 1960s' Britain.

Planchon recently made a clarion call in support of the arts in
Europe.[47] With budgets being slashed everywhere in 1993, he
compared policy on European theatre and cinema 'to a dead dog
floating downstream'. The GATT talks almost foundered on the
rights of film-makers to preserve locally-made and locally-released
work. Even in the end, the money-lords of the US industry were
able to force an 'agree to differ' decision on Europe. 'It is at the
very time when an economic and moral crisis is deepening that
governments need to care most deeply for creations of the mind . . .
and to pursue a bold policy to promote the arts and defend them
as an absolute priority.' In Britain, as elsewhere, such sentiments
cry in the wind of a cynical and philistine attitude which does
not even know it is being cynical and philistine. In 1993, 'not
one of our politicians would consider that the defence of artistic
creativity is as important as defending the country'.

But it was much earlier – May 1968, to be precise – that dedicated theatre people in France, with ideas on the role and power
of theatre in society, realized that the 'events' of that month had
become a watershed. Yvette Daoust tells how 'Directors from

popular theatres right across France met at Villeurbanne, and after days of discussion, issued a joint statement.' Although it agreed on a 'progressive definition of culture', it also focused on the enormous difficulties and misconceptions entailed in the ideal of 'bringing culture to the masses'. 'After ten years of work at Villeurbanne, only 8 per cent of the audiences were working-class.'[48] Planchon follows neither what he calls the 'Mystico-Sacré' theatre of Artaud, Grotowski, Arrabal and the rest, nor that of political agitation, the agit-prop school of direct action for a cause, which in any case usually only preaches to the converted. 'I create political theatre,' he was saying in 1970, 'but I'm interested essentially in the problematical aspect of politics... For me, a situation in the theatre is true insofar as it has its roots buried deep in everyday life.'[49] In May 1971, Patrice Chéreau joined Planchon as co-director at Villeurbanne, having previously worked for three years directing a theatre in a dormitory area of north-west Paris. The two men 'seem to have decided that the ambitions of creating a theatre which would attract the working-classes in representative numbers is unrealistic in our present society'. With the cultural gap painfully there, 'our role is to keep the wound open'.[50]

Nevertheless, writing in 1991, Michael Kustow reported that Planchon

> was and remains driven by the search for a richer, fuller kind of theatre. 'Culture: a privilege to be shared so that there is no more privilege,' was an early slogan of his theatre, and he acknowledges that his taste for spectacle and baroque effects comes from a wish to give a popular audience the theatrical equivalent of a rich country meal.[51]

Daoust describes over two dozen of the famous productions at Villeurbanne, with an excellent body of photographs from their archives. She wisely observes that the dilemma of 'popular' theatre directors like Planchon is that 'even when they themselves have humble origins, the culture and education which they have acquired by participating in a theatrical endeavour separates them from their potential public'.[52] There follows from this the problems of repertoire and of subsidy; and these, in turn, involve questions of, in the first case, education, and in the second, charges of élitism (or some might say, inverted élitism, should money be found for Music Hall rather than Meyerhold). The situation has not changed much from France in 1973 to Britain's Arts Council problems in the 1990s. The French Minister of Culture infuriated avant-garde groups in 1973 by saying 'People who come to the door of this ministry with a begging-bowl in one hand and a Molotov cocktail in the other will have to choose.' In other words, revolutionary theatre has a right to exist, but not at the taxpayer's expense. 'To argue that "good" theatre should be able to pay for itself is to see theatre as a commodity for the few and not a service for all.'[53] But that, of course, is the crunch of the matter for directors like Planchon, Strehler and the rest; and not least, Richard Eyre of the Royal National Theatre. Yet the view that 'good' theatre should be good enough to pay for itself is, one suspects, the sort of statement favoured by the Conservative Minister for English Heritage in the early 1990s, Mr Peter Brooke (ah, the difference in an 'e'); and moreover, a view which he would encourage his Arts Council appendage to take, although the independent Lord Gowrie may resist it. As a footnote concerning revolutionary theatre, it is a familiar irony that the rich often pay eagerly to hear and see themselves abused. Caryl Churchill's *Serious Money* was a case in point.

The lessons which Planchon took from Brecht were both ideological and practical. Life had to be 'explained' as well as merely 'presented'; and in doing so, the *mise-en-scène,* the 'scenic writing', had 'an *equal responsibility* [his italics] to that of the dramatic text'.[54] We have returned here to the Brechtian concept of the *gestus*, mentioned earlier; and it was in Planchon's work with Shakespeare, Molière and Marivaux, as Whitton notes, that this influence predominated. One of the most famous productions of Planchon's maturity was probably that of *Tartuffe* in 1962, in which all his personal theatrical style found expression, combining 'the richness of immediate experience with an understanding of social, historical, and psychological causality'.[55]

On the other hand, Planchon's own plays – and he has been fairly prolific – have not achieved similar success, 'perhaps because of their multi-layered complexity, though they have attracted the admiration of critics ... Their approach is one of vivid but un-rhetorical descriptive realism, re-creating the material fabric of life in its detail while trying to preserve the human experience of which it is part. As such, they are unique.'[56] Kustow reports how Planchon himself spoke of his 'passion for what is concrete . . . I like life in its most elementary state, without heightening . . . I love garbage, potato peel, bits of broken wood, all the things left over from life – not the things themselves, perhaps, but the life they point to.'[57] The illusion-reality syndrome that is theatre could hardly be better expressed.

Together with a select few directors who have run their companies virtually as communes, Planchon's importance to the making of the professional actor in the second half of the twentieth century is the freedom he offers them in their craft; giving them their rein whilst controlling the direction of the play as a whole; respecting the principles of an ideology without being governed too rigidly by it. In this, he progresses beyond his mentor, Brecht. As with Mnouchkine's Théâtre du Soleil, his company is less a *création collective* than a number of *créations individuelles* brought together in the service of a given text. The casting process at Villeurbanne, at least in 1962, illustrates the point. Planchon discussed with each actor the role which most suited them in a play to be done. Nothing was laid down as settled until each could see their place in the whole and be excited by it. Finally, after about a fortnight of reading and working around the text, the obvious distribution of roles became clear and was made firm. It was probably the same casting as he had foreseen himself from the start, but now the company felt involved in the decision. 'Planchon has a way of leading an actor, through conversation, in time, to make the same discoveries that he himself made in his preliminary work.'[58] As one of his actors, Gérard Guillaumot, put it: the good director is a *provocateur*.

Planchon hated what he called 'pathos' in acting, which he saw as a kind of lying, of over-playing, of indulgence. Indeed, he called it 'pathetic' acting and was probably well aware of the English overtones of the adjective. His own style has been described as 'being between parody and realism . . . the actor's perspective on his role is essentially witty'. Certainly, photographs of him show an almost impish humour in the eyes, which must have reduced many a tension during the rehearsal process. Daoust reports that 'Planchon has even refused to direct actors in another language than French, because they would not understand his jokes.'[59] This charming Gallic characteristic is a welcome antidote to the often over-serious intensity of some gurus who seem interested more in the neurotic aspects of emotional memory, and can rarely find it in themselves to smile at the human condition.

Ariane Mnouchkine

After Madame Vestris in the early nineteenth century and Joan Littlewood in the 1950s and 1960s, Ariane Mnouchkine (b. 1934) stands alone as an internationally-famed woman director deserving the soubriquet guru. This is not to forget the distinguished work of Nuria Espert in Spain, of Irene Hentschel in 1940s' London, or of Cheryl Crawford and Judith Malina in the USA; nor a sad salute in passing to the ill-fated promise of Buzz Goodbody at Stratford in 1975. Nor is it to ignore the strong feminine contingent of theatre directors whose work has become known in Britain during the 1980s and early 1990s, none of whom (yet) quite qualify as guru-leaders. In both London and the provinces, their names make a distinguished list. With apologies to those inadvertently omitted, alphabetically the list might read: Sarah Pia Anderson, Pip Broughton, Annie Castledine, Jude Kelly, Jenny Killick, Brigid Larmour, Phyllida Lloyd, Nancy Meckler, Katie Mitchell, Deborah Paige, Di Trevis, Clare Venables, Glen Walford and Deborah Warner. It is doubtful whether other countries could field such a talented distaff team.

In France, Ariane Mnouchkine's Théâtre du Soleil has been one of the most exciting and inventive companies operating there during the last thirty years. Its work, whilst having similar aims and ideology to Planchon's TNP, has been even more radical. Or perhaps 'even more democratic' would be the apter phrase, since Mnouchkine, in her own words, seeks 'to give the actors control over their art'.[60] She sees herself as less autocratic than perhaps Planchon does, for all his tactful sensitivity. Nevertheless, the idea once held feasible that the Théâtre du Soleil could exist as a viable *création collective* without her is no longer convincing. The director's role remains crucial to the company. Yet in their

1992 publicity leaflets they maintain that their identity is distinguished through their existence as a collective. 'Irrespective of their status in the company, all members share in the everyday work of the theatre – building sets, sewing costumes, taking tickets – and all receive equal pay.'[61]

Le Théâtre du Soleil began as a semi-amateur company in 1964 when Mnouchkine was a psychology student at university. Neither their first production – Gorki's *The Smug Citizens* adapted by Adamov – nor their second two years later – a company adaptation from Gautier – brought them much notice. But with Wesker's *The Kitchen* in 1967, they found a big success, moreover in the novel venue of a disused circus (the Cirque Medrano). Wesker's play about difficult employment conditions for working people anticipated the social unrest in May 1968. Now a fully professional group, the company used the same circus venue for a Dionysian love-fulfilling version of *A Midsummer Night's Dream*, two years ahead of Brook's famous production in 1970. By that same year, 1970, they had found themselves a permanent base in a cartridge warehouse, La Cartoucherie, at Vincennes on the outskirts of Paris; and at the same time they were fortunate enough to find international fame with their exuberant and spectacular interpretation of the French Revolution, *1789*. In it, the famous historical events of that year were shown at one remove by using the device of imagining them being performed by eighteenth-century fairground actors to their contemporaries. The production was brought to London's Roundhouse in 1971. Later, there was a less successful sequel devoted to the year *1793*; also a modern follow-up presented in 1975 called *L'Age d'or, première ébauche* (The golden age, first draft), which being set in the year 2000 was intended to give once again an objective view of social problems, this time in the mid-1970s.[62] There were three highly-stylized, Eastern-influenced versions of Shakespeare's *Richard II* (1981), *Twelfth Night* (1982) and *Henry IV, Part One* (1984); and two very unusual plays by Hélène Cixous, both overtly Asian this time, in 1985 and 1987.[63]

Twenty-one years after their visit to London with *1789*, Le Théâtre du Soleil returned to England in 1992 – characteristically to the waste-land outskirts of Bradford in West Yorkshire – with what they described as 'possibly the best example yet of

Mnouchkine's concept of total theatre': *Les Atrides,* comprising a cycle of four plays describing the tragic history of the House of Atreus. Euripides' *Iphigenia in Aulis* was followed by the *Oresteia* trilogy from Aeschylus. At the Robin Mills Carpet Warehouse, Greengates, near Bradford, the author managed to catch up with one of the plays, *The Libation Bearers* (*Les Choéphores*, given in French).

It was a rare and impressive example of 'Ritual Theatre' which normally only has a counterpart in ceremonial religious events held in great cathedrals. Indeed, the Warehouse – especially in its bleak, upper-storey theatre space – was given a distinctly 're-ligious feel' from the moment the audience entered, having climbed one of the two scaffolded outer staircases erected for the occasion. This feeling was achieved by a low insistent background sound, the deep note of a large drum continuously reverberating like a heart-beat, and giving the sensation of some fateful action about to be given expression, a judgement of the gods, a sleeping tiger, an incubus made manifest, as indeed was to be the case. As the play began, this sound was taken over from the tape and developed to a frightening intensity by the live percussionists who provided a drum-equivalent for the French 'Les Trois Coups' and a slowly rising curtain. Sound was a vital and busy contribution throughout the action, with a large number of exotic musical instruments housed on a long raised platform to audience-right of the stage, and under the direction of a Rasputin-like figure, the composer Jean-Jacques Lemetre who, together with three other players, rushed from instrument to instrument in a frenzy of in-terpretive commitment. This was one of the most important elements in Mnouchkine's production concept of 'total theatre'.

The Greengates Warehouse was chosen because of its close approximation to the company's home base at La Cartoucherie. In costume, dance, and mostly formal speech in what used to be called 'the grand manner' (and which sounds even grander in the precision of French), the actors call upon Eastern and Oriental techniques associated with the Noh, Kabuki and Kathakali traditions. Make-up – which, incidentally, the public are allowed to watch being applied in a makeshift dressing-room area beneath the scaffolded seating – consists of a painted mask on a white base, echoing the ancient Greek usage as well as those mentioned above, and providing semiotic definitions of human character. Individuals are more than themselves, being archetypal images of happiness and suffering, caught inevitably in the tragic destiny of the royal house of Atreus in Argos. The force of dramatic irony, of foreknowledge in the audience, has an elemental simplicity and power in this seminal text. It works today as it must have done in 458 BC, both as technically adroit theatre and for the issues it addresses of the futility of war, of the dreadful call of vengeance in a blood-feud, of sex and power and waste and injustice.

The prime importance of the Chorus as a device through which Aeschylus may comment on all this is patently evident in this production. The Chorus comprises between twelve and fifteen members of the company at different times, male and female; but as all are meant to represent the Women of Argos, the men are suitably shaped, dressed and made-up accordingly. They were an extraordinarily agile group, not only in the energetic stomping of feet in rhythmic responses to the savage percussion, but also in the acrobatic leaps and vaulting with which some of them dispersed over, through and behind the wooden walls and stepped exits of the set. One female leader of the Chorus (Catherine Schaub) spoke for all, most of the time.

There were two major entrances and exits: the giant wood doors up centre – four in all, opening on cords behind each other – and a moving ramp down centre used to deliver or carry off a standing character or death-laden bed from the four-feet height of the main stage area. There were also two minor entrance/exits either side of the central doors, and one each half-way either side of the almost square stage. These all had steps up out of sight as if leading to the parapeted walls of Argos. The whole design (by Guy-Claude François) was reminiscent of a bull-ring, a corrida of human blood and death, an arena for tragedy.

The lighting rig was fairly sophisticated, having some seven spot-bars with twenty-five lanterns each, plus extensive floods and side battens. Some blue and salmon-pink gelatines were used, but mostly it was open white as for a boxing ring or open-air spectacle. A couple of fades to semi-darkness were used to punctuate the slight changes of place and time indicated by the text, although these could hardly be said to damage the three unities as the action proceeded successively from Agamemnon's tomb to outside and then inside the Palace of Atreus. There was little or no attempt to dramatize 'mood' or the time of day or any special effects by means of the lighting plot. These matters were handled by the musicians, and of course the actors.

Two of the leading players, Juliana Carneiro da Cunha (Clytemnestra) and Simon Abkarian (Orestes), despite their mutually livid make-up, gave an interestingly divided collation of acting styles from this century: a filtering of the Stanislavskian mode (Clytemnestra) with a strong dose of the Brechtian (Orestes). She gained in audience sympathy; he gained in tragic inevitability, where no amount of emotional pleading could alter the objective course of destiny. But it was Aeschylus and his play which won over any confusion which might have been felt between different cultures and modes; and more than anyone, Ariane Mnouchkine was the victor, with her devotion to the concept of a pure theatre, beyond any particular national bounds, offering us archetypes of the human situation, both through the observing Chorus of common citizens and the tragic high-born participants entangled by their naked passions.

When Michael Billington saw *Les Atrides* in Paris in 1990, he concluded that 'Mnouchkine's great achievement is to have married Oriental stylisation and Western realism and to constantly remind us, through the ever-reacting Chorus, that the private griefs and lusts of these murdering royals have a shattering public dimension.' Michael Coveney, too, reviewing the Bradford performance, saw that 'Mnouchkine's brilliant tragic pageant is mere prelude to the implicit catastrophe of modern civilisation.'[64] The programme notes at Bradford spoke of theatre as a total vocation for Mnouchkine, 'giving her the opportunity to confront injustice and despair with a positive example of dramatic art as a shared living experience'.

Those last three words are the keynote to the work of every great twentieth-century director we have mentioned here. It is one that we have seen grow more evident, consistently from Copeau onwards, as the making of the professional actor has been given shape at its highest level. As we might expect, the ideal was noted and every attempt made to follow it up in that most romantic of great new nations, the USA. But they walked into a problem which only this century could have thrown up.

13

The American Actor in Search of a World Role

In one very definite sense, of course, the American actor has found his world role in the twentieth century – only it has been on the cinema screen rather than on the stage. The names of the Hollywood pantheon are known everywhere, but essentially it is a different medium and a different art-form. Even more, much more, than in the theatre, money is the bottom line of the game. First and foremost, the cinema is an industry and a distributing organization. Actors come fairly low down the hierarchy, with just a few mega-star exceptions who are rich enough to call their own shots. Writers are even lower down the ladder, and there's the rub. Screen actors have given great performances with third-rate scripts and incredibly 'botched' collaborations, but whilst it may serve the reputation of the stars and the studio, it does little to create a national dramatic tradition. For the latter, the writer is essential; the 'live' occasion onstage is essential; and the unique ambience of a city-culture and population within the country's whole environment is essential. Without these three combining for the event – the author, the player, and the audience – a distinctive dramatic culture is difficult to achieve.

The venerable length of American stage history may surprise the casual observer. Long before the end of the colonial period around 1775, and the establishment of the new nation up to about 1820 when proudly independent theatre-lovers sought to create their own playhouses, there had been virtually indigenous dramatic activity, encouraged as in Europe by the Catholic Church.

There are records from the sixteenth century of religious plays in Mexico and New Mexico, and professional Spanish actors were presenting dramas in the New World colonies by the beginning of the seventeenth century. As early as 1606 a masque was performed in French at Port Royal; but it is from England, not Spain or France, that the American theatre stems. Near to Port Royal at Charleston, South Carolina, just under a century later, in 1703, the apparently notorious Tony Ashton can lay claim to being the first American professional actor, albeit as a solo performer without a company. Around the same time, a certain Richard Hunter, otherwise unknown, asked for a license to act plays in New York, then with a population of scarcely 4000.[1]

By the end of the century, in 1798, the Park Theatre, an innovatory building in stone, with three tiers of boxes, a gallery and a pit, and having a capacity of around 2000, had opened in New York. It was after starring there in 1809 that the American actor John Howard Payne (1791–1852), famous for his lyric of 'Home, Sweet Home', created another signpost by travelling to England to appear at Drury Lane, thus reversing the theatrical flow and, perhaps, marking a certain coming-of-age for the American theatre. American audiences for their part were shortly hailing the arrival on their shores of such British leading players as George Frederick Cooke and Edmund Kean. The period from 1820 to 1870 was one of swift theatrical development, particularly in New York, although still with an English emphasis. Following Cooke and Kean came Macready, Charles Kean and Charles Kemble. All the same, American actors were beginning to create their own legends: Edwin Forrest (1806–72) rose to become the most representative thespian of his age. His famous clash of egos with Macready, which led to riot and deaths outside the New York theatre where Macready was playing Macbeth on 10 May 1849, was the subject of Richard Nelson's splendid play *Two Shakespearian Actors*, staged by the RSC in 1990. Nicoll tells us that by 1885 'over 3500 towns, with a total of more than 5000 theatres' were active in the USA, yet despite the utilization in many plays of American scenes (by Boucicault and others), the dominating model remained stubbornly English.

The end of the nineteenth century saw many great American players alongside the visiting luminaries: William Gillette (1855–

1937), Richard Mansfield (1857–1907), Julia Marlowe (1866–1950), and Ethel Barrymore (1879–1959), to name but four who appeared at the time and on the same stages as Irving, Coquelin, Bernhardt and Terry. In 1900, there were forty-three theatres in New York; by 1928 the number had nearly doubled to eighty.

'To find the moment when there appeared an unequivocally American drama,' says Travis Bogard, 'is impossible.' As has been noted already, most great drama stems from city life. When we speak of English, French, Greek or Russian drama, we invariably mean the drama of London, Paris, Athens or Moscow. So it is with American drama. New York drama is mostly what we mean to imply, and until that city became the unchallenged theatrical cultural capital of the USA after the First World War, it is hardly possible to fix a specifically American school of drama.[2] However, from then on, the names of the dramatists begin to flood in: names like Sidney Howard, Eugene O'Neill, Robert Sherwood, Maxwell Anderson, Thornton Wilder, Clifford Odets, Elmer Rice, George Kaufman, Irwin Shaw, William Saroyan, John Van Druten, Lillian Hellman, William Inge; and equally impressively, such more recent giants as Tennessee Williams, Arthur Miller, Edward Albee, Sam Shepard and David Mamet.

But however healthily the American drama appeared to be growing, there was no specifically American acting style, apart from the hijacking of Stanislavski's 'System' and re-dubbing it 'The Method' (although, as Orson Welles pointed out, it was only *a* method). As seen by the world, American acting style was that seen in the cinema. The Hollywood 'greats', forged by the strict demands of their own industry – close-up technique, for example, and building the measure of an emotional role shot out of true sequence – have invariably been good actors as well: Spencer Tracy, Katharine Hepburn, Gregory Peck, Elizabeth Taylor, Paul Newman and, of course, Greta Garbo, to pick only half a dozen out of the hat. But the specific genre is confused by the fact that in America, as elsewhere, 'stage greats', ever since the 1930s, have also been seduced by the profits and fame offered by the silver screen: to make another invidious selection, we might mention the Barrymores, John Garfield, Lee J. Cobb, Frederic March and Florence Eldridge, Jason Robards, Uta Hagen, Helen Hayes, Julie Harris, Jessica Tandy, and the ubiquitous Orson Welles. Only the Lunts and Katharine Cornell seem to represent those top names who largely resisted the blandishments of any long-term studio contract. This may be because they preferred the strenuous business of meeting the largest number of 'live' audiences through touring. The Lunts were repeatedly 'on the road' in Theatre Guild sponsored productions. Katharine Cornell and her company toured frequently in the 1930s; on one exceptional occasion, it was for twenty-nine weeks with *The Barretts of Wimpole Street*, *Candida* and *Romeo and Juliet* in the repertoire, playing 225 performances to an estimated 500,000 persons, and travelling 16,853 miles![3]

The late 1960s produced an exciting 'new wave' in American drama and an explosive mushrooming of experimental theatre groups, mostly again starting in New York. There was the Café La Mama, founded in 1961 by Ellen Stewart, and run successfully for a while by Tom O'Horgan. One of its early and innovatory productions was the musical *Hair* (1967). An even earlier starter was Judith Malina and Julian Beck's Living Theatre, founded in 1951 (after an abortive start in 1948), among whose productions were Jack Gelber's *The Connection* (1959) about drug addiction, an Artaudian *Mysteries* (1964), a version of *Antigone* (1967) set during the Vietnam War, and the Grotowski-influenced *Paradise Now* (1968). The Living Theatre toured extensively in Europe but disbanded in 1970. Another provocative group was Joseph Chaikin's Open Theatre, founded in 1963, which staged such convention-breaking writers as Jean-Claude van Itallie with *America Hurrah* (1966) and *The Serpent* (1968). The group lasted for ten years. The Actor's Studio had already been going twenty years by the late 1960s (founded by Elia Kazan and Lee Strasberg in 1947 – the year of Kazan's direction of *Streetcar* with the young Brando) and remained a powerful influence on American acting. Richard Schechner's Performance Group was set up in 1967 and achieved a notorious 'hippy' fame in 1968 with *Dionysus in 69*, which used *The Bacchae* as a political argument for free sex and the drug culture. The Group reformed in 1970, becoming the Wooster Group (still active), while Schechner, now doyen of the American avant-garde, started work again in 1994 with East Coast Artists (see Chapter 15).

A final mention in this brief round-up must go to Peter Schumann's Bread and Puppet Theatre, created on the streets of

New York in 1963. He was aiming at a non-sophisticated working-class audience with his parades of giant puppets and short plays on contemporary subjects, but rather like Brecht before him, he was almost embarrassed when taken up by the cultural élite. He made no charge unless performing indoors, for theatre, he said, is not a commercial transaction but more like a religion – 'a necessity like bread'. In the early 1970s his company, in the main non-professionals, turned up on tour in England, but not, I believe, in London. I caught up with them on a unique occasion in the small market town of Street in the West Country. For all its 'roughness', the performance was both poetic and spiritual.

With all this experimental activity, it seemed at last that America was taking a lead on the world's stage. The then new young critic, John Lahr, was excited by it all:

> The theatre is faced with the task of putting mystery and resonance back into the word at a time when language has been debased by Government to oppress and betray the public, and eviscerated by the mass media. It has also re-discovered the silent language of gesture, an aesthetic which aspires to show exemplary actions and also to incarnate the yearnings for transcendence and rebirth that linger in our songs and in our obsession with drugs.[4]

Those heartfelt words, written in 1971, and coming out of the American experience of the late 1960s, have a prophetic ring which still sounds meaningful today. We shall be returning to their message.

It was in 1972 that the Off-Off Broadway Theatre Alliance was established as a co-operative organization for something like sixty-five member groups. This New York initiative in trying to support experimental work alongside an increasingly rigid commercial field was also emulated by much regional theatre in the USA, thus fulfilling the latter's early promise as being the truly vital element of a national ideal.

America obviously has as many good actors, and in proportionate numbers, as any other civilized country. Likewise, her dramatists can match any others, whether in English or in translation. But she arrived comparatively late on the scene, and in this century the goal-posts for a national classic drama, and the recognition of a connected acting style, have been moved considerably, if not altogether. The 'game' is now in a global context only; the world has shrunk in size and cultural boundaries with it; and the cinema and television have made a special contribution to this.

Ultimately, for any actor or any national theatre to have a world role today, a world-class dramatist has to have articulated uniquely, in that country's language and social *mores*, the human situation, showing 'the very age and body of the time his form and pressure'. For more than 400 years now, England has been more than fortunate in having Shakespeare to speak for its theatrical place in the world, and giving its actors such supremely challenging roles to play. France has Racine and Molière; but as Copeau confirmed somewhat mournfully, in view of his failure to find a modern dramatist to match them for the Vieux Colombier as great as Chekhov had been for the Moscow Art Theatre, the actor has to rely on the 'poets' of theatre to give him or her roles in which to display the highest art and craft. (Irving in *The Bells* remains a classic exception to the rule.) For Copeau the tragedy was that despite the contemporary presence of the unclassifiable Paul Claudel, the more accessible work of Obey, Giraudoux, Cocteau and Anouilh was to arrive just too late for him. It was the Compagnie des Quinze and the Cartel des Quatre who mostly had the benefit. But what of the USA in the twentieth century – now indisputably the most powerful country in the world? Where, and to whom, are her actors to look for their national poet of the theatre?

We have already mentioned a flood of contenders, yet it is mostly too early to say which of them might still be world famous in a hundred years. Williams and Miller, perhaps; but the name which is invariably quoted, and which for most of the century has had to carry the heavy responsibility of being Number One, is Eugene O'Neill. The trouble has become increasingly obvious, however, that this cultural burden has been rather too much for the actual universality of his work to support. He is not easily revived. It is true that he wrote one or two late masterpieces, but these are not really sufficient to feed a great nation's soul beyond their time, nor even to speak through the personal pain which undoubtedly created them to all mankind for all ages.

It is sad to say, perhaps, but his particular distinction has been rather forced upon him by a nation desperate to have its own 'classic' representative (a role which O'Neill himself was dangerously conscious of trying to fill).

When the 1930s' theatres of the Left faded away at the close of the decade, Joseph Wood Krutch, a distinguished American critic, summed up rather despondently by saying: 'The fact remains that no playwright who has emerged since 1918, not even O'Neill, has produced an impact even remotely comparable to that produced by Ibsen or Shaw'.[5] So many 'best plays of the year', he notes, though vital and interesting, fail to achieve 'any permanent place in dramatic literature'. But he might well have changed his mind a little later on with the appearance of such major work as Wilder's *The Skin of Our Teeth* (1942), three more late plays from O'Neill – *The Iceman Cometh* (1946), *A Moon for the Misbegotten* (1947) and the posthumous *Long Day's Journey into Night* (1955), Williams's *A Streetcar Named Desire* (1947) and *Camino Real* (1953), Miller's *Death of a Salesman* (1949) and *The Crucible* (1953), Albee's *Who's Afraid of Virginia Woolf?* (1962), and perhaps even Mamet's *Glengarry Glen Ross* (1983) or *Oleanna* (1994). Nevertheless, over fifty years after Krutch's remark, despite its many achievements, the American drama (and her actors with it) still awaits 'what it wishes to do spiritually with its technical skill'.[6]

The nearest attempt in the early 1990s to help fill the void and fulfill the dream is probably Tony Kushner's breathtaking, politically-charged, seven-hour 'Gay Fantasia on National Themes' *Angels in America*. 'Was this to be "the elixir that might re-vitalize the nation's theatrical corpus" – strangled in scope and aspiration by commercial factors?' asked the *Plays and Players Yearbook for 1993*. Whether it proves to be or not, somewhere out there in the community, in the real world of real pain and joy, the new American dramatic genius is at work (or has been, or will be at work); and it is surely certain that, sooner or later, borne into the spotlight, their work will astound the world, and American actors will have found those roles in which to claim their special place in theatrical history.

14

The Nineties in Britain:
Actors at the Mercy of Market Forces,
but the National Theatre Dream Comes
True

Working conditions for actors in the Western world of the 1990s do little to favour the ideals promulgated by the gurus whose work was considered in Chapter 12. The delicate art of the theatre, and those who serve it, is as much in danger at the end of this century as some pioneering forebears recognized in 1900. The role of the theatre in life as opposed to the entertainment business; and the role of the actor as opposed to the media or showbiz personality – the slightingly dismissed 'luvvies' – has yet to be made generally clear. As always, the commercial concern of making a living governs the life of the professional theatre worker; and whatever lip-service may be paid to cultural standards and the non-partisan supremacy of art by Ministers and Councils, success with a paying public is still the name of the game. This certainly applied to Shakespeare in his day, and it applies to the running of a National Theatre in our own times.

The chequered history leading up to the realization of the National Theatre on the South Bank in 1976 has been well documented. The theatre itself has published several pictorial records of its work; and with the original 'Scheme and Estimates' of William Archer and Harley Granville-Barker in 1904–7, plus two more books from the latter, two from Geoffrey Whitworth, and further accounts from Judith Cook in 1976, John Elsom and Nicholas Tomalin in 1978, Olivier's *Confessions* and Hall's *Diaries* in the early 1980s, and from Peter Lewis in 1990,[1] the long gestation and final birth of a dream held since 1848 need only be summarized. Its achievement is all the more remarkable in a country whose government, for the most part, has not given much attention to theatrical matters. Lyttelton, Cottesloe and Olivier are rightly commemorated in the National's three auditoria; but it would be equally just, were there a fourth to be named, to call it the Hall, in recognition of the fine legacy handed on to the present Director.

The first definite suggestion for a National Theatre was made in 1848 by a London publisher called Effingham Wilson. The idea was subsequently greeted with enthusiasm by such leading figures as Dickens and Irving, also Charles Kemble and Matthew Arnold. It was the latter's famous plea in 1880 which Archer and Granville-Barker quoted at the front of their detailed plans published in 1907 (after private circulation in 1904). The plea concludes: 'The people *will* have the theatre; then make it a good one ... The theatre is irresistible; organize the theatre!' Also at the front of the book was a list of those giving their support, headed by Sir Henry Irving, together with Squire Bancroft, J. M. Barrie, Helen D'Oyly Carte, John Hare, H. A. Jones and A. W. Pinero. Bernard Shaw, later so notably in support, is conspicuous by his absence on this occasion. Certainly he had expressed some pertinent criticisms at the time to Granville-Barker, undoubtedly prompted by the omission of his own plays from a specimen repertory: 'no one with the youth and energy to get such a theatre started would do a hand's turn for the sake of such a musty list of plays as you put down'.[2] Back in 1906, nevertheless, even Winston Churchill had got excited about the idea in a speech to Parliament; although by the time he came to have more power, and two wars later, it seems to have slipped his busy mind.

Most of the work on the Estimates, according to Granville-Barker, was done by Archer. He said the project would cost £330,000, which by 1976, when it was opened though still unfinished, would have represented some £3.5 million. The actual final figure was over £10 million. The site, like the cost, had also constantly changed. When building finally started in 1969, it was on the fifth choice of venue. Completion then was forecast for 1973, but it took a further three years before a desperate Peter Hall opened the first completed auditorium to the public, the

Lyttelton, whilst the builders were still working on the Olivier and the Cottesloe. It had been in June 1970 that Olivier had accepted a life peerage, the first ever offered to an actor. In his maiden speech to the House of Lords he memorably put it on record that 'a great theatre is the outward and visible sign of an inward and spiritual culture'.[3] But like the building itself, that ideal had a distance to travel yet.

Much of the National Theatre saga is to do with finance, with the choosing of the site, attitudes to architecture, the clash of personalities, the practical difficulties of running such a complex organization, the breakdowns of ambitious stage machinery, the strikes, the unpredictable dangers of critical reception, not to mention the serious offence that was taken at some of the repertoire. But the latter was mostly in earlier days, and often due to the anarchic influence of the theatre's then dramaturg, Kenneth Tynan. As a single later example, the adventurous scope of programming in January 1994 is worth noting. Unusually, perhaps, all the work is from this century (it would seem that the earlier classics were being left for the RSC to do). In the Olivier, *The Wind in the Willows*, adapted by Alan Bennett, and revived as a tried Christmas treat with its inventive production and set; also David Hare's uncompromising analysis of Labour politics, *The Absence of War*. In the Lyttelton, Sondheim's coruscating musical of *Sweeney Todd*; Tom Stoppard's elegant dance of intellect and wit, *Arcadia*; Bennett again with final performances of his much-acclaimed *The Madness of George III*; and perhaps one of the most staggering productions (by Stephen Daldry) ever seen in this auditorium, Sophie Treadwell's expressionistic *Machinal*. In the Cottesloe, an energetic production of *Mother Courage*, designed to tour; a new 'play with dance' by Caryl Churchill, *The Skriker*; and one of the most audacious projects to be attempted in this smallest of the three 'houses' – Tony Kushner's epic *Angels in America*. All these productions are in repertoire in the one building in the same month. Archer and Granville-Barker are surely smiling in their theatrical Elysium.

But what of the actors – the raw material at this interface of audience and artefact? Though the National may shine – and it *does* shine – as the titular head of the profession, what conditions pertain in the 1990s for the profession at large in Britain?

Market-force ideology affects actors in three main areas: their personal finances, the availability of work, and the nature and conditions of that work. Its influence on the training field was outlined in the Introduction. Once on the market, the young actor's first priority is to get work; his second is to survive whilst looking for it. In recent years the Inland Revenue authority sought to remove the actor's traditional Schedule D status under which he could claim the basic professional expenses incurred during work, and even more pertinently whilst looking for work: the photographs and c.v.'s, the stationery and postage, the telephone, the travel to auditions and agents, and so on. The legitimate list supplied by Equity is much longer. The Inland Revenue sought to deny the 'self-employed' category to actors and wanted them to be subject to PAYE like other workers who are directly employed by companies, managements, and independent producers, despite most engagements being only for a limited period. Only agent's commission would be allowed to be tax deductible. However, a test case challenging this decision was brought by two Equity appellants, a new young actor and an established star, and the case was won in July 1993, thus preserving the right to Schedule D status. The Revenue authority reserved the right to appeal, but finally conceded the case in August 1995. However, it was the attitude taken in the first instance which remains a significant one.

Actors have always recognized the need to cope with lengthy periods of unemployment – the euphemistic 'resting' – but here, too, their traditional financial rights concerning welfare benefits have been challenged, this time by the Department of Social Security and new Government legislation. From October 1996, so-called Unemployment Benefit will cease to exist and Income Support will no longer be available for the unemployed. In their place will be the Jobseekers Allowance, which is dependent as before on sufficient National Insurance contributions for at least two previous tax years, or on a means-tested basis.

In keeping with this new use of words, clearly a political expedient, the date on which you claim benefit is now to be called the first day in the period of interruption of employment (PIE). The claim is considered as continuous for any period where less than twelve weeks' continuous employment has occurred, which is obviously of great importance to actors who may frequently expect employment for much less than that time. Under the tough new rules, when a claimant signs on they have to complete and sign both a Jobsearch Plan and a Jobseekers Agreement. The upshot of this for actors is that they now have to keep (and show on demand) detailed records of all jobseeking activities, and after a mere thirteen-week period in which to get a job in their chosen profession, they are now required to be available for any work which they can reasonably be expected to do (such as teaching, modelling, or promotional demonstrations), or else to attend a training course to improve their employability. Refusal, or leaving the work, or dismissal for misconduct, incurs disqualification from the Jobseekers Allowance for up to twenty-six weeks. Jobplan Workshops are mandatory after signing on for one year, and Restart Courses after two years. There is a Social Security Appeal Tribunal to hear all appeals against virtually all decisions, where in some cases Equity will represent its members. Work during the twelve-week period has to be declared, of course, with appropriate deductions being made from the Allowance. Entitlement to the Contributory Jobseekers Allowance is limited to six months, after which there are requalifying rules and conditions concerning interim short jobs and insurance contributions. The legislation is particularly harsh for younger and less established actors seeking a foothold in the profession, and Equity is continuing its attempts to rectify injustices.

Perhaps the most damaging Government 'reform' of all for the future of the British acting profession, which is possibly a bitter response by civil servants to losing the schedule D tax case, is the proposal by the Department of Social Security that freelance performing artists be no longer allowed to pay Class 1 National Insurance contributions, thereby forcing them into non-eligibility or the acceptance of much lower and unrealistic basic 'safety-net' benefits.

Meanwhile, leaving the Benefit Office behind, what does the actor find the state of the market to be in looking for work? Availability of employment, always at a premium, has itself been under increasing pressure from underfunding, the closure of many theatres or studios, the virtual demise of Theatre-in-Education and of the film industry, the greed of bricks-and-mortar landlords owning surviving theatres, and the much more difficult-to-access market of independent producers for television ('Producer Choice') in which actors and their agents must sell their wares. Provincial Repertory theatres continue in much-reduced numbers (though some with grander 'City-profiles' than hitherto) providing the essential development ground for young actors and a solid employment base on minimal salaries for others. Even tighter minimums apply to Fringe theatres, often on a company-sharing basis where, without any box-office profits after expenses of the production have been paid, the actor will get nothing (or as at the old Theatre Workshop company, a few pounds to survive on). Some films, too, are made these days with no payment to artists or technicians at the time, reward being conditional on later successful release in cinemas or sale, for example, to Channel Four Television. 'Nothing will come of nothing . . .'

Television, of course, has become by far the most important market for the actor; and especially for those who need the higher rewards to keep a family and home-base going, wherever it may be. But television has its drawbacks too, which take us into the third area affected by market forces. Being an industry, television inclines to take the necessary industrial attitude of regarding actors as just another 'source input' serving the technological 'product'. It can ruin a good actor's artistic career by typecasting in a 'soap' as easily as it can make his reputation in the public view. It is always requiring more 'actor-fodder' for frequently screened series like *The Bill* – often excellent actors and good stories well produced – but the emphasis is strictly on a behaviourist style which rarely stretches any other acting talent. Commercials – always a lucrative source of income – exploit the actor even more dangerously, except perhaps in the area of voice-overs. There are, of course, exceptions to every rule, but the conditions under which actors now most often have to work is that of a 'hired source' providing a pre-judged 'image' and performance level, conducive to helping the complicated manufacture of a technical artefact become successful in the ratings chart.

There are also other instances of market pressure which press upon the actor, or would-be actor. There are now courses to get you *in* to courses at theatre school. There are brief 'workshops' for which the actor pays to be seen in a 'showcase' at the end, which itself charges casting directors and the like for entry. There are now no less than four full pages of advertisements in *The Stage* for various types of actor training, not only for newcomers, but classes of every kind for the 'resting' professional to keep in trim – all of course at a price. Yet what price all this preparation to be a good actor when on the previous page it can be suggested by an 'old pro' that BBC-TV accountants do not regard rehearsing as 'cost-effective' and would prefer something closer to 'instant' performing;[4] nor is it only accountants who quite often expect something of the sort during an over-rushed schedule. Concerning theatre schools, a few years ago the Bursar was mentioned in prospectuses at the bottom of the list of staff: now they are bracketed with the Principal at the top of the list because their earnings are comparably similar. It is much the same on theatre programmes where until recently, together with the Artistic Director, only the Manager, Box Office Manager and secretarial help were given credits. Now the list of company employees extends to the Administrative Executive, company accountant and assistant, marketing manager, PR assistants, fund-raising executive, educational co-ordinators, media consultant, and heaven knows who else on the pay roll who are not actually engaged in putting anything on the stage. The packaging is all, and quality of content takes second place.

Finally, a word about the effects of public subsidy, and especially sponsorship by commercial organizations. These may only be peripheral to the actor's work, yet their influence, for good or bad, is fundamental to the end-product. Not only the National and the RSC, but most provincial theatres now have to rely on a degree of both subsidy and sponsorship to support their programmes, and in most cases it is absolutely crucial to survival. Four of the plays in the National's repertoire mentioned above acknowledge sponsorship (by four separate industrial organizations). The RSC, in particular, looked like being in dire trouble after 1993 when their principal long-standing sponsor, Royal Insurance, withdrew from further support; but after 'seven nail-biting months' the artistic director, Adrian Noble, was fortunate in attracting another generous sponsor who offered £3.3 million over a three-year period which staved off the threatened cut-backs just a week after the previous money had run out. Such tensions cannot exactly help concentration on the director's main business of planning and putting on plays.

What do the sponsors get for so much money? In the RSC case it is a food and drink giant, Allied-Lyons; and their executives consider they have a bargain. For a business with profits of £505 million in 1993, '£1.1 million a year is a small price to pay for cultural credibility and one of the world's most up-market calling cards'. The 'Royal' in the title goes down well with overseas business contacts; 'Shakespeare' is both 'priceless' and 'not too élitist'; and Stratford-upon-Avon and the Barbican are ideal for corporate entertaining, not to mention workforce outings.[5] But the marriage of commerce and art is not always plain sailing; there are tensions on both sides, greater than in other sponsor partnerships such as those in sport. Almost five times as much money is pumped by business into sport as into the arts, but the figure for the latter is still an overall £58 million. However, for the RSC, despite logo-sharing, joint branding of products ('RSCXXXX lager'), discounted tickets and special backstage tours, there is no interference with artistic policy, however dangerously unpopular some productions might prove to be. The 'marriage' has a shotgun necessity whereby value-for-money binds each.

Government subsidy, as we saw concerning the TNP in France, is a rather different ball-game. For all the Government's claims that the Arts Council is at 'arm's length' from any interference, 'in reality the Heritage Department now tends to lean heavily on it from above. Although this is not necessarily for party purposes, relations between the two bodies can easily become tainted with political dogma or bureaucratic bias.' Thus speaks no less an authority than Sir Edward Heath, offering advice to the Council's newly-appointed Chairman, Lord Gowrie.[6] Sir Edward goes on to say that 'with the creation of the National Lottery, the arts in Britain are being offered a tremendous – indeed revolutionary – funding opportunity. The Arts Council must be ready for this exciting new development and able to use the substantial new funds wisely... For the Government's part, it must address the issue of direct funding for the arts and redress the decrease that was announced in the last Budget.' Sir Edward was referring to the £3.2 million cut-back in grants for 1994–5.

Philip Hedley, artistic director of the Theatre Royal, Stratford

East, has been frequently the lone David challenging the Goliath of English Heritage and the Arts Council (not to mention most other Government departments) in the letter pages of the national press. He is particularly alert to the mistaken ideology which applies market forces to the arts. In January 1994, he was noting that 'sixteen West End productions are directly from subsidised sources ... It is vital that the Department of National Heritage gets the message through to the Treasury that it will lose the high profits it makes from the theatre if it starves the subsidised sector.' He then points out to the Department of Education that 'there's no future for any form of theatre unless drama is restored to the national curriculum'; and to the Department of the Environment that 'cuts to local authorities are leading to irreparable damage to local theatres'. The two-pronged pincer movement of market forces is on buildings and on companies, each aggravating the other; death by attrition or death by starvation leading to 'no commercial demand' for either buildings or companies. The profession is being strangled with the argument that it must suffer cut-backs like everyone else; which is rather like asking the starving of the world to diet like the over-fed rest of us. Hedley concludes that 'You cannot have the West End or National Theatre without the nation's theatre.'[7] It is a lesson which the British Government in the 1990s has yet to learn. They appear to think that, for the most part, other perhaps than a few 'centres of excellence', the arts can be left to sponsorship and a National Lottery. Both, for all the virtues mentioned, are something of a gamble; and as Roger Planchon suggested, if we would not dream of gambling so drastically with our defence budget, why would we think it so right to gamble with the very heritage it is meant to defend?

These are value-judgements by which quality of living is defined. It is the business of the serious artist – and philosopher – to help define it, to tell us 'the way things really are', or at the very least, 'the way that they appear to be'. Poets, not governments, are in Shelley's famous phrase, 'the unacknowledged legislators of the world'. Perhaps he, in turn, had it from Dr Johnson who, in 1759, had said that the poet 'must write as the interpreter of nature, and the legislator of mankind, and consider himself as presiding over the thoughts and manners of future generations; as being superior to time and place'.[8] Whether the poet writes in verse or not, this is his noble vocation in the theatre, as the history of drama has demonstrated beyond doubt from Aeschylus through Shakespeare and Molière to Ibsen and Chekhov. It is the actor's highest calling to serve such poets.

PART THREE: The Future

(Lovborg shows Tesman the manuscript which is the continuation of his new book just published)

TESMAN: Why, my dear Eilert – doesn't your new book come down to our own day?

LOVBORG: Yes, it does; and this deals with the future.

TESMAN: With the future! But, good heavens, we know nothing of the future!

LOVBORG: No; but there is a thing or two to be said about it all the same . . .

Ibsen, Hedda Gabler (1890)

15

New Forms, New Language, Old Needs

In some five hundred years, actors have progressed from being rogues and vagabonds, the outcasts of society, to reaching the threshold of becoming not just the mirror of that society but also a hope for its advancement. Twenty years ago, Peter Hall was saying that 'A good theatre company is a metaphor of a possible society.' That is to say, if it works, it works as a creative enterprise. Around the same time John Elsom was already noting how our social structures were breaking down, especially regarding leisure time, and that 'not far ahead, the theatre will become the place where leisure is used creatively . . . The theatre will not reflect social change, but initiate it.'[1] In January 1994, drama critic John Peter was moved by a House of Lords debate on arts funding to see theatre as more than a metaphor by declaring boldly that 'The arts are the national health service of the spirit . . . it is wrong simply to turn them into marketable commodities . . . a nation's treatment of its theatre is an index of its civilization.' The sentiments echo those of both Hall again, and of Planchon in France. John Peter's article is well worth quoting more fully. He goes on:

A community can recognize itself in its theatre and see both its faults and its virtues. The theatre has a huge range. It is entertainment; it is a provider of consolation and relief; but it is also a source of moral stimulus, of questioning and debate, without which a society will soon decline into mere consumers,

211

obedient yea-sayers and mulish nay-sayers. The theatre is not a frivolous or effete luxury. At its best it can send you home in a state of emotional and moral turmoil which is the root of true maturity, both individual and communal.[2]

Such words convey the true significance of theatre as it has been seen by all the leading creative practitioners of this century. Moreover, as we have already noted, they are a signpost to the future, in which the ongoing history of the actor's place in the community is accelerating towards a full cycle.

The great new art form of the twentieth century, at once both popular and élite in its output, is the film. The dichotomy between illusion and reality, between the 'as if' and the actual, is even more pronounced in the cinema where it is mostly accepted that 'the camera cannot lie'. It does, of course. The 'magic lantern' deals in optical illusion by being selective. Even so-called 'documentary-style' filming and *cinéma-vérité* are still only recording an actuality which on the material screen itself becomes merely another *image*, and on equal ground with the constructed artefact, the fictional film, making its own artistic statement about reality. It is, in fact, a truism that fiction, because of its condensation, can be *more real* than actuality. Commenting on the new video-culture and what he dubs the 'video generation', film director Bernard Tavinier has rightly observed that it is becoming more important to *look* at something than to do something. The video recording of a wedding becomes more important than the wedding itself; taking pictures of your child playing may take precedence over playing with the child yourself; partaking in a ritual is subordinated to observing it. This is one reason why the communal experience of live theatre remains so uniquely important. Fiddling with reality and illusion, fudging the borderlines of actuality, confuses the judgement and ends by devaluating life itself. Reconstructing actual crimes to provide voyeuristic entertainment on television – programmes like *Crimewatch* or *Crimefile* – are cases in point. They are dangers to the health of the community despite their ostensible justification as a means of helping the police in their work. But there will be much more to be said about this particular illusion-reality syndrome when we come to consider the new technology of 'Virtual Reality'.

On stage as well as screen, the image may often speak louder and more powerfully than words. Over the last twenty-five years or so, stage design has advanced both technically and artistically to very high standards. No longer need designers complain, as Ralph Koltai did in 1985, of being treated like the tea-boy. Indeed, there have been occasions when, once the curtain rises and often before any curtain at all, the set 'says it all' about the play to follow. A design expressing vertigo may anticipate the Master Builder's fall from the start, but it can be rough on the actors trying to negotiate it for two and a half hours beforehand. A design sympathetic towards the production concept and practical for the action is, however, much to be desired. It can be an important and vital component in the success of a play; for example, with Ian MacNeill's awesome set for *Machinal* in the National's Lyttelton. Very often in musicals the set is better than the score, although as the composer said, 'No one goes home whistling the set.' Nevertheless, the designer today is rightly as prominent as he ever was in the days of Inigo Jones or Drury Lane spectaculars. His poster credit (and that of the Lighting Designer and Sound Designer, too) speaks as large as that of the Director. For an audience, though, there remains an essential difference between going to a theatre and going to an art gallery, or even to the wonders of a *son et lumière*.

The art galleries themselves however, and more especially those with an avant-garde policy, are inclined to regard themselves as pioneers of new theatre forms. Lois Keidan, director of live arts at the ICA, comments that 'The work done at places like the ICA has had a major effect on the way traditional theatre has developed – particularly in areas such as set design and movement.'[3] She is referring to the work of people like Robert Lepage and Neil Bartlett among several others; and to the rise of Performance Art, installations, and Live Art as forces to be reckoned with. Live Art in particular has been recognized as a genre by the Arts Council and a number of academic institutions. It has been defined as bringing creative intelligence to bear on 'a mixture of history, literary theory, film theory, philosophy, physics, medicine even, and poetry. It's a bit like the art school tradition where everything is significant, and where the object itself is of value.'[4] This post-modernist view whereby 'anything goes' and one can 'go anywhere' for cultural experience – what might be dubbed the Damien Hirst sheep syndrome – finds its current theatrical expression most notably in the Austrian dramatist Peter Handke. He has been questioning the fundamental elements of theatre since the late 1960s with plays like *Offending the Audience*, *Kaspar*, and *The Ride Across Lake Constance*. Reporting on his latest work on Berlin's Schaubühne stage in February 1994 (later seen at Edinburgh), Denis Staunton notes that 'Much of his work has been aimed at stripping away illusion, both in the theatre and in society and, especially in his early plays, he has been concerned with the socially manipulative effect of language.'[5] *Die Stunde da wir nichts voneinander wussten* (The hour in which we knew nothing of each other) is also 'about the powerlessness of speech and the helplessness of humanity'. Yet its 300 silent characters traversing the stage for an hour and forty minutes clearly have theatrical eloquence. It 'owes much to the culture of the circus ... and the magician ... and is a warm, funny and passionate play brought magnificently to life through Luc Bondy's production and Gilles Aillaud's astonishingly beautiful design, and closely observed and performed with great verve' by the thirty-five actors. The play was conceived 'while sitting at a café table in Italy one summer's day, and it retains the quality of an observation of the world passing by' but it is also 'a humane vision of a world at odds with itself and desperately in search of orientation'.[6]

Handke's post-Beckettian minimalism and juxtapositioning of different theatrical modes has been around for over a quarter of a century now, as has the notorious Wooster Group from New York which stemmed from Richard Schechner's radical Performance Group founded in 1967. In 1976, several members of the original company, led by Elizabeth Lecompte, took over ownership of the Wooster Street Performing Garage when Schechner left. This continued as a base from which to further develop the hypereclectic style which has been the hallmark of both groups. In June 1993 the Woosters were presenting their latest work in Brussels, *Fish Story Part II*, which 'blends Chekhov, Kabuki, rock concert posturing and Tom and Jerry slapstick into a remarkable theatrical Esperanto for the late 20th century'.[7] An earlier cocktail, deconstructing Chekhov's *Three Sisters* and re-titled *Brace Up!*, was seen at Glasgow's Tramway in October 1992. Kenneth

Rea, interviewing Lecompte for *The Times*, and trying to keep an open mind between being repelled or excited, wondered whether the Group might not 'be laying out the ground for the theatre of the future'. No attempt is made to 'act' anything; the actors do not look at each other because lack of eye-contact is often habitual to modern conversation; moreover, they talk deadpan like television reporters, at a distance from the most emotionally-charged information; and the whole mishmash of read stage-directions, microphones, interruptions and apparent ad-libs by a narrator, and off-stage videoing of roles seen in close-up onstage, is edited, cut and spliced as if the whole 'live' operation was actually a film in the making. All this iconoclasm 'goes well beyond Brecht' and 'overturns all received ideas of what constitutes good acting'.[8] It is not surprising to learn that Lecompte's background is from the visual arts, and that she avoids the term 'theatre' altogether 'except when applying to the National Endowment for the Arts'.

Richard Schechner himself, now the doyen of the American avant-garde, formed a new company, East Coast Artists, which toured the UK in early 1994 under the auspices of the Centre for Performance Research, Cardiff, with his own adapted text, *Faustgastronome*. It describes itself as being 'full of humour, inventive cross-gender casting, and "no-holds-barred" acting' – whatever that may mean. Why Faust*gastronome*? Well, the alchemy of food preparation and consumption is used as a metaphor for our appetite-driven world. In the event, this 'thick gumbo soup of perverse pleasures' (as *The Village Voice* called it) containing elements of the old Faustbooks, Marlowe, pantomime kitchen knockabout, Goethe's romantic text, Hitler and Albert Speer's rhetoric (much of it in German), lust and simulated sexual variations (mostly in the nude, of course), and political satire on market economics, seemed more like a rather self-conscious student jape than any cutting-edge for new theatre. This was a pity, because Schechner's ideal of an ensemble company dedicated to lengthy training, research and rehearsal is admirable; but it is better expressed in the long programme note than on the stage. It is often observable that the more avant-garde the piece, the longer the explanatory preamble by the director. Here, Schechner, in pointing to his 'cautionary tale' on 'our abilities to turn anything into entertainment', is both having his cake and eating it. The performance relies precisely on being salacious and unpleasant in order to warn us about falling into just such a trap. Or as Schechner justifies this: 'Perhaps I can use some of my own Faustian drives to counter the destructive aspects of Faustian striving', and further, 'I cannot condemn what I am attracted to; but I do wish to be conscious of what I am doing and to act from an ethical basis.' Now we know; although that basis has to be entirely inferred, and it is to be hoped that the audiences all had time to digest this essential rider in the programme before watching the performance. Such attention, however, is rarely the case.

The attempt to lead an audience towards accepting a different language in the theatre is very much part of the British avant-garde in the 1990s. But it has tended to create an unnecessary dichotomy between those who still favour the value of a good text and those who see the components of 'physical theatre' and design as being more important. Ideally of course, as we have seen several times in this century, the concept of 'total theatre' attempts to balance all the separate components of the theatrical experience in a unified artistic integrity. However, the arguments between text and non-verbal theatre, between the articulate mind and the articulate body, are worth looking at. The artist and anthropologist Susan Hiller scrutinizes words as mere objects: 'By making us acutely aware of their physical character, she seems to suggest that, in life, we always feel first, and words come later . . . though we often act as if it were the other way round.' Hiller insists that 'we know through the body'.[9] Julia Bardsley at the New Vic and Neil Bartlett's experimental work with the Gloria company would probably go along with that, and although both would say they value the textual component, they would both deny that it is in new play-*writing* that they see the future.[10] The point is underlined by Paul Blackman of the Battersea Arts Centre when it was hosting the Fourth British Festival of Visual Theatre in September 1993: 'Textual political theatre has been winded by the last 13 years. People are word-weary. They have started to forge a new kind of physical and visual theatre where they can make their own rules and are not tied down by a train of development in British theatre which runs from John Osborne to David Hare.'[11] He, too, notes that theatre is edging towards the art gallery.

In September 1995, the *Observer* sent its Art Critic and *The Sunday Times* its second-string Theatre Critic to review the latest work of the much-lauded avant-garde theatre director, Robert Wilson. Wilson, formerly an architect, had created an 'installation' with the collaboration of Hans Peter Kuhn, a sound and lighting expert, and of Michael Howells, a film art director: they called it *HG*, and build it in the 'found space' of the Clink Street Vaults in Southwark (part of the notorious medieval prison in the ironically-named Liberty of which the original Globe Theatre was built, and now within a stone's throw of its freshly-thatched phoenix). Neither critic felt particularly happy in their duty because *HG* confounded any formal categorization. Was it sculptural art or environmental sculpture? Was it static theatre or a museum mock-up? There were no actors, but Robert Hewison justified it as a legitimate subject for a theatre critic because, he inferred, the experience of being there was theatrical. It worked on the spectator's imagination. Whatever narrative it held – which seems to have been a very vague thread – derived from the props and settings to be found in such works as *The Time Machine* (1895) and *The Invisible Man* (1897) by H. G. Wells. William Feaver, the art critic, got rather bored, let in like the rest of the 'audience' after one-minute intervals through a street door having the initials 'H.G.' on a brass plate. The 'wonderland' he walked through eventually 'ran out of time and space and things to do'. 'The labyrinth has its moments; it keeps you guessing; but the theatricality becomes a liability.' His reference to a 'labyrinth' recalls Enrique Vargas's much more personally-orientated theatrical installation, *Ariadne's Thread*, in which many actors (mostly unseen) were employed. That performance is reported in Note 11 to Chapter 17.

The devaluation of language in our culture cannot be denied, yet in talking of its limitations – now the vogueish thing to do – few critics are inclined to comment on 'the relatively narrow vocabulary of movement'. One who does, in defence of textual theatre, is Michael Billington. He is against 'the new anti-intellectual modishness that makes exalted claims for physical theatre and assumes that text-derived work is both circumscribed and long past its sell-by date. It is a way of draining the performing arts both of social and political relevance and of denying language's unique ability to explore the nuances of thought, feeling, status and familial relationships.'[12]

As always, each of us will pay our money and make our choice, but meanwhile be always looking for that ideal amalgamation of the best in every form that goes under the label of 'total theatre'.

Not much has been said so far about the place of comedy – of laughter – in this exercise of looking forward to the possible nature of theatre and acting in the future. Back in the 1980s, playwright Alan Plater declared his belief that the theatre would become less an institution for putting on plays and more of an environment where the public could find vitality and fun; it would be less the description of a building and more of a place where communal activities took place involving role-games and the suspension of disbelief. Perhaps he had something like Joan Littlewood's ill-fated 'Fun Palace' in mind, but it was more than just a revival of Music Hall. The traditional jesters of the people would remain, of course, also the bards and their singers, and the storytellers before bedtime; but not just on TV. The sophistication of a highly complex, technically orientated society requires the balancing factor of live interaction, and simple delight in the non-technical, non-fabricated elements of our life. It might be called the 'village shop factor' in community togetherness, whereby we can constantly check our bearings, not only physically and mentally but even spiritually. It tells us where we 'fit in'. It was formerly the job of philosophers and artists to do this, reinforcing the social cement; but in this century we have seen what Scott Fitzgerald called 'The Crack-Up' with the casting adrift of value-systems and the ascendency of materialist economics, selfishness and cynicism. It is time for the artists and philosophers to return on the scene as the 'unacknowledged legislators' of our lives; but with the jesters as well, to see that they, and we, do not get too far above ourselves in cleverness and tragic hubris.

Acting is sometimes dismissed as 'not a real job' ('What do you do in the daytime?'), but by the next century 'real jobs' may be even more difficult to find than at present. The majority may well be asking themselves, not why acting appears such a shallow job, but why life itself is so shallow that we should be mostly acting it rather than living it. People, like actors, will be spectators of themselves and the human scene, and albeit vicariously, perhaps through the electronic magic of Virtual Reality – of which more later – they may attempt to experience ideal ways of living rather than simply watch ideal forms of art. Actors themselves may be more concerned with expressing their common dilemma with the audience-participators than with imitating unreal or fictional characters in a similar situation. They will be at one with their audience; and to some extent representing them as deputies, not as better persons, but as more expert communicators. In his days as Principal at the RADA, John Fernald defined acting as communication. All the techniques of simulation and diversionary entertainment will continue in use, but what is likely to change is the *attitude* to these techniques by both the profession and the public.

Talking of his film *O Lucky Man* in 1973, Lindsay Anderson commented that

> Normally we stumble through life so bemused and so assaulted by the barrage of news, the barrage of hideous events, that veils drop mercifully between us and reality. One of the functions, and I suppose, privileges of the artist is to strip the veils away ... If he can do it with healthy laughter, so much the better ... *Dad's Army*, at its best, is really much better than most of what is being given to us by the serious and the experimental theatre.[13]

He was right, of course. Twenty or so years on, we are even more the unwilling victims of an overstimulating environment, bombarding the senses with 'information overload' and 'decision stress'. The acceleration of changes in society tends to make psychotics of us all. The demarcation lines between illusion and reality are constantly being blurred by the media. This is why the scriptwriter and actor as communicators of these pressures, sublimated by understanding, whether through fiction or not, are in a privileged position. The responsibility is a serious one, even in the most popular comedy or TV 'soap'. This is because, however inadequately and even mistakenly, they reinforce the *status quo* attitudes of the audience, confirming their common experience of life, providing the comfort which may well be missing, even among friends and family. The comedians and 'all-licensed fools' we love above all, because they act as touchstones of an agreed sanity in an insane world, and allow us to give vent to our pent-up feelings in the joyous release of laughter.

In Ronald Blythe's brilliant sociological study, *Akenfield*, a farmer, Jamie McIver, comments that 'All England is changing, of course, too fast . . . We need to be told where we are.'[14] To be told where we are is the beginning and end of theatre. Informed theatre-going opinion today underlines the farmer's point: 'Drama explains us to ourselves, offers us information about others, decodes the mysterious workings of society. Above all, it brings shape and structure to the flux of daily experience.'[15] This function grew from religious roots and will find its apotheosis in a metaphysical flowering of non-sectarian blooms. From Babylon to Beckett, from Eleusis to Eliot, from Stonehenge to Stoppard, it is the mystery at the heart of things which is celebrated, though it be a mystery that cannot be touched and can never be recorded once and for all. It most often finds its expression in the experience of 'poetry' – what the old Chinese sage called 'flowers at the heart'. 'Poetry' here is put in inverted commas because it is not meant to imply verse-form, nor indeed any words at all. The word is used here as from its derivation in the Greek 'poesis' – a thing made. There is a 'poetry' of each and all the senses which may be offered theatrically, and of which literate expression, as we have just seen, may sometimes be the least part. Throughout the ancient world, hieratic mask-dramas attempted to convey the human situation. Some of them survive today, either in primitive tribes or in traditional folk and carnival rituals. The early history of man, it seems fairly certain, is recorded poetically in the oral recital of ancient myths; the myths themselves evolving from ritual 'performances' which attempted to control life and destiny. Although it may not look like it afterwards, ritual precedes myth as practice so often precedes theory. Primeval man's daily life was the illusion; whilst the cosmic conflict he saw around him, and which he expressed in ritual dramas, was the true reality. But from the time that the art of drama evolved into written texts and playacting, separating itself from religion, the vital relationship between life and theatre became inverted; consciousness was actual, imagination was not; perceived existence was honest, acted existence was hypocritical. It is now for modern man to re-learn where the illusion and the reality lie; to learn which things are hypocritical in his or her life and which things are honest. It is part of the function of theatre to give help in this personal and group exercise.

There is an atavistic sense of these rituals of the past remaining with us which renders the stage of a theatre a sacred place. We trespass on it as uncomfortably as the tourist 'trespasses' on church altars today. The first-night party held on stage can feel a sacrilegious affair, debasing it to a fun-factory floor. Where in ancient times the actor-priest interpreted gods and heroes in his sacred grove, the modern actor-person interprets men and women to themselves on what must be, however temporarily, hallowed space.

Drama is traditionally a fight – a contest, an *agon* – between good and evil in the shape of gods or men (from Horus and Set to cops and robbers); or else of separate individuals pursued by some sort of fate (from Everyman to the Master Builder, from Hamlet to Harry in *The Family Reunion*, from King Lear to 'K' in *The Trial*, from Queen Hermione to Hedda Gabler). In the West, drama has progressively moved to more materialist attitudes, whereas in the East it has tended to try and retain at least its traditional religious forms. The position is now in the process of being reversed, with the East coming under the domination of materialist attitudes and Western cultural forms whilst the West is more and more recognizing its need to adopt a 'new religious' viewpoint and the use of Eastern cultural forms. Allardyce Nicoll always said this had to happen; and now from Copeau to Brook, and Artaud to the American formalists, Richard Foreman and Robert Wilson, there have been increasing signs of a Zen-like minimalism reacting against the extreme naturalism of mainline film and TV. Western theatre is being almost forced to rediscover its ancient hieratic roots. The old conventions of the past 400 years are no longer sufficient for what is now required of them.

So what kind of theatrical expression and acting is most likely to occur next in the ongoing attempt to recognize the Mystery that is human life? For one thing, its language (the dialogos) will be multiple in form and function, applying as best it can to every person's level of understanding according to their experience. That is to say, it will speak the same truth as life itself speaks, albeit in diverse ways; yet always aiming to be a single work of art. It will offer in the one work wide opportunities of interpretation in the philosophical, scientific, religious and poetic modes; in addition to language, it will employ some or all of the communicative paths open to movement, posture, gesture and dance, to music and voice, to colour, line and shape, and perhaps also to scent and touch. The theatrical experience of the future will be total as life is total. But there will be no confusion between them. Theatre will remain a simulated environment, an illuson, in which experience is real whilst being vicarious. Whatever the siting, shape and organization of the theatre space and buildings, in presenting the mysteries of our being – the joys and laughter, the pain and the miseries – they will become again 'houses of myth'; and those myths, as in their ancient performance but re-expressed for contemporary participators, will be 'new models of the universe'. They will contribute to the fulness of life by expressing its 'form and pressure'. In them we shall be able to recognize our place and our function. We shall be enabled to see the human situation for what it is, and receive the benediction of meaning for our everyday lives.

The post-Christian, post-philosophical Don Cupitt (his description) argues that 'we need to start work on a fully-democratic metaphysics of ordinary life'.[16] The theatre of tomorrow will be doing something very similar. But the metaphysical theatre will also be a place to have fun; it will be performing analogical parables as well as fiction; it will not only mirror the age (as theatre has always done) but also help set its agenda. Moreover, with its classical revivals it will 'lend to the past the actuality of the present'[17] and probe with equal passion the possibilities of the future. It will not only be showing these things, but in doing so it will be sharing and illustrating one of the first principles of the drama – a movement from what is not clear to what is clear (Aristotle's *anagnorisis*). At the same time, it will nevertheless acknowledge what is essentially mysterious, purveying that sense of the supra-rational hinted at in so much personal experience, and for which only an empathetic response can be asked. Such a theatre will reflect the mystery of our own ultimate destiny when consciousness has expanded to levels unimaginable to our own minds.

Martin Esslin, that most lucid of theatre theoreticians, has neatly summarized the future role of theatre that we have been attempting to prognosticate:

> It is a matter of developing ritual actions capable of expressing the deepest emotions about the most profound psychic contents and archetypes through which actors and audience can merge in a collective act of communication at the very deepest level. This is where the theatre originated. This is the direction in which it is tending.[18]

16

'Controlled Environments', 'Virtual Reality', and 'Found Spaces'

Before we look at how 'ritual action' and ritual theatre might occur in the future, it is worth considering some of the physical and technological conceptions already with us in their infancy, and which depart from the currently held conventional ideas of a theatre.

Environmental theatre is by no means new, but it has been developing at a pace in recent years. Country house 'Murder Weekends' and 'Elizabethan Banquets' have proved popular attractions; a 'real' Ambridge has had to be created to satisfy *aficionados* of *The Archers* radio serial; despite the commercial difficulties of EuroDisney, theme parks of all kinds are finding favour in the better weather of Spain and other countries bordering the Mediterranean. There is probably a European backlash against the over-Americanization of Disneyland – of which more later – at places like Futuroscope at Poitiers which calls itself a 'theme park of the Moving Image'. The subtitle is reminiscent of London's MOMI (Museum of the Moving Image) on the South Bank.

Museums have become quite an important employment area for actors just starting their careers, looking for 'exposure' and something to do which at least uses a little of their training and meanwhile pays the rent. It can be moderately enjoyable and is more 'ongoing' than plays which so often close on Saturday night. There are two kinds of option in museum work. You can be a 'first person interpreter' who adopts a real or imaginary character and stays in that character when explaining the exhibits and chatting to the public, which happens at the MOMI, the London

Transport Museum and the Imperial War Museum. Or you can be employed to act in set pieces which still allow for some degree of improvisation, and in at least a couple of cases, pay Equity rates: these are at Wigan Pier and the National Museum of Photography, Film and Television at Bradford. At Wigan, the actors in character have half an hour's ad libbing with the audience before the show; and at Bradford, the museum's theatre company called Action Replay comprises four actors who research and write their own short plays.[1] Theatre in Museum Education (TIME) is another group which has been active touring for over twenty years devising programmes directly with the staff of more traditional museums and their education departments. A wide range of performance skills is required, and much research is done so that props, costumes and historical content is authentic. TIME, too, involves the audience in interactive decision making; for example, pleading the release of Sir Walter Raleigh to look for Eldorado (Tower of London Museum) or arguing whether refugees from Nazi Germany should be interned for the duration of the war (Imperial War Museum).[2]

The commercial realization of Virtual Reality (VR) headsets, control panels and 'skin-suits' is not yet sufficiently advanced to employ actors in VR scenarios of the viewer's choice, but the day will surely come for something of the kind, and probably sooner than we expect. One of the best definitions of VR for the non-scientifically inclined is to say that if television can be called a 'window on the world' then with VR you can walk through that window. The description was coined by Charles Grimsdale of a firm called Division Ltd, who have made VR computers as space simulators, architectural simulators (showing rooms yet to be built with colour-schemes and lighting possibilities to order), and in order to show three-dimensional models of giant molecules to allow greater understanding of their structure. These are typical of the current military, industrial and scientific uses of VR. But the future is an open book, with at least one expert talking of getting the thoughts out of his brain directly onto a computer.[3] To date, the nearest an actor has come to being in a VR theatre was when Robert Powell tried on a rather cumbersome VR headset which took him 'inside' a three-dimensional colour graphics reconstruction of Shakespeare's Globe whilst actually

standing in the as yet unfinished reconstruction on a Southwark
site near to the original location. He could sit or stand among
the audience, or play any role he liked upon the stage with his
lines 'printed in mid-air by a sort of virtual teleprompter' (not a
recipe for a considered performance!); and although he could move
about himself with some feeling, any character 'onstage' with him
would seem 'motionless and unfeeling'. The headset's creator,
Andrew MacRea of California, explains that 'most VR environments are incredibly static';[4] and computer-humans have yet to
develop beyond the Disney-cartoon level.

A high-resolution computer-generated scene in 3D 'is made up
of millions of basic geometrical shapes (polygons), the exact shape
of each having to be adjusted as the point of view changes'.[5] For
this to happen in 'natural time' takes enormous computer power
to a degree not yet achieved with any sophistication; although
landing an airliner on a simulated landing strip for a TV game is
already very impressive. But the fact is that in the mid-1990s the
true difference between reality and virtual reality is roughly the
difference between 80,000 polygons a second (VR) and 80 million a second in everyday life.

It may take anything between twenty and fifty years before the
implications of VR become part of that everyday life. One of its
most dangerous potentials, akin to that of TV today, will be its
ability to mislead. More naturalism, or realism, does not necessarily mean more *truthfulness*. VR could so easily teach people
to believe in things which have absolutely no truth in the real
world. As was noted earlier, the money for VR's development
has mostly come in the past from space research and industry;
yet originally, way back in the mid-1950s and before that in the
1930s, it was the entertainment industry that was interested in
enlarging the cinema screen into a more total sensory experience.
Aldous Huxley had the idea as long ago as 1932 in his *Brave
New World*, but the ideas were there ahead of the technology,
and ahead of the required risk in investment. Cinerama, 3D, and
Sensorama had their brief day; and Morton Heilig's 'Experience
Theater', patented in 1960, 'might have ushered in the cyberspace
age' all that time ago. Now once again, as Howard Rheingold
points out, 'the entertainment industry may come to be the largest
driving force in the future development of VR'.[6] The genie is out

of the bottle, he says, and there is no way to reverse it.

The negative potential of VR, for example in advertising, is very high; but so are the positive aspects of greater mental flexibility. We already create our own lives, says Charles Tart, and VR is 'a tool to help our evolution if we use it creatively and positively'.[7] However, it is rather a big 'if', especially when we are reminded by Douglas Adams that despite the fact that we already live in a kind of 'virtual reality' by creating our own world, 'our brains are essentially the same as those used by cavemen'.[8] Well, perhaps in structure, but the feed-in of information and experience to be processed today is vastly different. We have been given a tool which, like all tools, can only be as effective as its use. One of the nascent problems of VR is that, of necessity, it is mostly in the hands of boffins rather than artists. But the time will surely come when Experience Theatre displays the wonders of imagination as well as the wonder of science; and when audiences, perhaps quite small ones, will interact in it, more as a community than an *ad hoc* group, to discover who they are and what it means to be human.

For the general public, VR raises a number of crucial questions which relate to everyone's life. For example: 'What are the extent and limits of the artificial?' . . . How do we maintain contact with reality 'when the fake becomes indistinguishable from – and even more authentic than – the original?' . . . Or putting that in another way: 'How is it possible to hold a clear view of the distinction between reality and fantasy when the unreal is continually being realized?'[9] Benjamin Woolley reminds us that 'J. R. Hartley's "book" *Fly Fishing*' in the TV advertisement for Yellow Pages was actually created by a ghost writer Michael Russell after 'overwhelming public demand for it' and published with the photo of the actor who played the fictional 'Hartley' on the dust wrapper. Fiction becomes fact; simulation becomes actual; artificial reality becomes reality.

Mention of 'simulation' points to the vital difference in VR, not at once obvious, between simulation and imitation; for the difference refers to what is actually real (and is imitated) and what is not actually real (but is simulated). *Imitation* simply reproduces a real working model of something or someone; *simulation* actually re-creates a totally new working model or fictional character *as if* it was real – that is to say, virtually real. The latter does not actually exist except in cyberspace. That which is merely imitated, on the other hand, does actually exists somewhere in actual space.

Concerning 'artificial intelligence' in this context, Woolley suggests that 'there is a very serious possibility that computers will one day match the processing power and storage capacity of the human brain'. But this prognostication relies heavily on whether computers can *simulate* rather than just *imitate* intelligence; which in turn depends upon whether human intelligence is actually mechanical (that is, computational) or something more. Woolley then hedges his bet. Having mentioned the 'serious possibility' of matching the brain's computing ability, he goes on to suggest further that the quest 'to reproduce human consciousness and intelligence is not a sensible computational target'.[10] His caution is commendable, for the living interface of separate consciousnesses remains a mystery which, as yet, has been neither defined nor understood. It is this mystery which live theatre and live actors serve.

It seemed possible at one time, following on the psychologist B. F. Skinner's analysis of human behaviour, that plays and the theatre might become a sort of scientific laboratory, setting out the causes and effects of human actions and relations, illustrating what he called 'a technology of behaviour'. We shall be looking at something similar in the next chapter, but the theatre is no more a computer than actors themselves. Theatre does not answer to the description suggested by one academic as 'a complex aesthetic machine, dedicated to the representation of the imaginable through performance' and therefore capable of being 'used to reproduce intelligence'. This argument continues that as actors often play characters more intelligent than themselves, so 'a similar sort of representational mechanism' could be used to reproduce artificial intelligence.[11] It is an attractive idea, but the catch is once again between imitation and simulation. The actor is much more than just a 'representational mechanism' despite all the technical prowess required to present a role over and over again. He simulates reality rather than just imitating it; indeed, there may be no model to imitate in many cases, and even where there is (as, for example, with an historical character), the imitation of outward habits and behaviour has to be supported with the inward feelings, thoughts and compulsions which can only be simulated. A robot-computer can imitate intelligence; and it might even simulate a human model of circumscribed abilities capable of being programmed into its computer brain; but it can never actually *be* that intelligence, or be that simulated model in the same way as the conscious actor can be the role he is playing. The robot is a fixed shadow of its programmer; the actor interprets and varies the fixed shadow provided by the dramatic, both for himself and in response to different audience reactions. The *live* experience is the essence of theatre's perennial fascination.

Likewise, the point that must never be forgotten in considering VR is that the living interplay is absent. This is not to say that VR audiences cannot be asked to react and make personal choices as sometimes happens literally in live theatre (for example, in Ayckbourn's *Intimate Exchanges*). An American computer expert equally interested in the theatrical connections with VR, Brenda Laurel, comments that 'The Greeks employed drama and theatre as *tools for thought* [her italics], in much the same way that we envision employing them in the not-too-distant future.'[12] 'Mimesis' was the method of Aristotle's catharsis, a purification of the senses and the soul through watching and identifying with a play. The emotions of the audience are stirred to a dense experience by a vicarious participation and suspension of disbelief in a ritualized story. The components of the story, probably already well known, 'serve to invoke mental and emotional states' in, as it were, encoded form, from which by association we can learn about real choices in real life. From our theatrical past in the intoxicated Dionysian revels on the threshing-floor circle to the possible future of cyberspace entertainment at home (described by sci-fi novelist William Gibson as 'consensual hallucination'), the historical line is clear. Theatre remains what it has always been: a play, a game, an entertainment, an escape, an addiction, a means of education, a trying-out of alternative life-scenarios without danger, and ultimately a mystery not to be divulged.

It would seem that for over forty years, the media have successfully connived not to give away 'who dunnit' in *The Mousetrap*. A similar silence pertained in the ancient past over many of the secret initiation mysteries. Only in this century has the mythologist Joseph Campbell ventured to suggest the sort of thing that probably happened in them. In the case of Eleusis, he speaks of initiates being led, perhaps blindfolded and lightly drugged, from symbolic darkness to light. The initiate's experience was intended to occur as an almost literal revelation, a teaching about life and death, about nature and rebirth. Campbell cites the instance of a shiny metal bowl constructed to give a distorted reflection into which the young initiate is invited to look. He expects to see his own face reflected, but instead he sees

> the face of an old man, or the mask of an old man. The shock of realisation, the death and old age within youth, represents an opening of the mind to a logic dimension of existence ... the initiate is awakened to the whole course of his life. This kind of shock would not be experienced if the young man had been told by a friend who had gone through the mystery. That is why it was regarded as criminal to betray anything of the mysteries.[13]

Rheingold goes on to comment that the reflective bowl was a tool for creating a life-like visual illusion – in other words, an early instance of VR. But the analogy seems rather overstretched.

In addition to its power to mislead, the biggest danger of VR, of 'getting out of our minds', is that it could easily become addictive, as TV has become addictive for millions today. Moreover, the danger is compounded by the fact that, as with TV, such addiction can imply big profits for those in control. The main difference from TV is that VR calls the whole illusion-reality syndrome into question. In the past, life has often been compared to a play, and a theatre to the world; in the future, we may be able to sample and play in any life we choose. The theatre of our dreams will feel actual, and the world merely a theatre in which we choose our preferred existence. In any case, we are 'actors' all, and VR will simply underline the fact, forcing us to decide 'what it is we as humans ought to become'.[14]

This inherent drama has already been recognized and put on a real stage, the Contact Theatre in Manchester. Kevin Fegan's *Strange Attractors* shows the effect of VR on its leading character. 'The audience,' reports critic Michael Coveney, 'promenades through designer Angela Davies's topographic map of ramps, slopes and boxes' – a sort of three-dimensional sideshow of images on screens displaying the various locations in the play. But the VR happens to the character, not to the audience. The author 'counterpoints the surface hardware and 3D escapism with strong, lyrical writing about the prospects for passion in a private fantasy scenario'. Coveney concludes that 'the ethical consequences of virtual reality, in personal and political fields, will be immense'.[15]

Whether we like it or not, in terms of the new technology such as fibre optics, and the world information network, we shall all become active citizens of cyberspace. Cyberspace is a new word which has several synonyms: virtual space, dataspace, the digital domain, the electronic realm, and so forth. We are all already involved in the prophet Marshall McLuhan's 'global village' where 'the medium is the message' and determines not only what we see but how we are to make sense of it.[16] The computer itself is now a creator of scenarios, of what has been called 'hypertext' resulting from the old 'creative accident' techniques of collage and cut-ups arbitrarily brought together in thesaurus-like variations. Something called 'Storyspace' has already been tried out as an 'authorizing tool'. Texts are drawn together, restructured and navigated between, creating an original network of 'units' called 'spaces' and 'places'. The resulting text depends on the 'author's' or reader's response, thus creating an 'interactive novel'.

Turn 'Storyspace' into 'Theatrespace' and you have the beginnings of Star Trek's 'holodeck' (where the crew of the starship Enterprise go for their chosen entertainment and relaxation). Or you have what has already been called the Cyberspace Playhouse, the successor to today's cinema, where 'people will go to play roles in simulations'.[17] At present, it is still at the level of an arcade game or fairground exhibition, with 'players' wearing uncomfortable headsets and 'sitting in modules with joysticks embedded in the arm rests'; but its inventor envisages the front-room TV set becoming a cyberspace engine. 'Programming will be built up out of both data sent in over a fibre optic cable network ... and information held in the TV set itself (... personalized virtual bodies), and used to generate worlds for a newly uprooted generation of couch potatoes to explore.'[18]

That 'data' fed in through fibre optic cable implies a welcome augury for future employment in the acting profession. A very large number of acted variations on a theme or plot may be required in computer 'libraries' into which the couch potato simulators will interact, dialling their preferred scenarios. The interaction, it must be noted, is in a real dimension, where virtual reality scenarios, by definition, cannot be. 'Artificial reality,' says Benjamin Woolley, 'is the postmodern condition, and virtual reality its definitive technological expression.'[19]

The educational potential of all this fiction is enormous. Woolley reports Picasso as having said: 'We all know that Art is not truth. Art is a lie that makes us realize the truth, at least the truth that is given us to understand.'[20] That is the crux of the matter when VR is considered – and used – as an art form. Philosophers have long concluded in their different ways that there is only one reality: that of the individual's experience. The experiential playhouse could well become tomorrow's most important teacher, allowing the widest ranges of vicarious experience through which to learn who we really are, and even why we are here, and what we must do. In doing that, or merely attempting it, VR might assume the mantle of spiritual education so patently failing in a secular age; and be returning to the ancient example of the teaching story, with its narrative wisdom rather than intellectual discourse in élitist language.

But for the moment, it is the entertainment and tourist industries which have the new ball of VR at their feet. Hardly a month passes without some new project announcing this latest attraction. P&O are building the largest passenger ship ever, designed to carry 2,600 passengers in luxury around the Caribbean. It is due for completion in 1997 and will have 'the world's first virtual reality theatre'.[21] Also a new luxury hotel is planned in London which boasts 'a VR theatre amenity'. Other examples no doubt abound in major cities of the world. Still at the head of the investment tyros is probably the Disney Corporation with such concoctions as the Star Tours ride. It remains fairly infantile stuff, however sophisticated the technology (by today's early standards). Disney theme parks all peddle more or less the same 'Magic Kingdom' illusions, usually referring to the settings of blockbuster films, and in particular, to American nineteenth-century mythology. The French philosopher Jean Baudrillard sees them as 'the perfect model of all the entangled orders of simulation . . . Disneyland is presented as imaginary in order to make us believe that the rest is real, when in fact all of Los Angeles and the America surrounding it are no longer real.' America *is* Disneyland, and all the theme parks are there 'as a substitute for a diminishing sense of reality' in what we like to think of as the real world.

Actors employed to play Mickey Mouse, Cinderella, Wild Bill Hickock and the rest, will find little creative comfort in such doubly-removed roles. Nevertheless, such devalued employment prospects are on the increase as tourism (which some quote as becoming the world's biggest industry) imitates Disney by turning Europe's historical buildings and sites into imaginary venues, gaining ever-increasing revenue by re-enacting their past stories. The present is just not 'real' enough to attract the customers. We prefer being fooled by the artificial image to being bored by the actual thing. Daniel Boorstein once reported the convincing story of a mother and child in a supermarket. A friend greets them and admires the child's good looks, whereupon the mother is heard to reply: 'Yes, I know – but you should see his photograph!' Baudrillard again hits the nail on the head when he writes: 'The old saying, "reality is stranger than fiction" has been surpassed. There is no longer a fiction that life can confront, even in order to surpass it; reality has passed over into a play of reality.'[22]

This new kind of reality, half-way between imaginative possibility and actual realization, between the idea of a 'happening' and the happening itself, has found scientific expression in quantum mechanics.[23] The particle/wave duality encountered at subatomic levels has supported those philosophical doubts about the nature of any 'reality' outside the observing self. Things are rarely either/or, but more often both/and. The Quaker, Isaac Penington, saw as long ago as 1653 that 'every Truth is true in its kind . . . and the shadow is a true shadow, as the substance is a true substance'. The theatre is an arena for such shadows, and the insubstantial actor's truth is as real in its way as the substance which makes it. Person or actor, we are all fragmented holograms of David Bohm's one implicate order of the universe. Whatever world we make up as we go along with VR, there is another larger reality still there to which it refers. To keep a hold on the latter whilst enjoying the former will be a crucial responsibility laid upon all involved.

Cyberspace may have no precise location, but back on solid ground, theatre spaces have some very exact and exacting requirements.

Although some stage designers and directors, and fewer architects, have from time to time addressed the problem of establishing what an ideal theatre building might be, there remains something of a mystery as to its nature. The ideal concepts of Appia and Craig have had considerable influence throughout this century; in America, Norman Bel Geddes, Jo Mielziner and Robert Edmond Jones have left their mark; in England (and elsewhere) Guthrie and his designer, Tanya Moiseiwitsch, had a lasting effect, as did Stephen Joseph and, of course, that international guru, Peter Brook (especially at the Bouffes du Nord, with the collaboration of Micheline Rozan, Jean Guy Lecat, and more recently, Chloe Obolensky). But relative to the importance of the subject, the amount published about it is small. Apart from books by some of the classic names mentioned above, there are only some half dozen worth noting from the last thirty years or so: Richard Southern's *The Seven Ages of the Theatre* (1962), Stephen Joseph's *New Theatre Forms* (1968), and Richard Leacroft's *The Development of the English Playhouse* (1973) are the older ones. Leacroft's book with its distinctive isometric cut-away illustrations was later complemented and expanded in *Theatre and Playhouse*, 'An illustrated survey of theatre building from Ancient Greece to the present day' (1984), in which his wife, Helen Leacroft, collaborated. It has very extensive bibliographical references, including a number of specialist articles from architectural journals here and abroad, but other than Walter Gropius of the Bauhaus and his unbuilt Total-theatre project of 1927, and a new glossy volume (1994) about Denys Lasdun of the National Theatre, Leacroft is one of the few architects to have their work about theatre buildings published for the general public. In 1990 the Arts Council published their *Guide to Building for the Arts* by Judith Strong; but it was in 1993 that an overview of European and American theatre architecture and philosophy came out which at last filled a gap in the field. In particular, it took account of more than just the design of bricks and mortar, but included the

necessary participation of actors and audience, director and designers, multi-purpose flexibility and above all, the scale-factor.
Its author, Iain Mackintosh, is design director for Theatre Projects,
a renowned English consultancy, and also a theatre historian.
His book *Architecture, Actor and Audience* is unique in its current 'state of the art' expertise; and there is a specially helpful
focusing on essentials in his final chapter, and a fascinating introduction to the mystical principles of 'sacred geometry' in both
theatres and 'found spaces'.

Earlier histories of the theatre, like that mentioned above by
Richard Southern, have concentrated on what he usefully called
'the Line of Contact' – more often thought of as the dividing line
between actor-space and audience-space. But the concept has become
more and more complicated and strained with the amorphous
mixture of players and spectators employed in some modern productions of a 'promenade' nature, and also the extreme closeness
of actors in some severely restricted venues. The 'line of contact'
may now be seen to have more than just a dividing significance.
It relates more to 'aesthetic distance', to actual size and to the
precise drawing of shapes. Mackintosh concludes that 'Almost
all theatres . . . in which successful drama, opera and dance have
been created, have been small.' Moreover, it is a 'paradox that
good theatres have a proportion of seats with bad sightlines, while
theatres with uniformly excellent sightlines are invariably bad
theatres, disliked by actors and audiences . . .' The optimum audience number appears to be around 400 to 450, which is really
very low considering the demands of commercial viability; but
this number seems to have something to do with the demands of
'sacred geometry' and the normal and natural parameters of human sight and hearing which ideally require that 'nobody is further
than approximately 48 feet (14.6 m) from the edge of the stage'.[24]

The principles of sacred geometry – the interrelationship of
squares, circles and triangles – are familiar but complex. In theatre
space, they concern the *ad quadratum*, the *ad triangulum* and
the *golden section*. These control a dynamic spatial harmony of
proportions which is analogous to the harmonies of music, and
to composition in painting. They also relate to 'the universal principle
inherent in all growing things', where the next term in a math-
ematical progression is the sum of the two previous terms as 1,

2, 3, 5, 8, 13, 21, etc. We are looking here at the geomancy (now rather discredited except in China) which positioned and decided the dimensions of the Gothic cathedrals; which occurs as a mystical element in all architecture concerned with arranging human space; which is found in Wren's St Paul's and his Drury Lane Theatre of 1674 (the second to be built); also in the work of Erich Mendelsohn, another Bauhaus architect, whose 1927 cinema was later to be 'adapted' by Jürgen Sawade to become the New Schaubühne in 1981. Mackintosh summarizes his researches by saying that 'The chief purpose of theatre architecture is to provide a channel of energy . . . flowing back and forth between actor and audience.' Its nature is one of the many mysteries of the theatrical experience.

> That almost all successful theatres might be analysable in terms of fields of energy has not yet been proved but seems plausible. It is possible that the majority of theatres built between 1870 and 1915, which actors, directors and designers instantly recognized as marvellous tools for their trade despite being unable to say precisely why, can be resolved into geometric patterns of a recurrent 'sacred' sort involving *ad quadratum* and *ad triangulum*.[25]

This business of energy fields and unusual theatrical environments has led to the increasing use of the term 'found space'. Architects, understandably, are very dubious about avant-garde directors and their attachment to 'found spaces' – for example, Mnouchkine's ammunition factory, Guthrie's Edinburgh Assembly Hall, Schechner's Performing Arts Garage, and of course, Brook's Les Bouffes du Nord – but the fact is that 'the theatre director and his or her group find it easier to control the design of "found space" than the design of the purpose built'.[26] The very fact that these places are *not* connected with 'accepted' theatres helps the conscious break with tradition. The oft-quoted Brook-Lasdun confrontation at a meeting of the National Theatre building committee in the 1960s underlines the point: Lasdun suggests with some bitterness that Brook would probably prefer a Brixton bombsite to anything an architect could design, to which Brook simply replies 'Yes'. In fairness, it should be added that Lasdun's building *per se* is a beautiful structure, *pace* Prince Charles; but its three stages and auditoria present spatial and technical difficulties which often obstruct rather than help the presentation of plays. (The Olivier's hydraulic system was *still* giving trouble during the 1994 production of *Pericles*.) Brook is now renowned for his preference for spaces 'marked by life' (in David Williams's phrase), and has been responsible over the years for at least seven major venues around Europe, and one in New York, which were first created 'to host him for a matter of weeks, but survived to develop full-time artistic lives of their own. Tramway in Glasgow; Frankfurt's Bockenheimer Depot; the Mercat de los Flores in Barcelona: Kampnagelfabrik in Hamburg; the Majestic Theater, Brooklyn; Brussels' Les Halles de Schaerbeek; the Gesnerallee in Zurich, and the Ostre Gasvaerk, Copenhagen' are all buildings converted relatively cheaply, without resident companies, but 'often dedicated to international excellence and exchange, inspiring new work'.[27] London is notoriously absent from this list, despite Brook's use of the Chalk Farm Roundhouse for *The Ik* in January 1976. That old engine-shed, once such a hopeful 'living space' arena, is now defunct and unlikely to find performance use again.

What sort of future theatrical experiences can actors be expected to give in these 'found spaces', or for that matter, in the more conventional buildings while they last? *Les Atrides, The Man Who*, and *Faustgastronome* have already been mentioned among several examples of 1990s' avant-garde, but what is it about them and other performances which may, perhaps, point to the future? The most obvious factor would seem to be their almost ceremonial and ritual quality, and it is to this that we now turn for a final chapter of speculation.

17

Towards Ritual and a Renaissance of the Mysterious

In considering aspects of performance like rites of passage, behaviourism, ceremony, role-therapy and the mystery of the human situation, we shall be entering – not to say, trespassing on – the specialist fields of anthropology, psychology, sociology, philosophy and theology. By their very fascination, these areas are a minefield for the unwary layman, *mea culpa*, yet they are essential terrain in which to pursue the possible future of theatre and acting.

Because of its basic ingredients of participation and 'live-ness', it is ritual which would seem the most likely direction in which the evolution of play-acting might proceed. Indeed, James Roose-Evans has noted the rediscovery of ritual as 'the next major development in theatre'.[1] The point about ritual in its most ancient sense is that it *teaches us something*. It helps us to know who we are, and where we are, in the scheme of things; and it helps strengthen us in the business of everyday living. Moreover, by putting us in communal touch with the meaning of things at a deeper level – perhaps, the collective unconscious – it expands the boundaries of our individual imaginations and conscious existence. It was the visionary Edward Gordon Craig who was probably the first to point out as an aesthetic law of theatre that 'the very best part of amusement is akin to the best part of instruction' and that when they actually combine, the 'nobility' and 'beauty' of the experience tends to make one feel 'smilingly from top to toe' (what others have referred to as 'the tingle factor'). The same point was followed up by Granville-Barker and Brecht, who said respectively: 'though we start from a conception of theatre as school, this by no means rubs out, but should rather enhance the more entertaining use of it', and 'theatre remains theatre even when it is instructive theatre, and in so far as it is good theatre it will amuse'.[2]

In real life, a person may enact doing something in their mind, and then they may proceed to do it. But it will probably not work out to be quite the same action as they had imagined. The actual result will differ from the initial concept because in the working-out period it will have been qualified by a number of 'hidden' factors not at first envisaged. Similarly, an actor may imagine how to play a role, but in the process of rehearsal and final presentation the initial concept in the theatre of his mind is compromised and changed into something different. Both the actor and the person may try to fool themselves into believing that they have achieved what they set out to achieve, but actually it is only the best result possible for them in the particular circumstances, time and place. To be told this, or simply to realize it, either as person or actor, can be very hurtful. It usually produces a strong reaction of self-justification: and it is at just such a point that life and art align themselves as a teaching process.

The working aspects of this process, in both cases, concern the actual *doing of something*; and in this they relate to a ritual activity which juggles with both illusion and reality, in both life and art. The American sociologist Erving Goffman echoes the point succinctly: 'Underlying all social interaction there seems to be a fundamental dialectic. . . . A character staged in the theatre is not in some ways real, nor does it have the same kind of real consequences as does the thoroughly contrived character performed by a confidence man; but the successful staging of either of these types of false figures involves the use of real techniques – the same techniques by which everyday persons sustain their social situations.'[3]

The actor as 'scapegoat' and conscious performer. It is in ritual that the observable dichotomy of 'actor and characters played' and 'person and life-roles played' may be drawn together into a significant focus: 'the thing done' – drama – becomes a celebration of life with all its contradictions and intractability, its frustrations and its joys, its tragedy and comedy. The professional actor in this scenario becomes an intermediary, a facilitator, and to some extent, when the action of the story demands it, a scapegoat. The archetypal scapegoats of Western drama are the tragic heroes: Oedipus, Faust, Hamlet, Lear, Brand and Willy Loman. The scapegoat, it will be recalled, is the one who is blamed for the sins of others and is sent out; the sins of society are symbolically cleansed by such an action. He that plays the scapegoat does signal service to the rest of the community in taking on such a role. In primitive tribes the sacrifice was often real; in more civilized society it is clearly the job for an actor. There are also interesting overtones here with *tragos*, tragedy, and the 'goat-song'. Also with the 'cleansing' dramatic action of *catharsis*, involving both pity and terror at the fate of the one who is making atonement (at-one-ment); and with the process of *anagnorisis*, or moving through a story from what is unclear to what is clear. All this, of course, harks back to Aristotle's *Poetics*; in our past is our future; in the seed are the shape and size of the flower. Through ritual we may re-invent our culture.

James Roose-Evans argues that human beings need ritual – 'one of the neglected forms of theatre' – in order to live fulfilled and creative lives, but that Western people have come to deny themselves access to it, not least from being seduced by the 'easy-fix' offered by mechanical media. He quotes Anna Halprin, formerly leader of the radical Dancers' Workshop in San Francisco, and latterly of the Tamalpa Institute where she runs community workshops to evolve 'rituals and ceremonials out of authentic life situations', and who sees the work of the professional actor and dancer as 'a special guide who works to evoke the art within us all. This is the true meaning of seminal theatre.' She sees the art within us all as part of an enduring process because 'it touches on the spiritual dimension in a way that no other human activity does'.[4] Initially, she was associated with the post-Martha Graham style of contemporary dance, but her 'events' as she called her work relied much upon improvisation and could not 'be repeated in a precise pattern, but different pieces have different degrees of unpredictability'.[5] Much of her work in the 1960s was 'way out' but its significance as a nursery for the future is undoubted. Here is a description of a 1967 'experiment in mutual creation' in which she herself was involved:

One of Anna Halprin's groups spontaneously embarked on a ceremony that closely resembled a primordial ritual of birth, ordeal, sacrifice and finally triumph of life and vitality. The door to the room was blocked, so that each entrant had to be pulled through an opening. He was passed overhead from hand to hand by a line of men and then placed against an upright board covered with shiny plastic.

He then crept into a huge cardboard box, and people pounded on the outside of it. He escaped from the din to a convoluted tunnel made of paper, cloth and boxes. This led to a chamber in the centre of the room, underneath a tower, formed by scaffolding. At last, the 'initiate' (as the group came to regard each person going through the maze) went out by an opening and burst free of the enclosure.

When it was Anna Halprin's turn to go through the maze, the crowd shouted, 'Sacrifice! Sacrifice!' Recalls Miss Halprin: 'They held me against the wall, put me in the cave, and handed me up to the top of the tower. The whole room then broke into joyous dancing. The emotional result was tremendous exuberance and awe, which was frightening to some, for we had really participated in "mysteries"!'[6]

There are three definite stages in the creation of a ritual: the preparation, the performance and the dispersal (or closing, or 'undoing' of the energies and atmosphere engendered). The first and last are as important as the performance itself. Both Roose-Evans and the New Age writer Lorna St Aubyn, in her forty or so 'Rituals for Everyday Living',[7] stress this point. It is an element which has inclined to drain away from both theatre-going and church-worship during this century. For any significant ceremonial event, it is important to allow time 'to prepare the heart and mind' (as Quakers say), to dress appropriately, and to have time to readjust to 'normal life' after the event, if only with a drink and some discussion. Such ritual procedure is almost entirely confined now to christenings, marriages and funerals; and even then it is often 'skimped' to a minimum, as if such formalities were an embarrassment rather than essential to the occasion. Theatre-going has picked up the casualness of a visit to the cinema; whereas, whatever the entertainment on offer, a measure of formal coming-together should mark each uniquely live performance. Not that everywhere should imitate Glyndbourne or Gala Night at Drury Lane, but the same basic attitude would not be a fault. Even the Proms at the Albert Hall have their formal and traditional element as part of the event. The period of applause and collection of coats, or whatever, allows for something of an 'undoing'; but a longer period of readjustment is often necessary, and it may find its expression in a silent journey home, alone with your thoughts, whether literally or in company.

The trouble with the word 'ritual' is that it can mean so much in a wide variety of contexts that it ends up meaning very little to anyone. It can be attached as an adjective to a concept, a practice, a process, an ideology, a yearning, an experience, and a function; it can be applied (and usually is) to sacred activity, and at the same time it is used by the media to describe the most evil of satanic and sexual abuses; it is a rich field of research for ethologists, anthropologists and scholars of mythology; and not least, it can bring together not only education and entertainment, as has been noted, but also healing and the celebration or marking of important events in individual lives. A ritual provides a 'bridge' from one state of being to another (a 'rite of passage'), or it offers some sort of protection for the cohesion of a society against forces intent on disrupting it. At present, its most obvious theatrical demonstration is in the traditional British pantomime. Here, the audience finds itself bound together as a social unit against the individual anarchy shown on the stage when the Demon King (or it may be, the Ugly Sisters) maintain their wicked will. The ritual convention is understood by all when 'Oh yes I will!' and 'Oh no you won't!' are repeatedly shouted in opposition between stage and audience.

If, as Anouilh once suggested, acting were to become a compulsory part of future education – and not only of education, but part of everyone's normal social activity – then theatres, or 'theatral spaces', would become the houses of ritual and festival halls of health-giving myths. They would not be as we know them in cities now, darkened boxes separating actors and audience, where admission was only for commercial gain. They would be returned to their former significance as the 'holy places' where the life of the community was celebrated and renewed. They would re-express in the terminology of their day the fundamentals of our existence, our recognition of the cycles of nature and history, of birth, maturity and death – in short, the human situation. If every citizen was involved, at least to some degree, in such ritual activity as a real expression rather than an illusory counterfeit, then the significance would be for all, and bind all, much as a church service is meant to celebrate the same faith for priest and congregation alike. As the old religions required their hierarchies of priests and helpers, so each School of the Mysteries – as they might well become again – would require its theatrical director and such workers as necessary to effect the artefact. 'The artist of the future,' says James Roose-Evans, 'will have to come to recognize more and more his role as teacher.' The artist as teacher is inevitably a leader and healer as well, in that those who participate in his act are led towards a 'revelation' and an enhanced capacity for living. Perhaps, after all, the ritual mysteries of rebirth into the light at ancient Eleusis will be reborn themselves to new forms. Then the role of the actor will come close to that which he originally played: that of the shaman.

Schechner notes that 'The techniques and ambivalent social status of artist and shaman approximate to each other.' He observes how the masked trance-dancers of the Pueblo Indians dance for individual therapeutic reasons.[8] There is no 'audience' as such, and there is not 'a performance'; the dancing is simply done to mark some kind of connection for the individual with the spiritual world. The content of the dance often enacts one of the tribal myths or stories. It is an exercise in personal adjustment, a health-giving balance to the vagaries of material life. The dancing-floor, the stage, becomes a 'holy place' and the house of health-giving myths. It soon becomes the initiation hut in the dark forest and the 'Speak-House' at the centre of the village; the altar-stage of the sacred mysteries, the stone circle, a temple of the sun and moon and stars, a *Teo-Kalli*; the 'orchestra' for the Chorus where the dithyramb will be sung; a cathedral where flesh and spirit are joined together. It is a 'School of the Mysteries' – a place where life and art become one in a reciprocal experience. We are back again here with Grotowski's latest interest in occult private ritual performances, not for public viewing. In the late 1980s, Grotowski was searching for a universal or archetypal expression of 'reality' underlying specific rituals. He now differentiates the actor from the Performer (with a capital P). The Performer does not play another or different being; he is a 'doer', a man of action, a dancer, a priest, a warrior, and outside aesthetic genres. 'I don't want to discover something new,' says Grotowski, 'but something forgotten.'[9]

I have referred from time to time to something I have called 'a health-giving myth'. What exactly is meant by this? Myth is sometimes called a poetic form of history; it describes in non-scientific language the story of creation and our part in it; it is an illogical exercise of the imagination dealing with observable natural phenomena, and in particular, it uses personification to do so. It is this personification which puts myth so firmly in the story-telling and theatrical context. In more contemporary terms, 'a health-giving myth' is a 'teaching-story', such as those of Mulla Nasrudin in the Sufi tradition, or the parables of Jesus. It is by way of being Applied Psychology before such a term was known; it does not require academic preparation. It implies the kind of benefit received from so-called 'growth games' and other psycho-physical exercises by which a person can 'awake' and gain greater control over their destiny, and through which a group or community may become better integrated.

The principle of revelation through the acting-out of a myth (or merely the participation in the significance of a story told by others) is basic to both dramatic form and to social and individual therapy. But this does not mean – as it might with a professional psychiatrist – that the actor himself, or indeed any practising artist, must fully understand all that he does in his art. Indeed, it is probably impossible that he should do so, although this may sound like heresy to some modern acting teachers. It is most unlikely that Shakespeare, for example, was aware of all that has since been inferred in his work or interpreted in its performance. So it is with myths and their performance. They have an independent, archetypal existence; and in expressing them, an artist is merely responding as a sensitive instrument of communication, giving his or her particular understanding of them. Peter Brook comments that 'a great ritual, a fundamental myth is a door, a door that is not there to be observed, but to be experienced'.[10]

For each of us, the experience of an artist's work is equally personal and singular. Nor is it necessary for us that we should fully understand our own experience. The experience itself is everything (which is very much a tenet of contemporary visual art); and it is this which explains why 'the house of health-giving myths' is also 'a school of mysteries' and 'a school for being'. The theatre has been all of these, and will be again.

A modern practitioner who sees his work as stemming from the origins of theatre in ritual is Alessandro Fersen. This Italian drama teacher and experimental director is renowned in his own country and specialist field, but little known in Britain. His life's work has been to develop a set of techniques, going beyond Stanislavski's 'emotion-memory', to enable Western performers to enter into and return from states of trance. He is, as it were, moving in the footsteps of the Pueblo Indians. He calls his work 'Mnemodrama' ('the drama of memory'). For the performer it is a psychic operation, retrieving through the interior life memories of the past, pre-natal and ancestral dreams. He insists that it is not psychodrama; it is for the strong and mentally-balanced who are seeking to find their own 'deep identity'. As a technique, it is not actually about acting at all: actors in a trance cannot easily play together! Nevertheless, Fersen sees Mnemodrama as being 'of extreme value to the actor today' because the actor's psyche, or own 'identity', is his third instrument of interpretation after the body and the voice. He says he is trying to continue where Copeau gave up; as indeed is Eugenio Barba, with whom he has something in common. They are both interested in developing the spiritual life of the actor. Mnemodrama, says Fersen, 'is a technique of abandonment at which women, incidentally, are better than men'. There are many modes of trance, but the common denominator is the temporary loss of personal identity with the assumption of another identity. With that sort of definition, Fersen is half-way back to acting; but he comments that 'Mnemodrama is really only an exercise for use at the threshold of acting itself, rather like a footballer skipping to get in shape for the game.'[11]

Mnemodrama is a separate part of the normal two-year Acting Course at the Studio Fersen in Rome, and does not even involve the same students. Fersen started his Studio as long ago as 1957 when it was coeval with Grotowski's earliest work at Cracow.

The following year, on a visit to Brazil, he observed the Candomble ritual there, seeing it as a model of Dionysian experience. Mixing the ingredients of anthropology and ritual with the innovative theatrical work he had begun in the 1950s followed naturally on his encounter with this primitive shamanic drama. When working with his students on 'the drama of memory', which is both autobiographical and ancestral, Fersen uses particular props – objects for the actor to play with, and which help them go within themselves and explore the caverns of recalled visions and gestures. Like Kantor, he stays 'onstage' with them, not participating, but guiding and maintaining their safety, and after about fifteen minutes, indicating it is time to finish. Even this comparatively short length of 'performance' is very exhausting for the participants, and they need to sleep afterwards. But then, it seems, they experience everything bright and sharp, and have lots of energy. It is, we may suppose, what actors today might call 'a good warm-up'.

Mention of Grotowski and anthropology brings us to consider another seminal figure in the relationship between theatre and ritual. The subject was the lifelong passion of the anthropologist and comparative symbologist Victor Turner (1920–83). Although he never met Grotowski, they were aware of each other's work which ran towards similar objectives. Turner strongly 'felt the need to find a global basis for the ritual process'.[12] He noted that 'A performance is declarative of our shared humanity, yet it utters the uniqueness of particular cultures. We will know one another better by entering into one another's performances and learning their grammars and vocabularies.' This, of course, is the ideal of the Inter-Faith Movement and Hans Küng's concept of global responsibility based on dialogue between religions. It underlines the most useful and sacred role of theatre in societies of the future, as of the past; and it confirms the actor's ancient significance as simulator, healer, facilitator of mystery and 'identifier' of the human situation – the shaman-artist. It may turn out to be one of the stranger ironies of human history that where religions failed to have sufficient dialogue among themselves to establish some sort of peace between nations, or at least the establishment of Küng's 'world ethic', the theatre – so often maligned by religion in the past – will enable it to happen. Though the live experience of theatre will remain paramount, it may fall to the new technologies of satellite and fibre-optic networks to provide an instant global access, albeit at one remove.

In his article 'Are There Universals of Performance in Myth, Ritual and Drama?' Turner quotes the philosopher John Dewey saying 'True theatre at its height signifies complete interpenetration of self and the world of objects and events.' It is when this happens that, for actors and audience alike, there occurs an ecstatic sense of union: 'A sense of harmony with the universe is made evident, and the whole planet is felt to be communitas.'[13] This is the most precise expression of what a great theatre experience is about. It becomes a ritualized and communal rehearsal for living. It puts flesh on dreams and ideals. But it is still only a rehearsal. That most sophisticated of theatrical theorists and commentators, Herbert Blau, points out that 'Whatever the appearance or actuality of communitas, performance is a testament to what separates . . . There is something in the nature of theatre which from the very beginning of theatre has always resisted being theatre . . . [But] what is universal in performance is the consciousness of performance.'[14] These are most important observations, and they answer Turner's question. The whole point about myth, ritual and drama, is that they should be performed as *consciously* as possible. They are all exercises in controlled attention; and therein lies humankind's only hope of further progress from those automatic responses programmed into our minds and bodies in the jungle. It is at this point that life and its shadow, theatre, merge as it were at high noon.

Scenarios of behaviour as teaching-stories. If we accept that at least one future format of live performance is likely to be ritualistic, then what might its content be? What kind of scenarios will ritual theatre be celebrating? New social rituals are certainly required, as we have seen, to revivify and replace those formal ceremonies of ours which, like the endlessly repeated plots of television 'soaps', have become jaded, over-familiar and unexciting. The old scenarios tend to stereotype, alienate and separate different social groups rather than unite them in any common value-system; and they certainly tend to stress wayward behaviour and misery rather than understanding and happiness. This disenchantment inevitably encourages cynicism and disorientation. It becomes a serious loss and sickness for any society to suffer when its principal role-models mostly self-destruct. To find again, or perhaps for the first real time, a significant and meaningful centre to our daily community lives, it has been suggested by Clem Gorman that the reinstatement of 'ceremony' is essential. He sees the term as very similar to what we have been calling 'ritual' – 'Ceremony is the way men have always come back to seeing the phenomenal world. When we are lost, we turn back to the centre.'[15] Here, the word 'ceremony' is being used to include the inward meaning as well as its more usual connotation of describing the purely external manifestation of a formal occasion. However, Gorman's interpretation becomes quite clear when he observes a useful term used in New Guinea: 'Wantok'. Wantok means 'one-talk', which includes all those who speak the same spiritual language, without necessarily having the same cultural background. 'For a ceremony to be real and not just an alienating entertainment, all celebrants and participants must be Wantok. American tourists watching a Hopi Indian rain dance are not Wantok. But Hopi Indians watching the ceremony are. It is not necessary for people to have been introduced to Wantok; it is enough that they are of one mind.'[16]

Actors, in Gorman's terminology, may become the 'new ceremonialists' and carry with them something of the magical power of the old shaman. Just as the shaman and his vicarious activities on behalf of the tribe were central to that tribe's well-being, recalling its ancient myths, keeping it in touch and in harmonious collaboration with mysterious higher powers – so the actor keeps touch, on behalf of the participating audience, with those universal truths, archetypal symbols and analogical stories which give life meaning and lend it renewed purpose. The shaman was an exceptional person, one who not only had special knowledge but also took pains, and personally suffered, on behalf of his or her tribe. The actor, too, as a 'new ceremonialist' will have to be an exemplar, a leader, not only in the sense of playing a leading character, or as any character, all of whom reveal some aspect of the human situation, but as a man or a woman who take their audience with them, and actually share in the dramatic experience of the scenario being performed. It does not matter whether that scenario is tragedy, comedy, farce or something in between them all: in ceremonial or ritual terms, it binds audience and players together. Harley Granville-Barker once asked himself 'Upon what does the *power* of the actor over his audience rest?' He concluded that it rested upon something that the actor *is*.[17] Looks, technical skill, a magnetic voice – these mattered on the way, but ultimately the actor's power to give of himself, to share his experience with others, depends on his naked being, the spirit unmasked.

The actor-person, person-actor dichotomy is well known, of course, to those who practice dramatherapy as a means of healing the psyche. The modern Sufi philosopher Idries Shah observes that 'Because it is difficult for people to perceive their own problems, they can get some sense of them through seeing themselves as seen by others.'[18] It is this two-way action between life and theatre which makes the art of the dramatist such a vital one in cultural history. Novelists create marvellous characters, but to have them given real flesh on a stage is an added dimension. Just as a person is born and created with an essence – 'unseen' characteristics of the genes built into body, mind and spirit, and then built upon further according to cultural environment and circumstances into a multiple 'seen' personality – so the actor works in reverse to uncover that essence. Starting with the 'seen' character expressed by the dramatist, the actor works backward to understand the motives and reactions and conditioning behind that character in order to act the essence of it truthfully. The human coding that creates the person, and the actor's decoding that creates a role – this duality of procedure in life and art is what produces recognizable, if sometimes oversimplistic, scenarios of behaviour.

A dramatherapist, Robert J. Landy, has listed a large number of character-types observable in both plays and life, a classification he calls 'a taxonomy of roles'. He points out that the concept of role-playing is more than just a powerful and frequently-used metaphor: it 'provides coherence to the personality . . . it supercedes the primacy of the concept of self . . . and it is dramatic in its own right'.[19] The fact that role-playing as a conscious activity can go beyond the normally-inhibited self is an extremely useful adjunct to both healing and education. The actor proceeds on the assumption of 'as if' a certain role were true; a person can imagine how they might change from what they are to something better by saying 'what if' I were to assume such-and-such a role were true. Roles are the necessary and natural content of ritual stories; and as another anthropologist, Carol MacCormack, reminds us: 'Symbol-enriched ritual fuses together the world as we live it and the world as we imagine it.'[20] Of course, the point about role-playing, whether in art, in life, or in therapy, is that you have to *want* to do it for it to be in the least effective. Participation in the ritual, the event, the performance – whatever its context calls it – can never be forced. Force invalidates the occasion. On the other hand, willing participation is not alone a matter of agreeing or disagreeing with a particular view of life. Most people seem to delight in vicariously experiencing compelling images about all kinds of roles in life (especially sexual images, and painful ones where they are not themselves sensitive to that pain), but the most important aspect of vicarious experience is that it sometimes surpasses mere observation and comes as a revelation.

Revelation usually implies that a totality of related images is recognized as being connected beyond the immediate experience of any one of them. It is this sudden apprehension of new relationships, especially through the 'living' analogy of a theatrical scenario or story, which brings a sense of new freedom, an exhilaration of the spirit. It is so much more than simply recognizing a common experience. Where an intellectual and emotional agreement with a scenario merely confirms our own previous observation of cause and effect, analogical theatre can lead us to a recognition of *processes* which may have been hidden before, but which had nevertheless been controlling our everyday life; and perhaps, beyond ourselves, unnoticed by groups and even nations. Such revelatory theatre can show us whole lifetimes of experience in an hourglass.

Take, for example, an observable concept at work in life which might be labelled 'the tragedy of fixed ideas'. Politically, it leads to situations like Suez, the Falklands and Northern Ireland; socially, to strikes and feuds of all kinds, and to institutionally-rigid religion, education and all manner of moral intolerance; individually, to the set behaviourism of old age, the blind preoccupations of busy middle age, and the simplistic idealism of youth. It is one of the functions of the drama to illustrate the principle of untenable fixity at work; and perhaps to show the inevitable processes of resolution, whether tragic or comic. The function is expositional rather than partisan; although any statement of a situation, however enlightened and balanced, will carry some degree of propagandic force. In a fast-changing society, reference-points giving some kind of social foundation or security assume great value and importance. They become, like the myths and rituals of old or medieval-style religious faiths, cornerstones of stability; and the theatre – or whatever its future manifestation may be called, 'the house of stories' perhaps, as well as 'health-giving myths' – the theatre will be at the centre of the community, as the church used to be, and as the pub or club are now, maintaining the welfare of the 'man and woman in the street' in terms of 'belonging' and behaviour. It will probably be supported by a mixture of the commercial, the self-subsidized, and the state-subsidized, much as the Medical Services and the Arts and Heritage foundations operate today. Although the theatre deals with life vicariously (and here we must include the mechanical media as well), it nevertheless offers the very real opportunity of seeing things objectively, of suspending judgement from fixed ideas, and giving alternative scenarios the chance of expression. By means of dramatic dialogue, in particular, the actions of people and their principles may be seen with the inevitable processes which accompany them. Dialogue (dialogos) admits of all possibilities for change; and in the context of fiction and drama, by suspending real time and space, it can experiment with consequences without paying any real price for them. Rigid labels in life too often spell tragedy, but in the theatre, the distraught plea of Faustus 'O God, turn back Thy universe and give me yesterday!' may be granted. J. B. Priestley used the device to moving effect in *Time and the Conways* and other of his 'time plays'. We have all experienced those 'dangerous corners' when, if only we had known, we might have behaved differently. In role-playing, whether through ritual theatre, virtual reality machines, or mere imagination, the opportunity is offered from which to learn without fear of retribution.

The old dichotomy of theatre *or* life, as being mutually exclusive images of reality, is slowly resolving back to its original unified existence as being theatre *and* life. The duality is retained and not denied, but the same images of reality are beginning to serve both once again, as it did in the ancient mysteries. The images have the same significance whether in life or art. Only the mode is different. In both we may discover the ground of our being. In the theatre we may rehearse our individual salvation in safety; only in life are we obliged to work out the scenario of our choice, and take the consequences. We are what we do; and the real being and the real shadow are equally true in their way.

The leading theatre gurus of this century have all sought to find in the theatrical context the nature of a true experience, rather than a mere collusion in the game of 'as if'. The personal experience of truth, for both actor and audience-participator, brings life back into the theatre, where for too long in the history of the written drama it has become separated, on the assumption that vicarious truth could not be real truth. The canvas and tinsel of 'as if' is giving way to the theatrical reality of real materials and unmasked design, but the common denominator of them both remains the written word. Whatever the advances in 'physical theatre', dialogue will always be a prime instrument of expression, with its usage, both written and spoken, requiring the most rigorous of training. We looked at this subject in the chapter on 'new forms', including Billington's defence of textual theatre, and concluded that, in any case, the ideal of 'total theatre' would include all modes. Way back in 1964, the dramatist Friedrich Dürrenmatt made an eloquent defence of dialogue worth quoting for its relevance here:

> The human being of the drama is, after all, a talking individual, and speech is his limitation. The action only serves to force this human being on stage to talk in a certain way. The action is the crucible in which the human being is molten into words, must become words.

> The purpose of dialogue is not only to lead a human being to a point where he must act or suffer; at times it also leads into a major speech, to the explanation of some point of view. Many people have lost the appreciation of rhetoric since... some actor who was not sure of his lines discovered naturalism. That loss is rather sad. A speech can win its way across the footlights more effectively than any other artistic device.[21]

The word 'footlights' sounds almost archaic now; but the argument is no less up-to-date for that. Whatever the 'found spaces' of the future, words, speech and dialogue will have their essential place in the concept of a 'total theatre'.

The merging of actor and person in the art of being human. We noted earlier that the most important thing in performing a text, whether formal or behaviourist, was the attention paid to it – doing it as consciously as possible, rather than allowing habit and 'automatic pilot' to take over. Actors understand this very well. It is the reason that long-run plays have to be re-rehearsed every so often. The syndrome applies to real life also. A considerable amount of everyday living is performed by rote. Indeed, if it were not so, we should probably soon collapse from sheer exhaustion. Once our bodies (and our minds) have worked out how to do something (or think of something), it gets consigned to the subconscious and automatic recall. Once grown up, we do not have to think about running downstairs, for example; but if we then tried to make every muscle move consciously, we would soon trip up. And that is the problem. 'Man has reached his present point in evolution,' says Colin Wilson, 'by the aid of certain habit patterns. Now some of these patterns must be broken, and restored to the realm of conscious activity. The problem of consciousness must be attacked by consciousness.'[22] This is where participation in games and sport, in social rituals of all kinds involving attention to procedures, and especially involvement in the creative arts, is so important to both personal and social well-being.

The behavioural psychologist B. F. Skinner, referred to briefly in the last chapter, once called for a conscious 'technology of behaviour' as the only thing to control our major social diseases.[23] He is now somewhat in disrepute with his peers, yet with a bio-feedback machine in every classroom, his diagnosis and remedy just might have been productive. Most people, though, would agree that his ideas were too prescriptive. However, there remains the observable field of 'scenarios of behaviour'. Despite the prospect of each generation being faced with the same infantile and bestial mechanisms of mind in trying to cope with the ever-increasing complexities of technological society, the element of choice and free-will is crucial. It is this 'x' factor in human

nature that can never be scientifically predictable. It has invariably confounded politics and economics. In their respective ways,
the dramatist and the philosopher and the psychologist have always dealt with it, although their necessarily limited, selected and
sporadic observation has rarely, if ever, been able to definitively
pin it down. Their works, as a result, from Plato to Shakespeare,
from Chekhov to Jung, have only given a partial sketch – albeit
with genius – of those scenarios of behaviour which describe being
human. The 'x' factor remains an enigma. Perhaps the future
will be able to consciously develop a fuller picture. The more it
is completed, the more art and life will become one. Actor and
person will merge in the art of living, and being will become its
own artefact.

Gaston Baty of the Cartel des Quatre had a utopian vision of
a theatre 'once again functioning as the focal point of the collective life and beliefs of the community', a theatre which 'would
resemble the "dream of an expressive universe", reaching beyond
man to embrace all that exists . . . the great forces of the natural
world . . . and beyond these forces of the natural world . . . and
beyond these mysteries to the still deeper mysteries of invisible
presences, of death and infinity'.[24] We can see, as in a mirror,
what we might become. Reverse ourselves with that image – step
like Alice into the looking-glass that is theatre – and it may be
that through a little play-acting and role-identification, like children, we could be rehearsing the reality. The final vision, like
Baty's, is mystical. The systole and diastole of all living matter,
that archetypal rhythm, will continue to give form and meaning
and infinite variety to our consciousness of existence; and its theatrical enactment in the house of mysteries will aim to do the
same. Life will be celebrated with ritual thanksgiving when we
can reside, at last, in 'the still centre' where 'energy is eternal
delight'. Our material bodies will be the vulnerable vehicles they
have always been, yet then joyfully containing 'the whirlpool in
pure intelligence'. That is Lilith speaking in the great final coda
of *Back to Methuselah*. Beyond this, says Shaw, for once reaching a last word, thought cannot reach. 'It is enough that there is
a beyond.'

There have been many hints and guesses in this chapter, but
one thing about acting in the future is for certain: it will speak

single person to single person. From Thespis to Burbage, through Bracegirdle and Betterton to Siddons and Kean, with Bernhardt and Coquelin, Irving and Terry, down to Ashcroft and Gielgud in our own times – the list is unavoidably invidious – but single actor speaks to single spectator (and also, of course, in doing so, to the audience as a whole). The living ritual of theatre is like a love affair, a sensitivity of common feeling and togetherness between performer and participator in which truth, as far as we can know it, is the broker.

It is said that trial and tribulation can be the 'making' of a person. The self-knowledge, self-discipline, imagination and application demanded in order to achieve another's spiritual identity on stage – or wherever the space may be – is similarly creative. It serves a community by showing it to itself, free of illusion. That is feared, especially by those in power, but it does happen. Many of us have been privileged to see it happen; and ultimately, that is what the making of the professional actor is all about.

Notes and References

Introduction

1. Kenneth Rea analysed the situation in the *Guardian*, 19 March 1991, with an article headed 'First, rehearse your credit-worthiness'. In another *Guardian* article, 25 February 1992, Simon Williams argued that only mandatory grants for drama students could halt the return of middle-class bias. In March 1993, the Arts Council's then Secretary-General, Anthony Everitt, said that 'The situation is now so serious that Britain's acknowledged capacity for producing some of the finest actors and dancers in the world is in danger of being undermined.' He went on: 'The system discriminates against young people from certain geographical areas and lower socio-economic groups, regardless of talent' (*Guardian*, 9 March 1993). Since then, there have been frequent letters and articles in the press repeating the same points.

2. Clive Barker, 'What Training – for What Theatre?', *New Theatre Quarterly*, No. 42, May 1995.

3. The Report reviewed is: Jackson, Honey, Hillage and Stock, 'Careers and Training in Dance and Drama', Brighton: Institute of Manpower Studies, Report No. 268.

4. Yoti Lane, *The Psychology of the Actor*, Secker and Warburg, 1959, p. 40.

Various parts of this Introduction were contained in articles written for *The Stage*, 15 October 1992, and for *Plays International*, September 1993.

PART ONE: The Past

1. *The Religious and the Secular in Medieval Acting*

1. This trope (from the Latin *tropus*, meaning an 'added melody or words') comprised four lines of dialogue sung antiphonally before Mass on Easter morning. Translated it reads:

> Whom do you seek in the tomb, O Christians?
> – Jesus of Nazareth, the crucified, O heavenly being.
> He is not here; he has risen as he foretold.
> Go and announce that he is risen from the tomb.

From the singing of this verse by priest and choir, it was a short but very significant step – the first in English drama – to introduce an impersonation of the Angel asking the question, and of the three Marys who reply, employing appropriate costume and gestures; although it took many years for even this to be allowed to happen. For a scholarly account of this vital seed of development, see Glynne Wickham's *The Medieval Theatre* (1974).

2. John Allen, *A History of the Theatre in Europe*, Heinemann, 1983, p. 77.

3. John Barton, *The First Stage: A Chronicle of the Development of English Drama from its Beginnings to the 1580s*, BBC Publications, 1956.

4. Ibid.

2. *The Elizabethan Actor Turns Pro*

1. Edwin Duerr, *The Length and Breadth of Acting*, Holt, Rinehart and Winston, New York, 1962, p. 110. I am very much indebted to this comprehensive study, as will be seen. Another seminal work detailing the Elizabethan period in particular is M. C. Bradbrook's *The Rise of the Common Player: A Study of Actor and Society in Shakespeare's England*, Chatto and Windus, 1962.

2. Duerr, op. cit., p. 112.

3. Ibid., p. 150, quoting G. E. Bentley, 'Shakespeare and the Blackfriars Theatre', in *Shakespeare Survey 1*, edited by Allardyce Nicoll, OUP, 1948, pp. 40, 47.

4. Ibid., p. 153, quoting Alwyn Thayer, 'Minor Actors and Employees in the Elizabethan Theatre', *Modern Philology*, Vol. XX, 1922, p. 50.

3. *Enter the Actress*

1. These had been classified by one John Bulwer in his *Chirologia: or, the natural language of the hand*, and in *Chironomia: or, the art of*

manuall rhetorique, published together in 1644. An account, with illustrations from Bulwer's treatises, is to be found in B. L. Joseph's *Elizabethan Acting*, OUP, 1950.

2. Duerr, op. cit., p. 185.

3. Ibid., pp. 195–6.

4. Ibid., p. 204. It was not until 1720 that England saw its first theatre periodical, *Theatre*, No. 1, also produced by Steele.

5. Gildon quoting the Duke of Buckingham. Once again, the source is the indefatigable Edwin Duerr, who gives a much more detailed account of Gildon's book, op. cit., pp. 205–9.

6. Thomas Davies, *Memoirs of the Life of David Garrick, Esq.*, 1808, p. 18.

7. Duerr, op. cit., p. 226, quoting Melville, *Stage Favourites*, p. 65.

8. Ibid., p. 250.

9. Ibid., p. 228.

10. Ibid., p. 242.

11. Allen, op. cit., Note 4, pp. 218–19.

12. Diderot's *Paradoxe sur le comédien* (c. 1770–78) was first published in Paris in 1830, and translated as *The Paradox of Acting* by W. H. Pollock, London, 1883.

Diderot is seen as the pivotal figure in the transition between ancient and modern theories of acting in an intriguing study by the American academician Joseph R. Roach, *The Player's Passion: Studies in the Science of Acting*, University of Delaware Press, Newark; and Associated University Presses, London and Toronto, 1985. Professor Roach examines acting styles from the seventeenth to the twentieth century, and measures them against the prevailing psychobiological paradigms. His illustrations include items from Bulwer's *Chironomia* and *Chirologia* (1644), Descartes' *Treatise of Man* (1666), the painter Charles Le Brun on *The Method for Learning to Design the Passions* (1734), Franciscus Lange's *Dissertio de actione scenica* (1727), David Garrick's gesture as Hamlet (1754), Charles Bell's *Anatomy and Philosophy of Expression* (1806), Henry Siddons' *Rhetorical Gesture and Action* (1822), Darwin's *Expression of Emotion in Man and Animals* (1872) and three of Meyerhold's biomechanical exercises.

Currently in London there is a School of the Science of Acting whose Principal, Sam Kogan, frequently writes to *The Stage* challenging the methods of leading drama schools. Whether his curriculum includes an emphasis on Diderot, I do not know; but it almost certainly stems from Stanislavski's self-questioning as to whether the creative process can consciously follow scientifically established laws of physiology and psychology, a matter which much occupied theorists of the eighteenth century.

13. John Philip Kemble's *Prompt Books* were reproduced in the USA in 1972 at a cost per copy of about £70. They show his directions written down with great neatness.

4. *The Early Nineteenth Century*

1. Ernest Reynolds, *Early Victorian Drama*, Heffer, Cambridge, 1936, p. 62.

2. Duerr, op. cit., p. 338.

3. *The Drama Review*, March 1972.

4. Alec Clunes, *The British Theatre*, Cassell, 1964, p. 130.

5. *The Oxford Companion to the Theatre*, edited by Phyllis Harnoll, OUP, 1951, p. 443. Several subsequent editions.

6. Ellen Terry, *The Story of My Life*, Hutchinson, 1908. p. 13.

7. T. W. Robertson, 'Theatrical Types', *Illustrated Times*, 1864, reprinted by A. M. Nagler in *Sources of Theatrical History*, Dover, New York, 1952.

8. Edward Gordon Craig, *The Art of the Theatre*, 1905; included in *On the Art of the Theatre*, Heinemann, 1911, with many subsequent editions.

5. *The Fin de Siècle Foundations of Modern Acting*

1. G. M. Lewes, *On Actors and the Art of Acting*, London, 1875, p. 90.

2. Ibid.

3. Antoine cited in Waxman's *Antoine*, p. 175, quoted by Duerr, op. cit., p. 374.

4. Duerr, op. cit., p. 385.

5. James Alberry (1838–89) was a disciple of T. W. Robertson, and Allardyce Nicoll saw him as making advances which 'definitely lead the comic stage towards the plays of Wilde' (*XIX Century Drama 1850–1900*, Vol. 1, CUP, 1946, p. 155). *Two Roses* was first performed in June 1870 at the Vaudeville, where Alberry received a flat sum of only £3 a performance (Nicoll, op. cit., p. 69). The play survives in print today as one of those chosen by George Rowell in his anthology of *Nineteenth Century Plays*, OUP, 1953, second edition 1972, with many impressions.

6. For a fuller description of this subject, see Michael Sanderson's excellent 'social history of the acting profession 1880–1983', *From Irving to Olivier*, Athlone Press, 1984. Chapter 5 covers 'The Actor in Trade Unionism and Politics 1890–1914'.

7. Constant-Benoît Coquelin, *The Art of the Actor*, Paris, 1894; translated with an introduction by Elsie Fogarty, Allen and Unwin, 1932, third impression 1954, p. 30.

8. Hugh Hunt, Kenneth Richards and John Russell Taylor, *The Revels History of Drama in English*, Vol. VII, *1880 to the Present Day* (General Editor: T. W. Craik), Methuen, 1978, pp. 71–3 on 'Acting 1880–1918'.

9. C. E. Montague, 'F. R. Benson's Richard II (1899)', quoted by Duerr, op. cit., p. 387.

PART TWO: The Present

6. *The Edwardian Theatre*

1. Allardyce Nicoll, *English Drama 1900–1930: The Beginnings of the Modern Period*, CUP, 1973, p. 5.

2. *The Revels History, Vol. VII*, p. 73.

3. Sanderson, op. cit., p. 37.

4. One of the 'Old Bensonians' who later published her memoirs, *Chameleon's Dish* (1973), was Nora Nicholson. I had the pleasure of working with – and learning from – her during my first professional engagement as an actor with the Oxford Playhouse for the Season 1942–3.

5. Sanderson, op. cit., p. 37.

6. Ibid., p. 38.

7. Ibid., p. 41.

8. Ibid., p. 42.

9. Ibid., p. 45.

10. Jean Benedetti, *Stanislavski: An Introduction*, Methuen, 1982, p. 26.

11. *A Living Theatre*. The Gordon Craig School. The Arena Goldoni, The Mask. Setting forth the aims and objects of the movement and showing by many illustrations the City of Florence, the Arena. Florence, 1913.

12. *Copeau: Texts on Theatre*, edited and translated by John Rudlin and Norman H. Paul, Routledge, 1990, p. 22.

13. 'Ernest Marriott' was almost certainly Craig himself who was notoriously fond of using several different pen-names in his magazine *The Mask* to disguise the fact that most of it was written by himself. 'Who is this Mr Marriott?' asked Copeau. 'I don't know, but I have some reservations about him' (op. cit., p. 20).

7. *The French Avant-Garde*

1. Copeau: Texts on Theatre, Introduction, p. xiii.

2. Ibid., p. 27.

3. Ibid., Notes, p. 226. Camus was writing in a brochure for a Copeau exhibition in 1959.

4. Ibid.

5. John Rudlin, *Jacques Copeau* (Directors in Perspective Series), CUP, 1986. This monograph, almost incredibly the first in English, is called by its author a useful 'primer' – and indeed, it paved the way for the later more expansive work mentioned in Note 12 of the previous chapter, which is such a valuable sourcebook of material hitherto mostly unavailable in English.

6. David Whitton, *Stage Directors in Modern France*, Manchester

University Press, 1987, p. 68. Actually, from a *Theatre Arts* 'Letter to Jacques Copeau' in October 1929, it would seem that it was Granville-Barker who said this to Copeau; although it is just possible that here he was quoting Copeau's own words back at him!

7. *Copeau: Texts on Theatre*, pp. 102 and 149.

8. Ibid., pp. 31–2.

9. Ibid., p. 255.

10. Ibid., p. 42.

11. This was Jean Dorcy (1895–1978) who in 1947 founded his own school of dance training, which numbered Marcel Marceau among its pupils. See *Copeau: Texts on Theatre*, Appendix H, p. 239.

12. A more detailed description of these courses is given in *Copeau: Texts on Theatre*, pp. 43–7.

13. These notes about Granville-Barker and the performance of the Noh *Kantan*, translated and adapted by Copeau and Bing from Arthur Waley's English version, were supplied by Copeau's daughter, Marie-Hélène Daste. They have been shortened slightly from the Note in *Copeau: Texts on Theatre*, p. 258. In October 1929, as referred to above, Granville-Barker wrote an interesting 'open letter' to Copeau, published in the American *Theatre Arts* magazine, in which he recommended acceptance of a directorship at the Comédie-Française should it be offered. It was not, despite a press campaign; but he eventually became an interim director in 1940, only to be discharged by the German occupation authorities in 1941 for anti-Nazi sympathies. Michel Saint-Denis commented that 'Our performance of *Kantan*, which left the impression of a spirited dream, was for me the incomparable summit of our work in Copeau's School/Laboratory' (*Training for the Theatre*, Heinemann, 1982, p. 33).

14. *Copeau: Texts on Theatre*, p. 49.

15. Benedetti, op. cit., p. 72.

16. *Copeau: Texts on Theatre*, pp. 51–4.

17. Ibid., pp. 81 and 87.

18. The Frontispiece to Craig's *The Theatre Advancing*, 1921, is of a 'Design for a theatre open to the air, the sun and the moon'.

19. *Copeau: Texts on Theatre*, p. 137.

20. Ibid., pp. 188 and 191.

8. *The Russian 'Revolution'*

1. Constantin Stanislavsky, *My Life in Art*, Geoffrey Bles, London, 1924. Chapter xlix is devoted to Sulerjitski, and Chapters lv and lvi to the First Studio.

2. Jean Benedetti, *Stanislavski: A Biography*, Methuen, 1988, p. 163 (quoting from the hitherto unpublished Stanislavski archive). As far as I know, the only other English translation to date of some of the archive

papers can be found in Konstantin Stanislavsky, *Selected Works*, compiled by Oksana Korneva, Raduga Publishers, Moscow, 1984. Methuen plan a ten-volume Collected Works, translated by Benedetti, between 1995 and 1998, based on the uncensored, unabridged Russian archive. Benedetti is also the author of the concise *Stanislavski: An Introduction*, Methuen, 1982.

3. Benedetti, *Stanislavski: A Biography*.

4. Ibid., p. 173.

5. *My Life in Art*, p. 537.

6. Benedetti, *Stanislavski: A Biography*, pp. 180 and 189.

7. *My Life in Art*, p. 525.

8. Benedetti, *Stanislavski: A Biography*, pp. 198–9.

9. In writing of emotion and the voice, in particular, Stanislavski tells a story which remarkably forestalls the experience of Alfred Wolfson and the establishment of the Roy Hart Theatre in the 1950s. He was walking in the Caucasus with an actor who had a very weak voice which no normal training had been able to help. Suddenly they were attacked by sheep-dogs. 'My comrade shouted so loud in his fright that he could be heard a mile away. He had a very strong voice, but only nature could control it' (*My Life in Art*, p. 429).

10. Ibid., p. 430.

11. Edward Braun, *Meyerhold on Theatre*, Methuen, 1969 (reissued, 1995), p. 41.

12. *My Life in Art*, p. 434.

13. Ibid., p. 435.

14. Braun, op. cit., p. 40. From Meyerhold's own account of the Theatre Studio, which describes in some detail its ideals and work. One of his more interesting conclusions was that 'An acting school must exist *independently* [his italics] and must not teach the current style of acting.' The complicated and emotional internal politics *vis-à-vis* the Moscow Art company and the Theatre Studio and Meyerhold are given full description in Chapter 12 of Benedetti's *Stanislavski: A Biography*.

15. Benedetti, *Stanislavski: A Biography*, p. 151.

16. Braun, op. cit., p. 40.

17. Ibid., p. 20.

18. *My Life in Art*, p. 483.

19. Benedetti, *Stanislavski: A Biography*, p. 197.

20. *My Life in Art*, pp. 531–4.

21. Ibid., pp. 538–9.

22. Ibid., p. 540.

23. Benedetti, *Stanislavski: A Biography*, p. 199.

24. Ibid., p. 221.

25. *My Life in Art*, p. 558.

26. Sonia Moore, *The Stanislavski Method*, Viking Press, 1960; later revised in 1965 as *The Stanislavski System: The Professional Training of an*

Actor, Digested from the Teachings of Konstantin S. Stanislavski. Her Russian source material was the most up-to-date and comprehensive at the time, though Benedetti's researches superseded it. Then in 1991, she published *Stanislavski Revealed: The Actor's Guide to Spontaneity on Stage*, Applause Books, New York.

27. Stella Adler, *The Technique of Acting*, Bantam Books, New York, 1988.

28. Evreinov, rather like Sulerjitski, was a man of many parts: a playwright, an actor, a circus performer, a composer, a painter, a novelist, a critic, an historian, a philosopher, a psychologist, a biologist, an archaeologist, and a graduate of law. He had also been a government official, a teacher and a world traveller. It seems that the Russian temperament early in this century produced such Renaissance men. His plays included two comic satires, *Revisor* (1912) and *The Fourth Wall* (1915), a monodrama defining his understanding of the art called *The Theatre of the Soul* (1912), and a play which found itself in the opening season of the New York Theatre Guild, *The Chief Thing* (1921). His theatrical credo, *The Theatre in Life* (Harrap, 1927) provided what Oliver H. Sayler describes in his Introduction as 'the first adequate statement of the psychological foundations of the revolt against dramatic realism'.

29. Braun, op. cit., p. 80.

30. Ibid., p. 211. Braun devotes the whole of Part Six of his book to the production, giving detailed descriptions and photographs. Braun has also published in *New Theatre Quarterly*, No. 33, February 1993, an account of 'Meyerhold: the Final Act' drawing upon new revelations from the opening of the KGB files on 'Case No. 537'. This material is updated and included in Braun's new edition of *The Theatre of Meyerhold: Revolution on the Modern Stage*, Methuen, 1995. In October 1995, at Aberystwyth, the Centre for Performance Research held a symposium devoted to Meyerhold and to his biomechanical exercises.

31. James Roose-Evans, *Experimental Theatre*, Studio Vista, 1970, p. 28. Fourth edition, revised and updated, Routledge, 1989, p. 33. The new edition has a useful and much more comprehensive bibliography; also new and extended chapters.

32. Theodore Komisarjevsky, *The Theatre and a Changing Civilization*, John Lane, The Bodley Head, 1935, p. 122. He goes on to say that the best actors at the Moscow Art Theatre did not follow the System to the letter, but nevertheless a positive *inner* ensemble was created in the best productions. It is interesting to note that long before American 'Method actors' were called 'mumblers', the 'old school' of Moscow actors used to call the Moscow Art Company 'whisperers'. Of the work of the Studios in Moscow, Komisarjevsky comments: 'Trained by Stanislavski's pedantic acolytes, lacking imaginative experience, these young actors gave weak reproductions of their own inner selves in intimate productions done in small

rooms.' John Gielgud writes at some length of Komisarjevski in Chapter 4 of *An Actor and His Time*, Sidgwick and Jackson, 1979. He worked with Komisarjevski, first in 1926 playing Tusenbach in *Three Sisters*, and finally in 1947 when Komisarjevski directed *Crime and Punishment* in New York, Gielgud playing Raskolnikov. 'Komisarjevski was a fascinating character, who looked like a little monk, completely bald and with the most enchanting smile. He had an impish, rather wicked humour, but was prone to "Russian moods" when things were not going well, when he would maintain a grim silence. He loved young people, especially if he thought they had talent . . . The stage hands all liked him and worked hard to please him.'

33. To those American books already mentioned, the following deserve noting in the context of Stanislavski's influence there:

Richard Boleslavsky, *Acting: The First Six Lessons*, Theatre Arts Books, New York, 1933.

Michael Chekhov, *To the Actor*, Harper and Row, New York, 1953.

Michael Chekhov, *Lessons for the Professional Actor*, Performing Arts Journal Publications, New York, 1985.

Robert Lewis, *Method or Madness*, Samuel French, New York, 1958. (This was the first book in America to seriously query the 'Method'.)

Lee Strasberg, *A Dream of Passion*, Bloomsbury, 1988. (Strasberg's shortcomings in his approach to the 'Method' have already been mentioned in the text. There is further comment when discussing Harold Clurman and his 'Fervent Years' with the American Group Theatre in Chapter 5.

34. Benedetti, *Stanislavski: A Biography*, pp. 316–17 gives details of this summary.

35. V. O. Toporkov, *Stanislavski in Rehearsal: The Final Years*, Theatre Arts Books, New York, 1979.

36. Verbatim comments noted by the author.

9. *The German Twenties*

1. From 'Objective Acting', an essay written for *Actors on Acting*, edited by Toby Cole and Helen Krich Chinoy, New Revised Edition, Crown, New York, 1970, pp. 301–2. This is an invaluable sourcebook for the history of acting. A much more recent sourcebook addresses this century alone, with key texts from creative practitioners. However, *Twentieth Century Theatre: A Sourcebook*, edited by Richard Drain, Routledge, 1995, is a rather inadequate anthology, omitting anything from Copeau or the Cartel des Quatre, and from Barrault, Guthrie, Strehler or Planchon.

2. These form a unique Appendix to *Max Reinhardt* by J. L. Styan, Directors in Perspective Series, CUP, 1982.

3. Gottfried Reinhardt, *The Genius: A Memoir of Max Reinhardt by his Son*, New York, 1979, p. 365 (quoted by Styan).

4. John Willett, *The Theatre of Erwin Piscator: Half a Century of*

Politics in Theatre, Eyre Methuen, 1978, p. 43.

  5. Edward Braun, *The Director and the Stage: From Naturalism to Grotowski*, Methuen, 1982, p. 145.

  6. Erwin Piscator, *The Political Theatre*, translated with introduction and notes by Hugh Rorrison, Eyre Methuen, 1980, pp. 121–2 (quoted by Braun, p. 153).

  7. Quoted by Duerr, op. cit., p. 456.

  8. Roose-Evans, op. cit., pp. 66–7.

  9. C. D. Innes, *Erwin Piscator's Political Theatre: The Development of Modern German Drama*, CUP, 1972, pp. 113–17 and 95–7. Following the Arts Council Exhibition at the Hayward Gallery, this book was a timely defence of Piscator's importance and originality when so many commentators seemed to have dismissed him because of his attitude to the actor (e.g. Norman Marshall in *The Producer and the Play*, 1957, and even Willett and Esslin in their books on Brecht).

  10. Braun, op. cit., p. 154.

  11. John Allen, *A History of the Theatre in Europe*, Heinemann, 1983, p. 288.

  12. These comments occur in Brecht's *The Messingkauf Dialogues*, composed between 1939 and 1942 in the USA, and published in a translation by John Willett (Methuen, 1965, p. 67). Perhaps it should be added that he prefaced the comments by calling Piscator 'one of the greatest theatre men of all time'.

  13. Willett, op. cit., p. 188; also quoted by Braun, op. cit., p. 168.

  14. Braun, op. cit., p. 161.

  15. It is interesting to relate this remark to that of Stanislavski reported by Anatoly Efros in Chapter 8.

  16. *Brecht on Theatre: The Development of an Aesthetic*, edited and translated by John Willett, Methuen, 1964, p. 283.

  17. John Willett, *The Theatre of Bertolt Brecht: A Study from Eight Aspects*, Methuen, 1989, third edition revised; Univeristy Paperbacks, 1967, pp. 112 and 124.

  18. Willett, op. cit., p. 145.

  19. Willett, op. cit., p. 148 (with photos on pp. 171 and 173).

  20. *Brecht on Theatre*, pp. 53–6.

  21. Braun, op. cit., pp. 173–4.

  22. Tony Cottrell, *Evolving Stages: A Layman's Guide to 20th-Century Theatre*, The Bristol Press, 1991, p. 37.

  23. Braun, op. cit., p. 168.

  24. *Brecht on Theatre*, pp. 200–1.

  25. Ibid., pp. 26–7.

  26. Ibid., p. 138.

  27. Richard Eyre, 'Confessions of a Failed Actor', *Observer*, 14 March 1993, extracted from his book *Utopia and Other Places*, Bloomsbury, 1993.

28. *Brecht on Theatre*, pp. 186–7. A 'long overdue assessment' of Brecht is made in John Fuegi's *Life and Lies of Bertolt Brecht*, Harper-Collins, 1994.

29. Ibid., pp. 202, 204.

30. *The Times*, 12 February 1993.

10. *The 'Turbulent Thirties'*

1. J. C. Trewin, Raymond Mander and Joe Mitchenson, *The Turbulent Thirties: A Decade of the Theatre*, Macdonald, 1960.

2. John Gielgud, *An Actor and His Time*, in collaboration with John Miller and John Powell. Based on a series of BBC Radio interviews. Sidgwick and Jackson, 1979, p. 78. Gielgud thought that Baylis never saw a play right through and doubted whether she 'had any real understanding of Shakespeare'.

3. Foreword to Michel Saint-Denis' *Training for the Theatre Premises and Promises*, Heinemann, London; Theatre Arts Books, New York, 1982, pp. 13–15.

4. Michel Saint-Denis, *Theatre: The Rediscovery of Style*, Heinemann, 1960, p. 41.

5. Ibid., p. 34.

6. *Training for the Theatre*, p. 46.

7. *Theatre*, pp. 54–5.

8. *Training for the Theatre*, p. 49.

9. *Theatre*, pp. 61–70.

10. Ibid., p. 92.

11. *Training for the Theatre*, p. 11.

12. Sally Beauman comments that, invited by Peter Hall to 'bring Europe into the company', Saint-Denis' Studio training was severely curtailed by his ill-health. *The Royal Shakespeare Company: A History of Ten Decades*, OUP, 1982, p. 249.

13. *Theatre*, Introduction, p. 12.

14. *Training for the Theatre*, p. 66.

15. Tyrone Guthrie, *In Various Directions: A View of Theatre*, Michael Joseph, 1965, p. 19.

16. George Rowell, *The Old Vic Theatre: A History*, CUP, 1993, p. 123.

17. *In Various Directions*, p. 21.

18. Tyrone Guthrie, *Theatre Prospect*, Wishart, 1932, p. 62.

19. Irving Wardle, *The Theatres of George Devine*, Cape, 1978, p. 138.

20. John Elsom and Nicholas Tomalin, *The History of the National Theatre*, Cape, 1978, p. 100, quoted in Rowell, op. cit., p. 143.

21. *Tyrone Guthrie on Acting*, Studio Vista, 1971, pp. 30–1.

22. Ibid., pp. 8, 9, 29.

23. Rudi Shelly, doyen of acting teaching at the Bristol Old Vic Theatre School, always defined acting as 'the art of reacting'.

24. *Tyrone Guthrie on Acting*, p. 14.

25. Ibid., p. 32.

26. Ibid., p. 94.

27. Harold Clurman, *The Fervent Years: The Story of the Group Theatre and the Thirties*, Dobson, London, 1946, p. 5. Clurman's book is obviously an authoritative source; but a full and much later study was published in 1990 by Knopf, New York. This is Wendy Smith's *Real Life: The Group Theatre and America 1931–1940*.

28. Ibid., p. 7.

29. Ibid., p. 32.

30. Ibid., pp. 87–8.

31. Ibid., p. 42.

32. Ibid., p. 148.

33. Ibid., p. 149. 'Awake and Sing' was revived in the spring of 1994 by the Birmingham Repertory Company, directed by Bill Alexander.

34. Ibid., p. 62.

35. Ibid., p. 158.

36. Ibid., pp. 193–6.

37. Ibid., p. 297.

38. John Allen, in his Foreword to Michael Sidnell's *Dances of Death: The Group Theatre of London in the Thirties*, Faber, 1984.

39. Sidnell, op. cit., p. 62.

40. Ibid., Appendices C and D.

41. Antonin Artaud, *The Theatre and its Double*, translated by Mary Caroline Richards, Grove Press, New York, 1958, p. 133.

42. Martin Esslin, *Artaud*, Fontana/Collins, 1976, pp. 12, 14.

43. Ibid., p. 38.

44. Ronald Hayman, *Artaud and After*, OUP, 1977, pp. 41, 50. This book was the result of Hayman's work on an exhibition of the same name held at the National Book League, London, from October to November 1977. It is rich in detail from both the life and works of Artaud, plus interpretive comment; and from the exhibition, of course, there are some very interesting photographs. Hayman comments that 'Thirty years after Artaud's death [in 1998 it will be fifty years], it is still hard to draw up a balance-sheet of what was progressive and what was retrogressive in his thinking. Though the use of the word "signs" for the component elements of theatrical language may seem to anticipate semiological analysis, what Artaud was expounding was not a science of signs but a metaphysic of signs' (op. cit., p. 79).

That Artaud retains his fascination for students in the 1990s is indicated by the publication of a new full-length biography of Artaud by Stephen

Barber, *Antonin Artaud: Blows and Bombs*, Faber, 1993.

45. Hayman, op. cit., pp. 135–6, where a fuller account of the poetry reading is given.

46. Esslin, op. cit., p. 9.

47. Ibid., p. 44.

48. Ibid., pp. 28 and 78.

49. Ibid., p. 116.

50. Hayman, op. cit., p. 101.

51. Jean-Louis Barrault, *Souvenirs pour demain*, Paris, 1972, translated by Jonathan Griffin in 1974 and published by Thames and Hudson as *Memories for Tomorrow: The Memoirs of Jean-Louis Barrault*, pp. 80 and 83. In both his earlier books, *Reflections on the Theatre* (Paris, 1949; translated by Barbara Wall, Rockliff, 1951, and Theatre Book Club, 1952), and *New Reflections on the Theatre* (Paris, 1959; translated by Joseph Chiari, with a preface by Armand Salacrou, as *The Theatre of Jean-Louis Barrault*, Barrie and Rockliff, 1961), Barrault presented those ideas and comments which found their more considered repetition in his memoirs. All three books are excellent and most readable accounts, and all three are subsequently quoted from here, but obviously most material has been taken from the most recent in composition. The title of the memoirs derives from Barrault's observation that he does not wish to talk about himself so much as to recollect himself so as not to be lost: 'The memory of yesterday exists only so as to serve tomorrow.'

52. *Memories for Tomorrow*, pp. 47 and 45.

53. *Reflections on the Theatre*, p. 18.

54. *Memories for Tomorrow*, p. 75.

55. *The Theatre of Jean-Louis Barrault*, p. 36.

56. Ibid., p. 38.

57. *Memories for Tomorrow*, p. 151.

58. Ibid., p. 268.

59. Ibid., pp. 294, 296.

60. Ibid., p. 325.

61. Ibid., p. 328.

62. *The Theatre of Jean-Louis Barrault*, p. 56.

11. *A Note on the Fifties' Watershed*

1. John Elsom, *Theatre Outside London*, Macmillan, 1971, quoted by Howard Goorney (see below), p. 184.

2. John Osborne, *Almost a Gentleman*, Faber, 1991, p. 15.

3. Ronald Hayman, *British Theatre since 1955*, OUP, 1979, p. 131. Howard Goorney's *The Theatre Workshop Story*, Methuen, 1981, is probably the best account of Joan Littlewood's work. She is the only woman director mentioned in the otherwise male-dominated historical compendium

Directors on Directing by Cole and Chinoy (revised edition, Peter Owen, 1970). In it, various actors from the Theatre Workshop company describe what it was like working with her. It took her until 1994 to publish her own autobiography, nearly 800 pages of it, as *Joan's Book*, with the idiosyncratic subtitle of 'Joan Littlewood's Peculiar History As She Tells It'. This was reviewed by John Peter in the *Sunday Times* for 27 March 1994 as 'an exuberant but ultimately sad book, a disappointing account of what should have been a triumphant life. . . . Littlewood is a fighter who never knew how to win. Even when she did win, she did not know how to hold the fort.'

4. Whitton, *Stage Directors in Modern France*, p. 220.

5. Saint-Denis, *Theatre: The Rediscovery of Style*, pp. 87–8.

6. Whitton, op. cit., p. 222.

7. Ibid., p. 223.

8. Ibid., p. 228.

9. Irving Wardle, *The Theatres of George Devine*, Cape, 1978, p. 226.

10. Ronald Hayman, *The Set-Up: An Anatomy of the English Theatre Today*, Methuen, 1973, p. 160.

11. Richard Findlater (ed.), *At the Royal Court: 25 Years of the English Stage Company*, Amber Lane Press, 1981, pp. 7 and 29.

12. Joan Plowright in *At the Royal Court*, pp. 32 and 34.

13. Wardle, op. cit., p. 261.

14. Ibid., p. 279.

12. *The European Gurus*

1. From the article 'Theatre's Conjuring Spirit' by James Woodall in the *Sunday Times*, 8 November 1992. Nick Dear is the author of *The Art of Success*, and adaptor of Tirso de Molina's *Last Days of Don Juan* for the RSC, and Ostrovsky's *A Family Affair* for Cheek by Jowl. His most recent work is *Zenobia* for the RSC (August 1995). Peter Brook's new presentation at the Bouffes du Nord, Paris, in January 1966, *Qui Est Là*, appears to resemble an interim essay towards *Signals Through the Flames*. Michael Billington described it as 'an extraordinary mosaic in which scenes from Hamlet are interspersed with passages from Stanislavski, Meyerhold, Brecht, Craig, Artaud and the Noh master Zeami. The result is spare, economical and illuminating: a meditation not just on Shakespeare and the mystery of theatre but on life, death and the transforming power of the imagination' (*Guardian*, 10 January 1966). In many ways, Billington says, he was reminded of Brook's previous production, *The Man Who*, where the stage 'took on the role of a research laboratory'. Here again, the theatre's empty space becomes an arena for enquiry, both intellectual and emotional. 'What he is exploring is the whole meaning of representation, of how the theatre

accommodates life and of how the symbolism of gesture varies between cultures.'

2. From the article 'Disability as a Family Affair' by Michael Billington, *Guardian*, 13 March 1993.

3. Yoshi Oida, *An Actor Adrift*, Methuen, 1992, pp. 158–9, 162 and 94.

4. Peter Brook, *There Are No Secrets: Thoughts on Acting and Theatre*, Methuen, 1993, pp. 16–17.

5. Ibid., p. 66.

6. Ibid., p. 72.

7. Ibid., p. 50.

8. Ibid., p. 54.

9. From 'Marginal Notes', a pamphlet by Tadeusz Kantor, translated by Marein J. Dabrowski, and made available at performances of *The Cloak Room* given at the Traverse Theatre during the 1964 Edinburgh Festival.

10. Ibid., with adjustments made of layout and syntax to clarify the assessed meaning.

11. Ibid., from Wieslaw Borowski's 'Function of the Text in the Plays of T. Kantor', extracts of which were included in the pamphlet.

12. Ibid.

13. James Roose-Evans, *Experimental Theatre*, fourth edition, revised and updated, Routledge, 1989, p. 157. The book gives two chapters to Grotowski.

14. Christopher Innes, *Avant Garde Theatre 1892–1992*, Routledge, 1993, p. 149.

15. Ibid., p. 151. Roose-Evans gives a description of *Acropolis*, premièred in 1962 at Wroclaw but given in a revised 1967 version at Edinburgh in 1968, and at the Arnolfini, Bristol, as late as May 1984. The original play by Wyspianski was first produced in 1904 and was set in Cracow Cathedral on the eve of Easter Sunday. 'The statues and paintings in the cathedral come to life and re-enact various biblical and Homeric themes. Grotowski moved the action to Auschwitz ... relating it to the experiences of Poland during the Second World War [and testing] how far the classical idea of human dignity could withstand [that] insight into human degradation' (Roose-Evans, op. cit., pp. 149-50).

16. From a text known as 'Holiday', quoted by Jennifer Kumiega in *Laboratory Theatre/Grotowski/The Mountain Project*, Theatre Papers, Second Series, No. 9, edited by Peter Hulton, Department of Theatre, Dartington College of Art, 1978. Kumiega worked with the Laboratory Theatre in 1975 and 1977. In 1985 her definitive study in English, *The Theatre of Grotowski*, was published by Methuen.

17. Kumiega, *Laboratory Theatre*, p. 3.

18. Innes, op. cit., pp. 153–4.

19. Jerzy Grotowski, *Towards a Poor Theatre*, Odin Teatrets Forlag,

1968 (Methuen, 1970), p. 194.

20. Grotowski, interviewed by Claude Sarraute in *Le Monde*, weekly selection in English, 4 June 1969.

21. Quoted by John Russell Brown in *Effective Theatre*, Heinemann, 1969.

22. Grotowski in the *Los Angeles Times*, 1983, quoted by Richard Fowler in 'The Four Theatres of Jerzy Grotowski: An Introductory Assessment', *New Theatre Quarterly*, No. 2, May 1985.

23. John Allen, *Theatre in Europe*, Offord Publications, City Arts Series, 1981, p. 140. Allen's information was drawn from a programme note on the history of the Piccolo Theatre – *La Storia della Bambola Abbandonata*, 1976.

24. Michael Billington, 'The Magician and Mephistopheles', *Guardian*, 16 May 1990.

25. Luigi Pirandello, *The Mountain Giants: A Myth*, translated by Felicity Firth, *The British Pirandello Society Yearbooks*, No. 10, 1990, pp. 8 and 105. The final section of the play, although fairly fully described, was never finished by Pirandello. Charles Wood translated and completed his own version for the National Theatre, first performed in July 1993, and published by Methuen.

26. Andrea Bisicchia, 'Giorgio Strehler's Production of *I Giganti della. Montagna* in the Context of its Performance History', translated by Felicity Firth, *The Yearbook of the Society for Pirandello Studies*, No. 11, 1991, pp. 1–22. Since the first professional production in England with Charles Wood's version at the National, this essay is of particular interest to Pirandello 'buffs', with its fascinating description of the first open-air production in 1937, which linked with the painters Arnold Böcklin (whose 'Island of the Dead' painted in 1880 also influenced Strindberg) and Giorgio de Chirico with his objects in surrealist space akin to Pirandello's 'arsenal of apparitions'. Strehler, too, was partially guided by the pictorial link with the two painters. Bisicchia also gives a full description and commentary on Strehler's 1966 production.

27. Corrado Stajano and Neil Wallace, *Guardian*, 18 February 1993.

28. Billington, op. cit.

29. Ibid.

30. Wallace, op. cit.

31. *Plays and Players*, December 1992.

32. Christopher Balme, 'Giorgio Strehler's Faust Project: Signification and Reception Strategies', *New Theatre Quarterly*, No. 35, August 1993.

33. Ibid.

34. Italo Alighiero Chinsano, in June 1991, quoted by Balme.

35. Strehler in April 1991. All the quotations in this paragraph are from Balme, op. cit.

36. Simon Reade, 'Teutonic or Not Teutonic?', *Observer*, 15 August

1993.

37. Michael Patterson, *Peter Stein: Germany's Leading Theatre Director*, CUP, 1981, p. 7.

38. Stein, 18 October 1980, quoted by Patterson, op. cit., p. 156.

39. Patterson, op. cit., pp. 132–49.

40. Roose-Evans, op. cit., p. 71.

41. Denis Staunton, 'Trouble in the Riding School as Café Life Continues', *Observer*, 1 August 1993.

42. *Guardian*, 3 September 1993.

43. *Guardian*, 4 August 1993.

44. *Guardian*, 3 September 1993.

45. Yvette Daoust, *Roger Planchon: Director and Playwright*, CUP, 1981, pp. 5, 6, and 8.

46. Planchon, in an interview with Michael Kustow, 'Creating a Theatre of Real Life', *Theatre Quarterly*, January–March 1972, quoted by Daoust, op. cit., p. 9.

47. Roger Planchon, 'Killing Culture', *Guardian*, 21 July 1993.

48. Daoust, op. cit., pp. 10–11.

49. Ibid., p. 27.

50. Ibid., pp. 217–18.

51. Michael Kustow, 'The Country Cook', *Guardian*, 13 September 1991.

52. Daoust, op. cit., p. 213.

53. Ibid., p. 214.

54. From a 1964 interview, quoted by Whitton, op. cit., p. 243.

55. Whitton, op. cit., p. 255.

56. Ibid., pp. 251–2.

57. Quoted in ibid., p. 254.

58. Daoust, op. cit., p. 21.

59. Ibid. It is very appropriate, therefore, that Planchon's latest production should be at the Comédie-Française (where most French theatrical rebels eventually arrive) and should 'redefine' Feydeau (in this case, *Occupe-toi d'Amélie*) with 'impassioned human beings rather than whirling puppets ... more social comedy than heartless farce' (Michael Billington, *Guardian*, 10 January 1966).

60. Whitton, op. cit., p. 255.

61. From programme note, *Les Atrides*, Bradford.

62. These productions are reported fully by Whitton, op. cit., pp. 263–71.

63. The Hélène Cixous plays are described at some length by Innes in *Avant Garde Theatre*, pp. 211–13.

64. *Guardian*, 13 December 1990, and *Observer*, 26 July 1992. For students who wish to study Mnouchkine more fully, there is a monograph by Adrian Kiernanda, *Ariane Mnouchkine*, CUP, 1992; and for fifty years

of the French influence generally, David Bradby's *Modern French Drama 1940–1990*, updated edition, CUP, 1991, is to be recommended.

13. *The American Actor*

1. Allardyce Nicoll in *The Oxford Companion to the Theatre*, third edition, 1967, pp. 965ff.

2. Travis Bogard, Richard Moody and Walter J. Meserve, *The Revels History of Drama in English*, Vol. VIII, *American Drama* (General Editor: T. W. Craik), Methuen, London; Barnes and Noble, New York, 1977, pp. 43–4.

3. Ibid., p. 23.

4. John Lahr, *Acting Out America: Essays in Modern Theatre*, Pelican, 1972, p. 13.

5. Quoted by Nicoll in the *Oxford Companion*, p. 973.

6. Jack Morrison, ibid., p. 977.

14. *The Nineties in Britain*

1. William Archer and Harley Granville-Barker, *A National Theatre: Scheme and Estimates*, Duckworth, 1907; Harley Granville-Barker, *The Exemplary Theatre*, Chatto and Windus, 1922; Harley Granville-Barker, *The National Theatre*, Sidgwick and Jackson, 1930; Geoffrey Whitworth, *The Theatre of My Heart*, Gollancz, 1930 (revised, 1938). This book ends with a charming invocation:

Some seeds the birds devour,
  And some the season mars;
But here and there will flower
  The solitary star.
Such a star is the National Theatre. May it flower soon!

It was to take another thirty-three years for a company to be formed; and forty-six years before the building arose.

Geoffrey Whitworth, *The Making of a National Theatre*, Faber, 1951; Judith Cook, *The National Theatre*, Harrap, 1976; John Elsom and Nicholas Tomalin, *The History of the National Theatre*, Cape, 1978; Laurence Olivier, *Confessions of an Actor*, Weidenfeld and Nicolson, 1982; Peter Hall, *Diaries*, edited by John Goodwin, Hamish Hamilton, 1983; Peter Lewis, *The National: A Dream Made Concrete*, Methuen, 1990.

2. Granville-Barker's Preface to *The Exemplary Theatre*, p. vii.

3. Lewis, op. cit., p. 46.

4. Milton Johns, 'Letters to a Young Actor 36', *The Stage*, 20 January 1994.

5. Caroline Lees, 'Shakespeare and the Money Men', *Evening Standard*, 20 January 1994.

6. *Guardian*, 19 January 1994.

7. 'The Culture Forum', *Sunday Times*, 16 January 1994.

8. Samuel Johnson, *Rasselas* (1759), ch. 10.

PART THREE: The Future

15. *New Forms, New Language, Old Needs*

1. John Elsom, *Theatre Outside London*, Macmillan, 1971, p. 128.

2. *Sunday Times*, 23 January 1994.

3. Quoted by Lyn Gardner, *Guardian*, 9 November 1993.

4. Joanna Scanlan, Arts Council live art officer, quoted in an article by Andy Lavender in *The Times*, 1 December 1993.

5. Denis Staunton, 'Staging a Mute Point', *Guardian*, 17 February 1994.

6. Ibid.

7. David Gale, 'Wooster Source', *Guardian*, 23 January 1993.

8. Kenneth Rea, 'Who Cares Whose Line It Is?', *The Times*, 26 October 1992.

9. Susan Hiller, quoted by Guy Brett in 'That Inner Vision Thing at Freud's', *Guardian*, 16 April 1994.

10. Lyn Gardner, 'Let's Get Physical', *Guardian*, 22 September 1993.

11. Ibid.

12. Michael Billington, 'The Inarticulate Body', *Guardian*, 11 September 1993.

13. Interviewed by David Robinson in *The Times*, 21 April 1973.

14. Ronald Blythe, *Akenfield*, Allen Lane, 1969; Penguin Books, 1972, p. 320.

15. Michael Billington, introducing a *Guardian* supplement on Drama, in association with BBC Radio, 9 April 1994.

16. Don Cupitt, 'The Kingdom Is Coming – So Book Your Ticket', *Guardian*, 19 February 1994.

17. Harley Granville-Barker, *The Use of Drama*, Sidgwick and Jackson, 1946, p. 69.

18. Martin Esslin, *Brief Chronicles*, Temple Smith, 1970, p. 288.

16. *'Controlled Environments'*

1. Sue Corbett, 'Life upon the Museum Stage', *The Stage*, 26 May 1994.

2. Rosemary Linnell of Theatre in Museum Education, writing to *The*

Stage, 16 June 1994.

3. Paul Fisher, 'Serious Suits Get Lost in Space', *Guardian*, 7 January 1993.

4. Jack Schofield, 'Actor Performs in Virtual Reality', *Guardian*, 5 February 1994.

5. Benjamin Woolley, *Virtual Worlds: A Journey in Hype and Hyperreality*, Blackwell, 1992; Penguin, 1993, p. 240.

6. Howard Rheingold, *Virtual Reality*, Secker and Warburg, 1991; Mandarin Paperbacks, 1992, p. 46.

7. Charles Tart, 'Models of the Mind: Virtual Reality and Transpersonal Psychology', lecture to the Society for Psychical Research, 26 June 1992. (Available on cassette from J. and R. Recordings, 84 Herbert Gardens, London, NW10 3BU.)

8. Douglas Adams, author of *The Hitchhiker's Guide to the Galaxy*, speaking on *Desert Island Discs*, BBC Radio 4, 11 February 1994.

9. Woolley, op. cit., pp. 2 and 4.

10. Ibid., pp. 110, 114, and 119.

11. Julian Hilton of East Anglia University in an unpublished paper 'Theatricality and Technology: Pygmalion and the Myth of the Intelligent Machine', quoted by Woolley, op. cit., p. 118.

12. Brenda Laurel, *Computers as Theatre*, Menlo Park, California: Addison-Wesley, 1991, quoted by Rheingold, op. cit., p. 300.

13. Joseph Campbell, *Day of the Dead* (1988), quoted by Rheingold, op. cit., p. 299.

14. Rheingold, op. cit., p. 386.

15. *Observer*, 13 February 1994.

16. Woolley, op. cit., pp. 127 and 134. If proof were needed that we are already deeply involved in the technological pursuit of life in the 'global village', it is not only the high profile now being given to the Internet and World Wide Web in the daily press that underscores it. It is in the projected nature of future work indicated by such advertisements as the following which appeared in the *Guardian*, 18 September 1995:

> The University of the West of England has launched an innovative research programme in collaboration with Hewlett Packard Research Laboratories, Bristol... The Digital Media Research Group is now seeking prospective research students for [three projects]:
> *The Medium Formerly Known as Text*
> *True Stories and*
> *Virtual Stories*

The description for the latter project, Virtual Stories, reads:

> to research the potential for narrative development within virtual real-

ity environments and ways of blending recorded and real time images
in VR. This project builds on work by an existing multidisciplinary
team in the creation of populated virtual worlds. You should be interested in new forms of narrative and understand 3D graphics modelling.

This might almost be a job description for a dramatist, combined with the
talents of a Disney live actor/cartoon film maker (à la Bob Hoskins and the
Rabbit, only in virtual depth).

17. Randall Walser, 'Elements of a Cyberspace Playhouse', Proceedings of the National Computer Graphics Association '90, quoted by Woolley,
op. cit., pp. 161ff.

18. Ibid.

19. Ibid.

20. Ibid.

21. *London Evening Standard*, 6 April 1994.

Further advances in the field of the 'interactive movie' where 'the
only co-star is you' were reported in the *Sunday Times*, 17 July 1994 ('Casting
Couch Potatoes' by Tim Green). A software company has produced a de-
tective drama 'somewhere between a computer game and a film' in which
the player (he cannot just be called a viewer or contestant any longer) takes
on the role of a 'private eye' in the 'computer-rendered streets and buildings of San Francisco 50 years in the future'. The player 'grills the characters met ... and their responses determine the course of the adventure'.

The 'characters', of course, are actors who have recorded their scenes
'without props in front of a blue "chromakey" background which is edited
out later'. Already the American Screen Actors Guild have drawn up a
Standard Interactive Movie Agreement. 'After 11 months, 2000 SAG members had earned two million dollars from it.' In the UK interactive movies
are only just beginning to be made; and Equity reported its first Agreement
concluded in September 1995.

22. Baudrillard, quoted by Woolley, op. cit., pp. 201 and 209.

23. Woolley, op. cit., pp. 218ff.

24. Iain Mackintosh, *Architecture, Actor and Audience*, Routledge,
1993, pp. 159ff.

25. Ibid., pp. 172 and 169.

26. Ibid., p. 87.

27. Neil Wallace, 'The Conquest of Space', *Guardian*, 4 May 1994.

17. *Towards Ritual*

1. James Roose-Evans, *Passages of the Soul: Ritual Today*, Element,
1994, p. 155.

2. The sources of the three quotations are: Craig, *On the Art of the*

Theatre, 1911; Mercury Books, 1962, p. 248; Granville-Barker, *The Exemplary Theatre*, Chatto and Windus, 1922, p. 78; and *Brecht on Theatre* (trans. Willett), Methuen, 1964, p. 73.

3. Erving Goffman, *The Presentation of Self in Everyday Life*, Allen Lane, 1969; Pelican Books, 1972, pp. 220 and 225.

4. Roose-Evans, op. cit., p. 34.

5. Richard Kostelanetz, *The Theatre of Mixed Means*, Pitman, 1970, p. 77.

6. Howard R. Lewis and Harold S. Streitfield, *Growth Games*, New York, 1970; Souvenir Press, London, 1972; Paladin Books, 1973, pp. 263–4. Roose-Evans describes at much greater length a more recent and extraordinary ritual which Anna Halprin created, repeated over a five-year period, called 'Circle the Mountain' (1981–5). See *Passages of the Soul*, pp. 33–41.

7. Lorna St Aubyn, *Rituals for Everyday Living: Special Ways of Marking Important Events in Your Life*, Piatkus Books, 1994.

8. Richard Schechner, *The Future of Ritual*, Routledge, 1993, pp. 238 and 245.

9. Ibid., pp. 253–4. Schechner is quoting from *Workcentre of Jerzy Grotowski*, Pontedera, Italy, 1988: Centro per la Sperimentazione e la Ricerca Teatrale.

10. Peter Brook, *There Are No Secrets*, p. 87.

11. Alessandro Fersen's remarks were noted verbatim by the author at the International Theatre Conference, 'Points of Contact: Performance, Ritual and Shamanism', held at the Centre for Performance Research at Cardiff in January 1993. The CPR and its widely-informed and innovative artistic director, Richard Gough, were also responsible for inviting a visit by Enrique Vargas's company *Taller de la investigacion de la Imagen Teatral* (Investigation Workshop of the Dramatic Image), in October 1994. The company is based at the National University of Colombia at Bogotá, and has extensively toured its award-winning project *Ariadne's Thread – The Labyrinth* to festivals in Chile, Portugal, Spain, Italy, Brazil, Venezuela and the USA. This was its first visit to Britain, and its work parallels some of Fersen's ideas in Mnemodrama, especially in the tactile use of carefully chosen props, and in clearing the way for the arousal of memories, both personal and anciently racial.

The play – and they *do* call it a play – of *Ariadne's Thread* takes place in a real labyrinth set, a large and complicated installation which took five days to construct in the old gymnasium at the Howardian Community Education Centre in Cardiff. It takes its story from the Theseus and Minotaur myth and from Ulysses' journey to Ithaca, but its roots are deeply embedded in pre-Columbian cultures and the magical world of Latin America. It is very much a one-to-one theatrical experience which proposes a game to each individual member of its audience as they explore barefoot, alone, and in almost total darkness, the labyrinth's paths, crossroads and pass-

ageways, 'seeking the tracks of the Minotaur, the immemorial inhabitant of
its regions'. (The secret and very personal nature of its revelation is certainly a considerable *coup de théâtre*.) In the darkness of the labyrinth,
words – of which there are a few, mostly whispered – give way to silence,
to scents, to touches of the most sensitive and evocative kind, and to set
images of an almost surrealist nature. For each member of the audience,
the exploration takes about an hour; for the company it takes over three
hours at each performance. Being a very physical journey, all coats and
jackets, shoes and socks, loose coins or jewellery, are left in safe-keeping at
the entrance to the installation. It is, by the way, very much more than just
a rather sophisticated version of the fairground 'Ghost Train' ride. The
object is not to scare, or even shock, but to reveal ever so gently; not to be
violent, but softly to be led into unknown realms, as it were, by guardian
angels, unseen, but having warmth and skin and loving care. The experience has the nature of a true mystery-rite or initiation, and is reminiscent
of the kind of thing which must surely have been organized at Eleusis and
elsewhere in the ancient world; and as with those mysteries, the detailed
and precise secrets must be preserved.

Ariadne's Thread is a collective creation of the *Taller Imagen* company, founded in 1980, with a cross-section of Colombian University per-
sonnel including students and academics whose backgrounds may be in
physics, philosophy, anthropology, writing, painting – or performance. The
company are not actors in the usual sense of the word, either professional
or amateur: but they *are* performers, and there is a serious and accomplished
'making' of a theatrical artefact in their collaborative work. There are some
twenty-four artists, including their director and dramaturg, Enrique Vargas.
His background, not surprisingly, is that of both anthropologist and theatre
director. During the 1960s he worked with the La Mama company in New
York, and with the urban community of East Harlem. His more recent
work has been with South American Indian communities (the Fersen connection again), and with Andean ritual. The company's aim is to explore a
new theatrical language, non-textual, of a personal sensory interaction between artist and audience, encouraging new ways of seeing, listening, feeling, smelling and touching, that avoids the separation and passive witness
in most conventional theatre. It is the very antithesis of 'couch-potato' culture. The particularity of the labyrinth theme is the use of darkness as an
'image-detonator' and springboard for the personal imagination. 'Do you
dare to find the Minotaur in its lair?' reads the publicity leaflet: it is a fair
question with which to challenge new audiences who might never think of
going to a play about a Greek myth. Nor will they – indeed, nor can they
– be disappointed when they do so.

12. Schechner, op. cit., p. 256.

13. *By Means of Performance: Intercultural Studies of Theatre and
Ritual*, edited by Richard Schechner and Willa Appel, CUP, 1990, p. 13.

14. Ibid., pp. 268, 253 and 259.

15. Clem Gorman, *The Book of Ceremony*, third edition, Whole Earth Tools, Cambridge, 1972, p. 8.

16. Ibid., p. 17.

17. Harley Granville-Barker, *The Use of Drama*, p. 63.

18. Idries Shah, *Reflections*, Octagon Press, 1968.

19. Robert J. Landy, *Persona and Performance: The Meaning of Role in Drama, Therapy, and Everyday Life*, Jessica Kingsley Publishers, London and Bristol, Pennsylvania, 1993, p. 7.

20. Carol MacCormack, *Wisdom, Nature and Spirit*, Quaker Universalist Group Pamphlet, 1994, p. 12.

21. Friedrich Dürrenmatt, 'Problems of the Theatre', translated by Gerhard Nellhaus, as the Preface to *Four Plays*, Cape, 1964.

22. Colin Wilson, *Voyage to a Beginning*, C. and A. Woolf, 1968, p. 167.

23. B. F. Skinner, *Beyond Freedom and Dignity*, Pelican Books, 1973.

24. Gaston Baty, quoted by Whitton, op. cit., pp. 115 and 122.

Index